# THE NEW CATHOLIC
# EVANGELIZATION

## KENNETH BOYACK, CSP
### Editor

*With a Preface by Archbishop Edward A. McCarthy*

PAULIST PRESS
New York/Mahwah

The New Catholic
evangelization

Library of Congress Cataloging-in-Publication Data

The new Catholic evangelization/Kenneth Boyack, editor; with a preface by Archbishop
    Edward A. McCarthy.
        p.   cm.
    Includes bibliographical references and index.
    ISBN 0-8091-3310-5 (pbk.)
    1. Evangelistic work—United States.   2. Catholic Church—United States.
I. Boyack, Kenneth.
BV3773.N49   1992
266'.273–dc20                                                                 91-47721
                                                                                     CIP

Published by Paulist Press
997 Macarthur Boulevard
Mahwah, NJ 07430

Printed and bound in the
United States of America

# CONTENTS

# I
# NEW IDEAS

# II
# NEW STRATEGIES

# III
# NEW METHODS

# IV
# NEW FERVOR

Dedicated to

REV. ALVIN A. ILLIG, CSP

Born August 17, 1926; Died August 2, 1991

Pioneer Paulist Missionary and Evangelist

Founder and Director of the
Paulist National Catholic Evangelization Association
1977–1991

First Executive Director of the
National Conference of Catholic Bishops'
Ad Hoc Committee on Evangelization
1977–1983

Faithful and steadfast advocate for the
evangelization of the unchurched in North America

# PREFACE
## Edward A. McCarthy
## Archbishop of Miami

"Me evangelize? I'm a Catholic!"

People may not *say* this when I insist on the opportunity we have to share our Catholic faith, our Catholic way of life, with others. They are kind to the senior archbishop. But something of the sort very likely goes through their minds. Reluctance to speak of "the hope that is in us" is characteristic of American Catholics. Evangelization, or evangelism, is something Protestants do. Catholics are more private; we do not wear our religion on our sleeves.

This reticence is grounded in the turbulent history of Catholicism in the United States. In 1776, when the Declaration of Independence was fresh, only one percent of Americans were Catholic. In part because Catholics were identified with countries with which England had warred for centuries, in part because the founders applauded the reformation and accepted the skeptical, rationalist principles of the enlightenment, the Catholic Church was viewed with suspicion. Catholicism had been illegal in all the colonies but one (Maryland) and was therefore poorly developed. In the years after Yorktown, the American presbyterate consisted of twenty-five priests and a single bishop, John Carroll.

The great immigrant waves of the nineteenth century both strengthened the church and isolated it from general society. The Germans, Poles, Irish and Italians who flooded through American ports had strange ways, spoke strange languages. They worked for low wages, taking jobs from people already here. They kept to themselves, setting up separate parishes and schools, creating their own organizations, celebrating their odd rituals, owning loyalty to a "foreign potentate" in Rome.

One of the aims of such nativist groups as the Know Nothings, the Ku Klux Klan and the American Protective Association was to defend Americanism against these Catholic foreigners. In 1834 a convent was

1

burned in Massachusetts. The next year a pitched battle erupted between Catholics and Protestants over the use of the King James Bible in public schools. Churches burned and fifteen people died in the rioting. When the Washington Monument was erected, many nations sent commemorative stones to be built into the structure. Vandals stole the Vatican's stone and threw it in the Potomac, feeling, no doubt, that it had no place in a monument to freedom.

Happily, anti-Catholicism has faded over the years. By dint of hard work, sound living and loyalty to the flag, Catholics have won acceptance and now stand among the most prosperous and successful of Americans. The church is well known and generally well respected in this country for its contributions to health and education, its imposing charitable work and its defense of human rights.

At the same time, the liturgical and disciplinary reforms of the Second Vatican Council have brought the church into closer engagement with secular society. Catholics realize that the tendency toward self-isolation, however necessary it may have been in immigrant days, is no longer desirable or appropriate. Thus, both internal change and external circumstance have created a favorable climate for Catholic evangelization in the 1990s.

While the historical reasons for our reticence about sharing our faith no longer apply, psychological constraints still remain. Catholic evangelization in the United States is a spark. If it is to become a Pentecostal fire, Catholics must feel free and inspired to spread the gospel.

Certainly this is Jesus' desire. The Great Commission which closes Matthew's gospel ("Go and make disciples of all nations . . .") has the same force it did two thousand years ago. Moreover, it applies to all the members of the church, not just to "official" ministers like priests and sisters. Every Catholic by virtue of baptism has the duty and privilege of sharing the gospel of Jesus Christ with inactive Catholics and people not of our faith. While we bishops have begun the preparation of a national plan for evangelization, plans alone cannot lead people to salvation. Evangelization, in the words of Pope Paul VI, is "the essential mission of the church"—the whole church. All of us can and should be the faithful messengers of Jesus' "good news."

We have another motive for evangelization as well, one closer to the heart. The joy of Christian faith should overflow in us so that we want to share this great treasure with others, especially those near and dear to us. Spreading the gospel is not an imposition, something we force upon an unwilling listener. It is a gift, and a most precious one. We offer it in simple love.

How do we evangelize? Climb on soapboxes? Knock on doors? Get on TV? Some people may do so and be very effective at it. In practice, most Catholics will evangelize mostly by taking their faith seriously enough to live good Christian lives. They will not be perfect. But they will consciously obey what Jesus called the two greatest commandments, loving God and loving neighbor. They will work out their salvation by worshiping God in harmonious community, by observing the teachings of the church Jesus founded, by serving others, and by trying to make this world a more just, more peaceful place. Americans tend to have a skeptical, "show-me" mentality. They will notice when Catholics live genuinely good, peaceful, happy, productive lives. They will wonder about the power of the faith which can produce such results, and may be moved to explore it for themselves.

Living a good life, one which testifies to a hearty faith, is the most powerful tool for evangelization the church has. However, one thing more is needed. People have a right to know why we behave as we do. If we refuse out of shyness or the fear of "imposing our morality" to say we are committed to Jesus Christ and his church, how will others find the treasure we have found? St. Peter says in his first letter: "Always be ready to give an explanation to anyone who asks you for a reason for your hope, but do it with gentleness and reverence . . ." (1 Pet 3:15–16). Thus witness is supplemented by straightforward declaration, gently offered so as to be gently received. Effective Catholic evangelizers are not pushy, just honest.

And what is the message? Before answering this question, let us glance at the culture Catholics hope to evangelize. Americans are justifiably proud of their country which, over the past two hundred years, has fostered, protected and expanded human rights in ways consistent with Christianity. We are a pragmatic and skeptical people, reliant upon reason and empirical science, more interested in results than theories. We are an individualistic people which braved the rigors of the frontier and built a powerful industrial society. We are a proud people which has defended liberty around the globe and still serves as a model of democracy for other nations. We are, at least superficially, a religious people; about ninety percent of Americans profess to believe in God. Finally, we are free. If it were not for the rights our Constitution guarantees, the church might be unable openly to preach the gospel at all.

Unfortunately, in the years since World War II some of these virtues have tended to tip into unhealthy excess. Trust in reason, for example, has been pushed to the point where religion is virtually excluded from public life; our educational, judicial and legislative systems have become rigidly secular. We have elevated individualism to such heights that "doing your own thing" takes precedence over humble acceptance of religious teaching and undermines the Christian duty to serve others. In the last twenty years, the culture has carried individualistic thinking so far as to create a new "right to privacy." It is difficult to see how any sense of community, without which Christianity is inconceivable, can withstand such powerful ideological acid.

Responding to this degeneration of traditional values, Pope John Paul II said in his 1988 statement "The Vocation and Mission of the Lay Faithful": "Whole countries and nations where religion and the Christian life were formerly flourishing . . . are now put to a hard test . . . as a result of a constant spreading of an indifference to religion, of secularism and atheism. *This particularly concerns countries and nations of the so-called first world, in which economic well-being and consumerism . . . inspires and sustains a life lived 'as if God did not exist' *" (34) (emphasis mine).

The holy father does not retreat before this secularized first world. Rather, he insists that the apparent triumph of secular values creates an opportunity to evangelize. Many commentators on modern society have noted a spiritual hunger bred by the hollowness of utilitarian, rationalist morality, a hunger which people attempt to satisfy through various fundamentalisms, through exotic "new age" practices, even through satanism and witchcraft.

Meanwhile, the progressive atomization of society has bred its own anxieties. President Jimmy Carter was criticized a decade ago for pointing to a "malaise" in American life, but the intervening years have proved him right. Society is troubled about many things: continuing racial tension, drug abuse, violence in our cities, apathy and lack of commitment, a failure of idealism, financial failure and corruption, potentially explosive foreign entanglements and, perhaps most disturbing, the apparent paralysis of our political system in the face of all these difficulties.

This background should make it clear what the Catholic Church has to offer America, and why its message, the message of Jesus Christ, should be welcome. First and foremost, the church offers a living faith that God created us, that the Son of God died and rose again so we might have eternal life, and that the Holy Spirit guides us in seeing that God's will is "done on earth as it is in heaven." This faith is founded firmly on the Bible and on Catholic tradition. It is the gospel, the great "good news" of salvation in Jesus Christ.

What does the word "secularism" mean, as the holy father uses it? Simply put, that people live as though the everyday realities of work and home, money and sex, friends and foes *are all that exists.* Secularized people may profess to believe in Christ, but they do not *act* as though they realized that Jesus has redeemed them out of his great love and that they are on a journey that leads through death to new life. America is secular in that it seems to have lost any solid sense of the transcendent, the sense that God is a true and present reality.

Faith in God is a touchstone issue for any culture because it affects everything else: family life, economics, politics, even art and popular entertainment. Catholics evangelize American culture when they respect the spiritual dimension of human existence, when they live, to quote Pope Paul VI, "as though they could see the invisible."

Beyond this fundamental realism, Catholicism offers American society an alternative to the harshness and fragmentation which increasingly plague it. Christianity is an incarnational, lived religion which links this world with the next. The church teaches that Jesus, through his life, death and resurrection, established the kingdom of God here on earth, a kingdom of peace, joy and harmony which will find fulfillment on the last day. It is the evangelizer's duty not only to preach eternal life, but also to help God's kingdom emerge ever more clearly in the here and now. Christian love is God's own cure for excessive individualism and the basis for genuine community. How great a gift to our native land if we could help make this vision of harmony part of the American dream! Only universal love of neighbor, without regard for race or culture, makes possible a community formed "one from many"—*e pluribus unum.*

The evangelist calls for and helps realize a new "civilization of love" based on respect for all people, respect for life and for human rights; on freedom from loneliness, bitterness, fear, mistrust, hatred, turmoil, violence, misery, guilt; on the healing of family life and all sinful and destructive human relationships. Such a civilization, in turn, flows from accepting the Lord Jesus Christ as the way, the truth and the life, from listening to him who came that we might have life to the full, from heeding the wisdom of the ages.

A new spirit is stirring in the Catholic Church in America. There is much good in American democracy, much that received its original impetus from Christianity and would benefit from reconciliation with these roots. It is time for a spiritual call to action, time for immersing American culture in the spirit of Christ, time for building that civilization of love of which Christ is the keystone.

My friends, it is a magnificent challenge. Pope John Paul II declares: "The church today ought to take *a giant step forward* in its evangelization effort, and enter into *a new stage of history* in its missionary dynamism. . . . The church community [must] commit itself . . . to a unique and common mission of proclaiming and living the gospel" ("Vocation and Mission," 35).

May the Catholics of the United States respond with joy.

My heart is steadfast, O God,
My heart is steadfast.
I will sing and chant praise.
Awake, O my soul;
Awake, lyre and harp!
I will wake the dawn.

(Ps 57:8–9)

# INTRODUCTION
## Kenneth Boyack, CSP

"So whoever is in Christ is a new creation: the old things have passed away; behold, new things have come" (2 Cor 5:17).

This book is rooted in a fundamental Christian belief: the resurrection of Jesus Christ brings about a new creation. The witness of the empty tomb and the testimonies of the disciples who saw the risen Lord marked the beginning of a new promise: all sin, suffering and sadness will be wiped away; all will be made new in Christ.

For all who have faith in this promise, the question arises concerning the ways in which the Holy Spirit is bringing about God's kingdom now, in this time, in this generation. We can see ample evidence of the Spirit's activity today, especially in the areas of Catholic evangelization. We witness an increased awareness of the role of the laity in the life and mission of the church, the emergence of evangelization committees in parishes, the development of schools of evangelization and training institutes, and certainly a greater comfort and ease with Catholics using the term "evangelization." Even in the midst of hardships and struggles stemming from budgetary restraints and differing understandings of church, we can still identify specific activities and attitudes in Catholic evangelization, present now, which were not part of our consciousness or vocabulary twenty years ago. The Spirit of the resurrected Christ is alive and at work!

The essays in this book shed light on one aspect of evangelization within the Catholic Church—and that is what Pope John Paul II defines as "the new evangelization." Tracing the development of this term will identify its specific meaning for the United States in the 1990s and will show why "the new evangelization" holds great promise and hope for American Catholics today.

The foundation for the new Catholic evangelization began with Vatican II and with the subsequent 1974 Synod on Evangelization in which the bishops in attendance kept these three questions in mind:

—In our day, what has happened to that hidden energy of the good news, which is able to have a powerful effect on [the human] conscience?
—To what extent and in what way is that evangelical force capable of really transforming the people of this century?
—What methods should be followed in order that the power of the gospel may have its effect?[1]

Pope Paul VI presented an answer to these questions in his inspiring and insightful apostolic exhortation *On Evangelization in the Modern World*. This meditation—the first comprehensive understanding of Catholic evangelization in a post-Vatican II context—has provided rich guidance to numerous readers since its publication in 1975. As many Catholics attest, they find their own experiences and intuitions regarding evangelization validated through reading this teaching document of the church. This fact affirms, at least on one level, the presence and activity of the Holy Spirit in the life of the church.

Pope John Paul II advanced the understanding of evangelization when, in a 1984 speech entitled "Building a New Latin America," he urged Catholics to promote "a new evangelization: new in its ardor, its methods, its expression."[2] The pope announced this call in the context of the advent of the V Centenary—five hundred years of the gospel of Jesus Christ coming to the Americas. The call for a renewed zeal for the gospel as well as new language and methods to tell the story of God's love in Jesus reflects the basic goal of Vatican II: to equip Catholics to proclaim and live the gospel with a deepened sense of holiness and mission.

Recently—in December 1990—the holy father presented a more developed understanding of the new evangelization in his encyclical *On the Permanent Validity of the Church's Missionary Mandate*. The pope states, for example, that "it is in commitment to the church's universal mission that the new evangelization of Christian peoples will find inspiration and support."[3] The term "new evangelization" refers to the missionary activity needed in countries in which people already have heard the gospel. The pope insists that new zeal, new language, new expression, and new methods are needed at this time in order to overcome Catholic complacency in the midst of a secularized culture. Despite contemporary challenges to the gospel, the pope asks Catholics to consider new ways which will enable the resurrected Christ to exercise a still greater transforming impact on individuals, the family, work situations, and in all society. Similar to Pope Paul VI, Pope John Paul II seeks to implement the

Vatican II goal that Catholics live and preach the gospel of Jesus with a deep faith, unwavering conviction, and in the power of the Holy Spirit.

The term "new evangelization" defines a movement of the Spirit shaping the decade of the 1990s. But what is the shape of this new evangelization in the cultural context of the United States? And what are potential future developments? This collection of essays provides some answers to these questions. Thanks to the dedication and expertise of the contributing authors, we present in this book a collection of sixteen articles which illustrate the ways in which new zeal, new language and new methods are needed to preach the gospel competently and effectively in the fast-moving, secularized culture of the 1990s. Each essay was commissioned and written specifically for this volume.

The book is divided into four sections which explore different aspects of the new evangelization. The section entitled "New Ideas" presents articles which highlight issues affecting the content of the gospel message and the ways in which that message impacts on the people, history and cultures of our country. The second section, "New Strategies," looks at the areas of the laity, church structures, the family, the work environment, and social justice—all from the angle of inviting the reader to consider the evangelizing dimensions of these areas of life. The third section, "New Methods," presents new methodologies which focus on the Bible, the parish, the training of evangelizers, and using the media to proclaim the gospel. The final section, "New Fervor," highlights the spirituality of the new Catholic evangelization through essays on the Holy Spirit, the eucharist, and a review of one worldwide effort to promote the gospel in this "Decade of Evangelization"—the 1990s.

We intend the essays in this book to advance the cause of the gospel in the United States. For this reason each author has included a set of questions for discussion and has recommended other resources "For Further Reading." Individuals and groups can profit by thinking about these questions and by consulting the multiple resources listed. We trust that the Holy Spirit—the source and power of the new evangelization— will be at work in the hearts and minds of those who read this book.

I am deeply indebted to Archbishop Edward McCarthy and to the other authors who contributed to this work through their original thoughts and insights. They help to bring about the new evangelization. I am equally indebted to Fr. Alvin Illig, CSP, former director of the Paulist National Catholic Evangelization Association, who encouraged and supported me in this work. I also want to express my appreciation and gratitude to Mrs. Monica Theis Huber whose expertise and skill proved invaluable in the preparation of the manuscript. Finally, I am grateful to Fr. Kevin Lynch, CSP, the president of Paulist Press, and to Fr.

Lawrence Boadt, CSP, associate editor at Paulist Press, for their encouragement and commitment to this project.

As a work of the Holy Spirit, evangelization is primarily a work of faith. With this conviction, I conclude this introduction with quotes from two great leaders who have helped Catholics to develop a new evangelizing consciousness: Pope Paul VI and Pope John Paul II.

> It must be said that the Holy Spirit is the principal agent of evangelization: it is he who impels each individual to proclaim the gospel, and it is he who in the depths of consciences causes the word of salvation to be accepted and understood. But it can equally be said that he is the goal of evangelization: he alone stirs up the new creation, the new humanity of which evangelization is to be the result, with that unity in variety which evangelization wishes to achieve within the Christian community. Through the Holy Spirit the gospel penetrates to the heart of the world, for it is he who causes people to discern the signs of the times—signs willed by God—which evangelization reveals and puts to use within history.[4]
>
> —Pope Paul VI

> With the torch of Christ in your hands
> and full of love for all people,
> go forth, Church of the New Evangelization.
> —Pope John Paul II

## NOTES

1. Pope Paul VI, "On Evangelization in the Modern World" ["Evangelii Nuntiandi"] (Washington, DC: USCC Office of Publishing and Promotion Services, 1975), n. 4.
2. Pope John Paul II, "Building a New Latin America," *Origins* 14:20 (Washington, D.C., November 1, 1984), p. 308.
3. Pope John Paul II, "On the Permanent Validity of the Church's Missionary Mandate" ["Redemptoris Missio"] (Washington, DC: USCC Office of Publishing and Promotion Services, 1990), n. 2.
4. "On Evangelization in the Modern World," n. 75.

# I
# New Ideas

# DISTINCTIVE QUALITIES OF CATHOLIC EVANGELIZATION

## Robert J. Hater

A parishioner recently commented, "Why are Catholics now discussing evangelization? That's for Protestants, not us." Actually, the contrary is true. Evangelization forms the heart of Catholic life and mission.

Catholic evangelization begins before people come to church. A childhood story illustrates this point:

> Our family eagerly awaited Thanksgiving dinner on a warm November day. My sister, Mary Ann (age 5) and I (age 6) heard the doorbell ring and ran to answer it. A boy (about 10) and a girl (about 11) asked for money. The girl held a baby covered with a light blanket. We called Mom. The girl said, "We are poor and have no money for food. Please give us some money."
>
> Mom told them that we did not have much money, but we had plenty of food. We offered to share Thanksgiving dinner with them. The children hesitated. Then Mom said she would make three meals for them to take along. The children said, "Okay."
>
> Dad, Mary Ann and I helped Mom prepare the containers of food. We gladly shared our food with these less fortunate children. They accepted the food and left. Mary Ann and I watched them walk up the street.
>
> When the children got to the corner, the girl threw the baby to the boy. He tossed it up and down. We called Mom. She came quickly to see what was happening. Then the children tossed the food down the sewer, laughed and disappeared around the corner.
>
> Mary Ann and I cried, thinking they hurt the baby. We cried harder when they threw the food down the sewer.

13

Mom called us to her and said, "I have something important to tell you. That wasn't a baby; it was a doll. The children tricked us. They only wanted money. But we will have a fine Thanksgiving, for we gave with a good heart. That's the most important thing. The value of a gift doesn't depend on whether someone appreciates it. Its value comes because we gave out of love. God will bless us because of our gift. God gave his Son, Jesus, and people rejected him. Our gift of food is like God's gift of Jesus."

We had a great Thanksgiving, one I will never forget.[1]

Was my mother an evangelizer? The answer to this question depends on one's view of evangelization, for Catholic evangelization differs from Protestant, fundamentalist evangelism. This essay explores the differences in three sections: Brief History of "Evangelization"; Evangelization, Kingdom and Culture; Distinctive Qualities of Catholic Evangelization.

## BRIEF HISTORY OF "EVANGELIZATION"[2]

"Evangelization" has an interesting history, which sheds light on the meaning of Catholic evangelization.

"Evangelization" comes from the Greek verb "euangelizo," meaning to "convey good news" of a wedding, party, athletic victory or suchlike. The Septuagint (Greek version of the Hebrew Bible) uses it in 2 Samuel, Psalms, the prophets, and historical writings. Psalm 40:9 states, "In the assembly of all your people, Lord, I told you the good news ("euangelizon," the noun) that you saved me."

Jesus spoke Aramaic and probably used "sabar" (to announce good news) to refer to what was translated later as "euangelizo." The latter verb appears many times in the Greek version of the Christian scriptures.

Paul uses "euangelizo" primarily as a missionary term. It has the simple meaning of "announcing the good news of Jesus," as well as the broader meaning of "describing the whole activity of a Christian disciple."

Paul's usage reflects the early Christian practice of using "euangelizo" in a wide sense. It referred to Jesus' mission and ministry, his life and preaching. It also referred to activity of Christians, usually implying outreach to non-believers, but also including shared belief with Christians.

Many synonyms existed for "euangelizo." Christian scriptures use over thirty-five other Greek words to describe what "euangelizo" attempts to convey. These words imply preaching, witnessing, proclaiming and announcing the good news. John, for example, uses "marturein," meaning "to bear witness." Interestingly, words like "martyres" (witness) and "keruxate" (proclaim) were used instead of "euangelizo" during the period from Pentecost to Ascension. The Great Commission in Matthew 28:19—"Go, therefore, make disciples of all the nations . . ." does not use "euangelizo."

The multiple vocabulary used to express Jesus' good news indicates early Christian attempts to "share faith." This was their goal; they never canonized one word, like "euangelizo." Their wisdom contains an important reminder for contemporary evangelists. Catholic evangelization has happened from Jesus' time to the present, even though the word was not always used.

Early Christian writers (Clement of Rome, Justin Martyr, Irenaeus, John Chrysostom and others) used "euangelizo." The Latin fathers translated "euangelizo" as "evangelizo." St. Thomas followed the latter usage. In 1382 John Wycliffe introduced the word "euangelisen" (to evangelize) into what is sometimes called "Old English."

By the seventeenth century, "evangelize" meant "to win over to the Christian faith." Francis Bacon first used "Evangelisme" (evangelism) in *New Atlantis* (1626), while Thomas Hobbes used "Evangelization" (proclaiming Christ) in *Leviathan* (1651). During the nineteenth century these English words began to be used more frequently in some Protestant churches.

Catholics rarely used "evangelism" or "evangelization" before Vatican II. Cardinal Suenens in *The Gospel to Every Creature* (1956) linked "evangelization" with the whole process of Christianization. That book's preface was written by the future Pope Paul VI, whose "On Evangelization in the Modern World" became the "Magna Carta" of Catholic evangelization.

Four conclusions flow from this history of "evangelization":

1. Evangelization, focused on "sharing faith," can take many forms.

2. Other words—"witnessing," "proclaiming" and suchlike—can be used also, for the essential ingredient is "sharing faith," not what it is called.

3. Evangelization, while having a strong missionary focus (namely, sharing faith with non-believers), also includes a broad range of Christian activities.

4. Evangelization is a new word for an old reality, for Christians always shared their faith, even if they used other words to describe this process.

## EVANGELIZATION, KINGDOM AND CULTURE

This section considers the Catholic meaning of evangelization, its relationship to the kingdom of God, and the impact of contemporary culture.

### Meaning of Catholic Evangelization

Catholic Church documents describe holistic and restricted views of evangelization. The *wide* or *holistic* view is reflected in "On Evangelization in the Modern World" ("Evangelii Nuntiandi") and in "On Catechesis in Our Time" ("Catechesi Tradendae"). Seen in this way, *evangelization is an ongoing conversion process within the Christian community, a process that seeks to initiate people ever more deeply into the mystery of God's love (i.e., the kingdom), as it is manifested most fully in the dying and rising of Jesus.*

This evangelization process, inspired by the Spirit, is a response to God's call to proclaim the good news of the kingdom in word and deed. Mom proclaimed this message to Mary Ann and me on Thanksgiving by teaching about the real meaning of a gift. Business executives can evangelize in corporate board rooms. This is not a special vocation but one central to the Christian calling. Evangelization is part of a lifelong conversion process in which God's word is heard again and again. Seeing evangelization in this wide, holistic sense, my mother was an evangelizer on that Thanksgiving Day.

Evangelization is the lifeblood of Christian life and ministry. As an ongoing activity of the community, it includes the initial proclamation of the word, as well as various pastoral ministries which nourish this initial proclamation. Hence, various ministries (catechesis, liturgy, service activities) contribute to the church's evangelizing activity. The chief ministries of word, worship and service are key aspects of evangelization (Figure 1).

Family, church and world have vital roles to play in evangelization. The church must relate to family and world as subjects, not objects, of evangelization. The latter are not objects "out there" to be evangelized, with little to contribute to the dialogue. Evangelization means communicating among subjects, each manifesting a different face of God (Figure 2).

The *General Catechetical Directory,* the *National Catechetical Directory* and the Rite of Christian Initiation of Adults (RCIA) propose a *more restricted* view of evangelization. These documents describe evangelization (and sometimes pre-evangelization) as operative before a person makes a faith commitment. Evangelization is seen in terms of the initial proclamation of the gospel, which is directed toward conversion and is

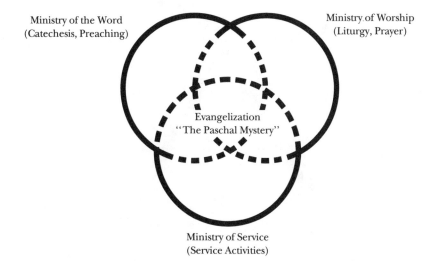

Ministry of the Word
(Catechesis, Preaching)

Ministry of Worship
(Liturgy, Prayer)

Evangelization
"The Paschal Mystery"

Ministry of Service
(Service Activities)

**Figure 1**

© Rev. Robert Hater, *Parish Catechetical Ministry,*
Benziger Publishing Company. Revised for this article.
Used with permission.

followed by catechesis. In this sense, people are evangelized before and catechized after their faith commitment.

Catholics today are opting for the holistic view of evangelization, also called the "convergence" model of evangelization. Both Catholic views differ from a more fundamentalist approach which emphasizes hearing the word of God and accepting Jesus Christ once and for all, in a definite moment of being converted or saved.

In proclaiming the lived reality of Jesus' dying, rising and sending of the Spirit, evangelization energizes Christian endeavors, reminding Christians of their mission to live out God's kingdom message. Christian life is rooted in the life-blood and marrow of evangelization. Without it, individual or institutional efforts to proclaim God's word, celebrate it, or serve others lack the dynamism promised by the good news.

*Evangelization and the Kingdom of God*

What is the good news that Jesus proclaimed? Answering this question involves the heart of the Christian message, namely, the kingdom of God. All evangelization centers around this message.

Jesus' kingdom message is reflected clearly in his words in the Naza-

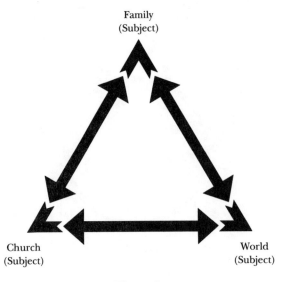

Family
(Subject)

Church
(Subject)

World
(Subject)

**Figure 2**

© Rev. Robert Hater, *Parish Catechetical Ministry,*
Benziger Publishing Company. Revised for this article.
Used with permission.

reth synagogue, "He has sent me to bring good news to the poor, to proclaim liberty to captives and to the blind new sight, to set the down-trodden free, to proclaim the Lord's year of favor" (Lk 4:18–19).

Jesus proclaimed the good news of the kingdom and promised peace in this life and blessedness in the next for those who follow him. In so doing, Jesus is the model for all evangelization.

The Christian scriptures reveal the components of Jesus' evangeliz-ing activities. In his apostolic exhortation "On Evangelization in the Modern World," Pope Paul VI describes them as Jesus' incarnation, his miracles, his teaching, the gathering of the disciples, the sending out of the twelve, the crucifixion and resurrection, and the permanence of his presence in the Christian community (nn. 6–13). These seven compo-nents remind Christians that evangelization is much more than "words." It presupposes the witness of faith, hope and charity.

Pope Paul VI describes two distinctive yet related aspects of Jesus' evangelizing activity: the kingdom of God and liberating salvation (nn. 8–9). Mark links these activities by quoting Jesus, "The time has come . . . and the kingdom of God is close at hand. Repent and believe the good news" (Mk 1:15). To embrace the kingdom, repentance is necessary, for a person's relationship to the kingdom is linked with liberation from sin. The church's Ash Wednesday liturgy implies this connection in the words used while ashes are administered, "Turn away from sin and be faithful to the gospel."

The Christian community continues Jesus' mission and ministry which focuses on the kingdom. Christian efforts make little sense if their dynamism does not reflect the kingdom. To ensure fidelity to Jesus' command the church receives the Spirit, whose actions are discerned in light of scripture, tradition and magisterial interpretations.

An event at Eastertime challenged me to look more deeply into the meaning of evangelization. It happened during the Good Friday liturgy.

> St. Clare parishioners narrated the passion account in words and actions. I sat on the side of the church, reflecting on the gospel story, when suddenly Jesus' words to Pilate, "Mine is not a kingdom of this world" (Jn 18:36), pierced my soul. This expression struck me as it never did before.
>
> In a few moments, I stood beside the life-size cross that I had just carried up the aisle to the altar. I began my homily, "Mine is not a kingdom of this world."
>
> These words remained with me, as later I reflected on the biblical understanding of the kingdom of God.

No description adequately expresses Jesus' teaching on the kingdom of God. Some people translate it as the reign, rule or sovereignty of God. Others prefer the presence of God. The latter is appealing because God's kingdom is wherever God is present. It is an action, not an abstract concept.

Although the kingdom of God is elusive and paradoxical, it has several levels of meaning, rooted in Jesus' words, "Mine is not a kingdom of this world."

Jesus believed in the imminent coming of God's kingdom, seen as a radical, even cataclysmic event. He taught the disciples to get ready for its arrival. When he called Peter, Andrew, James and John, he said, "The time has come and the kingdom of God is close at hand" (Mk 1:15). His death must come first, and his resurrection would testify to the immediate coming of the kingdom. After Jesus' ascension the disciples waited anxiously for his return in glory to initiate this kingdom.

Jesus also announced the kingdom's presence on earth in his role as a servant. He taught that God is present now, working to heal the broken and forgive the sinners. Paul reflects this by saying, ". . . because the kingdom does not mean eating or drinking this or that, it means righteousness and peace and joy brought by the Holy Spirit" (Rom 14:20).

Jesus predicted his resurrection; it happened. He also spoke of the imminent coming of the kingdom; it did not happen. In this mystery rests the great unfinished symphony of Christianity and its greatest paradox. If belief in Jesus' resurrection requires faith, belief in his second coming requires absolute faith.

Consequently, to appreciate the kingdom of God means to live the kingdom "now" through ministry to economically, psychologically, spiritually and physically poor people. This focuses on healing, forgiveness and reconciliation of weak, sinful people, while anticipating the future kingdom of God.

This future kingdom, which Jesus predicted, has a universal, communitarian scope. It is not limited to the union of a person with God in the afterlife. It is for all good people. When it comes, heaven and earth will be transformed. Then all members of God's kingdom will rise from the dead, as Jesus did, and a new era will begin.

The kingdom of God means God's radical presence here on earth, yet always beyond this world. It is mysterious, transcendent, and can best be described in stories and parables. When Christians lose sight of the apocalyptic aspect of the kingdom and regard it as some kind of a "heaven on earth," or stress "what is to come" and neglect the "now," they miss the full dynamism of Jesus' message.

A balanced stance for Christians in God's unfinished symphony involves living with faith in a paradoxical world of sin and tension.

The Catholic view of the kingdom shows how the evangelist John, near the end of his life, after waiting in vain for Jesus' second coming, gave his disciples a symbolic blueprint for faith in the book of Revelation. This book is the final piece of the kingdom's paradox, which always reminds Christians of the need for faith in a mysterious, yet loving God.

Catholic evangelization must always maintain belief in God's radical presence and the consequent process of the overcoming of sin. Any other posture means living on the surface of Christianity, never probing its depth.

### Evangelization and Contemporary Culture

Jesus proclaimed the good news of God's kingdom within a Jewish culture. Early Christians reinterpreted his message within a broader culture (Greek, Roman, African and more). Today, United States Catholics struggle to refocus Jesus' teaching in a materialistic, technological world.

"Culture" is viewed here from a double vantage point, namely,

United States culture and world culture. Both perspectives offer significant challenges for Catholic evangelization.

## United States Culture

The mix of wealth and poverty in United States culture bears many resemblances to the culture of Jesus' time. Gradually the middle class is thinning out, as the gulf widens between rich and poor. At the same time, technological advances offer many promises for the future. The current situation brings blessings and challenges to the Catholic evangelist.

On the *positive* side, contemporary culture presents wonderful blessings, such as television, radio, rapid transportation, computers and suchlike. These make possible advances in medicine, health care, food production and worldwide distribution of goods. The Catholic evangelist recognizes God's presence in these scientific developments.

The *negative* side of modern culture includes greed, materialism, immorality, secularization of values, and the abuse of technology. Today's evangelist must face the great challenge of a sinful, hedonistic world and challenge it with gospel values. The kingdom message can never be accommodated to materialistic culture without destroying the spirit of Jesus' teachings.

## World Culture[3]

Jesus' kingdom is broader than the church; it exists wherever God's presence is manifested. Consequently, wherever people strive to live good, upright lives, regardless of their religion or culture, God's kingdom exists.

Jesus' first disciples were Jewish, but soon his message spread to the Gentile world. At the Council of Jerusalem (50 A.D.) Christianity was liberated from the Jewish culture, and no longer were Christians obliged to observe Hebrew rituals, like circumcision or dietary laws, to be faithful disciples of Jesus. Gradually, his message was reinterpreted within various cultures (African, Asian, Roman). In time the western cultural model took over, as terms like substance, nature and person replaced Hebrew expressions. For nineteen hundred years westernized Christianity predominated. Christian missionaries brought it to other cultures and changed them in light of western ways.

Vatican II effected a major shift in acknowledging God's presence among all great world religions and cultures (e.g., Buddhism, Islam, Judaism). No longer can a westernized form of Christianity be imposed upon other cultures. Future Christianity will be changed in light of non-western cultures as Buddhism, Islam and native religions bring fresh insights to Christianity. Just as westernization changed Jewish Christianity, so will world cultures bring new insights, vocabulary and spirit to contemporary Christian understandings of Jesus and the kingdom.

Catholic evangelization must acknowledge the rich soil of dialogue inherent in world cultures, as they begin to interact more dialogically with western Christianity.


## DISTINCTIVE QUALITIES OF CATHOLIC EVANGELIZATION

The meaning and history of evangelization and its relationship to kingdom and culture imply ten distinctive qualities of Catholic evangelization.

1. *Catholic evangelization is rooted in life itself.*

Evangelization begins in the *family* (integral, divorced, single parent). Witnessing my family's love through a lifetime taught me how birth, growth, joy, sorrow, success, failure, life and death root human relationships with God. Families are challenged to see their critical role in God's plan of evangelizing all people.

The *world* (friends, workplace, technology, culture, neighbors, business offices, civic associations) can also reflect God's presence. At the same time it can lead people away from God, for today's amoral, materialistic culture is the greatest challenge to Christian faith.

Catholic evangelization invites all Christians to see their work as a vital aspect of their calling by God and to respond to this calling by evangelizing their workplace through good example, just business practices and wholesome, moral conduct.

The *church* plays a special role in evangelization. Parishioners gather to hear God's word, celebrate liturgy, pray, learn, support one another, and serve needy people. When family evangelization is absent, other Christians can significantly influence children, youth and adults. Many people are Christians today because a friend, teacher or church minister encouraged them. Breakdowns in many families today—drugs, divorce, latchkey children—indicate that Catholic evangelization within the church must focus strong efforts on the family.

2. *Catholic evangelization is directed toward the kingdom of God.*

The goal of evangelization is to share faith, and, in so doing, to further God's kingdom of charity, justice and mercy. The church helps bring God's kingdom to completion. Whenever Christians support, love and forgive hurting people, God's kingdom is present.

Catholic evangelization acknowledges Jesus' unfinished symphony, knowing that someday he will come again, and that believers will rise from the dead as he did. This radical awareness calls Christians to live their everyday lives in God's mystery as their absolute future. At the same time, Catholic evangelization acknowledges God's presence in other Christian denominations, world religions and cultures. It sees the need to reinterpret the Christian message within these cultures, as the planet moves closer to becoming a world culture.

3. *Catholic evangelization is always related in some way to the Christian community.*

Catholic evangelization presupposes a communal aspect and never reflects the "me and Jesus" focus of many TV evangelists. Catholics believe that God calls them as a people to follow Jesus. Usually this begins in the family and lasts a lifetime.

Evangelization that does not include a communal aspect is one-sided and incomplete. Community creates a climate where people feel at home, supported and able to appreciate the presence of God's spirit in their everyday lives.

Evangelization, however, includes more than participating in church-related ministries, inviting lapsed Catholics back to church, and welcoming new church members. It includes all activities directed to the kingdom of God.

4. *Catholic evangelization recognizes all church members as partners in furthering God's kingdom.*

God's spirit is manifested most fully in a healthy relationship between laity, sisters, brothers, priests, pastoral ministers, deacons, theologians, bishops and the pope. The Catholic approach to evangelization acknowledges different yet complementary gifts existing in the church.

Jesus' work on earth continues through all church members under the guidance of the magisterium. A healthy give-and-take within the entire church community guarantees fidelity to God's revelation and avoids one-sided interpretations, sometimes characteristic of individual-centered evangelists.

5. *Catholic evangelization energizes Christian activities and church ministries.*

Rooted in God's kingdom, Catholic evangelization provides dynamism for the ministries of word, worship and service. These ministries are aspects or moments in the evangelization process; each presupposes initial acts of evangelization occurring in the family, workplace or church.

These ministries merge at many points and cannot function effectively apart from one another. Catechesis, liturgy and social activities, for example, interpenetrate one another, although they focus respectively within the context of the ministries of word, worship and service.

Catholic evangelization is one process with many aspects which become one dynamic whole. To evangelize as though proclaiming God's word has little or no relationship to prayer, eucharist, community worship or social concern is not the "Catholic" way. Evangelization efforts flow from the paschal mystery and are unified in a holistic vision of God's word experienced and celebrated in a vibrant faith life.

Every church organization, structure and activity must help teach people God's word and celebrate life. Religious education (catechesis), liturgy, sacramental preparation programs and St. Vincent de Paul societies are good ways to evangelize. Concern for the poor and financial priorities speak volumes about a parish's commitment to evangelization.

"Welcome" is the first requirement for successful evangelization. Baptisms, funerals and weddings provide wonderful occasions to evangelize. Impersonal answering machines never enhance a parish's reputation as a welcome place.

Effective evangelization means all church ministers accept their call to further God's kingdom.

6. *Catholic evangelization interprets scripture in a rich way and does not limit the Bible to its literal meaning.*

Catholics accept the Bible as God's word, written in human language. The Bible includes literal accounts, poetry, parables, hymns and suchlike. Catholic evangelization interprets biblical passages (e.g. Adam and Eve or magi stories) in light of why they were written, their literary forms (poetry, historical) and church tradition. Since a passage's meaning is not always clear, Catholics get help from church tradition, magisterial teachings and scholarly research.

Some biblical evangelists insist on the literal interpretation of all scripture passages. This approach is inadequate. It makes no more sense to interpret every scripture passage literally than to demand literal interpretation for every newspaper account (news, editorials, comics).

Catholic evangelization encourages people to study scripture, pray with it, and allow God's word to touch their lives.

7. *Catholic evangelization is optimistic, but realistic.*

Catholic evangelization believes that the world is basically good, but admits the presence of sin and evil. God created a good world. After sin entered the world (depicted in the Adam and Eve story), the world remained good but wounded.

Catholics reject evangelical efforts that say creation-after-the-fall is evil. This approach concentrates on sin and corruption and minimizes basic human goodness. While admitting sin's allurement, Catholic evangelization focuses on God's promise of hope and freedom.

8. *Catholic evangelization is a lifelong journey to God.*

Catholic evangelization is a continuous process, not a once-and-for-all event, as many TV evangelists claim.

Biblical evangelists say that conversion, a once-and-for-all event, happens when a person is "saved." While Catholic evangelization admits that one event (sickness, death, a joyous occasion) may trigger conversion, it teaches that conversion is a lifelong journey to God, not a single isolated event. On this journey both faith and good works are necessary for salvation.

9. *Catholic evangelization happens in the midst of everyday living.*

Catholic evangelization stresses the need to discover God in ordinary life. This happened when Mom taught Mary Ann and me the value of a gift on Thanksgiving. It can happen many times each day if people are open to God's presence in everyday life. Prayers such as the Morning Offering are excellent ways to acknowledge daily opportunities to share Christian faith.

10. *Catholic evangelization offers a firm anchor and clear direction in an uncertain world.*

Catholic evangelization gives people a two thousand year faith tradition, definite beliefs, deep spirituality and vibrant liturgical life. It does not shift with the latest whim. At the same time, while rooted in basic beliefs and practices, Catholic evangelization is ever fresh, because the Spirit constantly invites Christians to apply God's word, especially scripture, to their ever-changing world. This means maintaining the basics of scripture, Catholic beliefs and practices, while remaining open to personal and cultural changes.

"Evangelization" is a Catholic word, deeply rooted in the Christian heritage. Our family's early Thanksgiving experience, and many like it, symbolizes the deep significance of evangelization. Just as our family was drawn closer on that day, so will God's help strengthen all people on their common journey to the kingdom of God.

## NOTES

1. This story originally appeared in my book *Holy Family: Christian Families in a Changing World* (Allen, Tex.: Tabor Publishing, 1988), 67–68, and was adapted for this essay.
2. The source for much of the information in this section was *Evangelize! A Historical Survey of the Concept* by David B. Barrett (Birmingham: New Hope, 1987).
3. See address given by Karl Rahner, "Towards a Fundamental Theological Interpretation of Vatican II," trans. Leo J. O'Donovan, SJ, *Theological Studies*, vol. 40, December 1979, 716–27.

## DISCUSSION QUESTIONS

1. What do Catholics mean by "evangelization"? How does it differ from many Protestant, fundamentalistic approaches to "evangelism"?

2. Discuss the implications of making Jesus' message of "the kingdom of God" the central motivation of all Catholic evangelization, especially in regard to: (a) family life today, (b) ministry in the marketplace, and (c) the parish.

3. What changes will be necessary if Catholics (parishes, religious communities, dioceses, individuals) are to become an evangelizing people?

4. Discuss the chief characteristics of Catholic evangelization as these apply to one's personal and professional life.


## FOR FURTHER READING

David B. Barrett. *Evangelize! A Historical Survey of the Concept.* Birmingham: New Hope, 1987.

Kenneth Boyack, CSP, ed. *Catholic Evangelization Today.* New York/Mahwah: Paulist Press, 1987.

Robert J. Hater. *Holy Family: Christian Families in a Changing World.* Chap. 4: "The Family as Domestic Church." Allen, Tex.: Tabor Publishing, 1988.

Robert J. Hater. *News That Is Good: Evangelization for Catholics.* Notre Dame: Ave Maria Press, 1990.

Pope Paul VI. "On Evangelization in the Modern World." Washington, D.C.: United States Catholic Conference, 1975.

# CATHOLIC EVANGELIZATION IN THE UNITED STATES FROM THE REPUBLIC TO VATICAN II

William L. Portier

Drawing "On Evangelization in the Modern World" to a close, Pope Paul VI gathered inspiration from "the greatest preachers and evangelizers, whose lives were devoted to the apostolate" (n. 80). Throughout American Catholic history, people of faith have been raised up who were highly conscious, in their particular circumstances, of the church's missionary nature. Catholics in the U.S. today with a new sense of their call to be salt and light and leaven in American culture can draw like inspiration from our rich but largely untold history of evangelization. This essay's purpose is to recover some of that history.

## THE EARLY REPUBLIC AND THE IMMIGRANT CHURCH, 1776–1908

*Evangelization as Nurturing the Faithful*

Today it is hard to imagine just how tiny the Catholic community was when the United States began. With the majority living in Maryland and Pennsylvania, Catholics made up less than one percent of the entire population. No parish structure was possible with less than thirty priests for the whole country. Until John Carroll's election by the clergy in 1789, there had never been a bishop. The Catholic Church in the U.S. was itself a mission, having begun in the seventeenth century as the Jesuit Maryland Mission. Until 1908 it remained under the jurisdiction of the Sacred Congregation for the Propagation of the Faith.

Penal laws forbidding public worship and restricting the activities of priests consigned English Catholics in colonial Maryland to life in a domestic church. They worshiped in homes rather than parish churches. Their religious lives were family-oriented, their spirituality personal and interior. Republican Catholics had just begun to take advantage of the new religious toleration to build a more public church. Their religious witness to the culture was understandably reserved.

Carroll was a missionary bishop whose diocese included the entire country. Like some of the Jesuit missionaries in colonial Maryland, the clergy of the new republic often assumed the style of the circuit rider, undergoing great hardship to nurture the Catholic faithful. With Bishop John England (1786–1842) a notable exception, most clergy did not present an aggressive witness to the wider culture. Dialogue took the form of defending the faith when it was attacked.

But republican Catholics did not lack an awareness that life in Christ ought to be shared with those outside the church. Maryland native Leonard Neale (1746–1817) has been called the "first American foreign missionary." This future bishop of Baltimore (1815) spent three unsuccessful years (1780–1783) in South America (present-day Guyana) as a missionary. In the early 1840s three American Catholics undertook an equally unsuccessful mission in Liberia on Africa's west coast.[1]

The republican era also saw the beginnings of evangelization as the conversion of America. John Thayer (1758–1815), a Boston Congregationalist who became a Catholic in 1783 and a priest in 1787, was the first Yankee to dream of a Catholic America. Though the story of his conversion, first published in 1787, went through numerous editions, Thayer's efforts as a Catholic evangelist in New England proved relatively fruitless.[2]

By the mid-nineteenth century, immigration had transformed the Catholic Church in the U.S. from a tiny minority to the nation's largest single denomination. Missionary consciousness focused primarily on preserving the faith of the immigrants. Three factors contributed to this focus. First was the enormity of the task of building a church out of such a diverse population in a voluntary pluralist environment. Without state aid, American Catholics cast their church into the form of parish and diocese and met the needs of transplanted people from diverse ethnic and national backgrounds. Parish pastors and bishops scrambled for personnel, money and a place in the priorities of the people. As a mission church, U.S. Catholics received considerable financial support from mission-aid societies in Europe. Today's parish structure testifies to the achievement of the immigrant church.

The second factor contributing to their internal evangelization emphasis was the predominant religious orientation of immigrant Catholics. They developed a parish-centered, devotional spirituality. It tended to focus their religious energies on what one scholar has called the "household of faith."[3] One of the most effective means used by the immigrant church to nurture and reconvert the faithful, bonding them to a parish-based form of Catholicism, was the parish mission of Catholic revival. A mainstay of religious renewal in Europe, the parish mission lent itself well to the environment of American voluntarism. Traveling in bands, mission preachers served as agents of renewal. Parish missions mediated conversion sacramentally through confession rather than through the revival altar call. Conducted by Jesuits, Redemptorists, Vincentians and later Paulists, missions thrived in the religious climate of the 1850s and thereafter became a staple of American Catholic life.[4]

American anti-Catholicism was the third contributing factor. American culture responded to surges in immigration with periodic outbursts of nativism. Though the U.S. offered Catholic immigrants unprecedented opportunities for religious freedom and economic advancement, most remained outsiders in an often hostile environment, in no position to make missionary overtures to the dominant Protestant culture. They learned to use their political strength to defend their interests. Eventually the experience of voluntarily building the immigrant church would help integrate them into the American mainstream. But in the nineteenth century most Catholics found themselves on the cultural defensive and, with two conspicuous exceptions, never adopted an evangelical posture toward American society. The first exception is the Negro and Indian missions. The second is the tradition represented by American Catholicism's premier advocate of evangelization, Isaac Hecker (1819–1888).

### Evangelization and Inculturation: The Negro and Indian Missions

African-American Catholics, most slaves or former slaves, had lived in British North America since the Ark and the Dove sailed into the Potomac in 1634. Nevertheless, after the Civil War, the newly emancipated freedmen became a mission field. Both the second and third plenary councils of Baltimore called for Catholic evangelization of southern African-Americans. One of the few to answer the call was John R. Slattery (1851–1926). As leader of the Josephites during the last quarter of the nineteenth century, he pioneered Catholic evangelization among African-Americans. He sought the answer to the "Negro question" of post-Reconstruction days in the conversion of the unchurched freedmen to Catholicism. He advocated a black Catholic clergy during the days of segregation and helped to integrate American seminaries. He believed that under the American arrangement of separation the church was most free to be her missionary self. He chided his fellow Catholics for lack of missionary spirit. Embittered by racism in the church and lack of support for the Negro missions, and shaken in faith by his encounter with modernist historical and biblical scholarship, Slattery publicly renounced the church in 1906. Nevertheless, his effort to raise the mission consciousness of American Catholics had no precedent in his day.

The work went on without Slattery. The struggle against racism and segregation in the church became part of the larger struggle in American society.[5] Though the work is far from done, the black Catholic bishops' 1984 pastoral letter on evangelization and the 1987 National Black Catholic Congress testify that the African-American Catholic community has become a powerful agent for evangelization in contemporary American society.

Studies of the Catholic missions among native Americans are "woefully scarce."[6] John Gilmary Shea's *History of the Catholic Missions Among the Indian Tribes of the United States, 1529–1854* remains important. With westward expansion, Catholics undertook new missions in the same spirit of evangelizing the heathen that brought the Spanish, French and English missionaries to the new world.

President Grant's "Peace Policy" of 1870 reversed some of the modest successes chronicled by Shea. Grant's policy took the responsibility for administering Indian agencies from the military and placed it in the hands of organized religion. Government procedures restricted 80,000 Catholic native Americans to reservations administered by Protestants.[7] The Catholic bishops responded by creating a Commissioner of Catholic Indian Affairs, and eventually in 1874 the Bureau of Catholic Indian Affairs. Most evangelization of native Americans took place through mission schools. Under Grant's plan they were financed in part by the government until 1900. In 1884 the Third Plenary Council of Baltimore established the annual collection for the Negro and Indian missions.

The most influential advocate of evangelization among native Americans was Blessed Katharine Drexel (1858–1955), the daughter of Philadelphia banker Francis A. Drexel. She was first introduced to the Indian missions as a young woman in the early 1880s. After her father died in 1885, Drexel devoted her life and her considerable inheritance to what she called the Negro and Indian missions. In 1891 she founded the Sisters of the Blessed Sacrament for Indians and Colored People. During the twentieth century, millions of dollars of Drexel money financed mission schools and churches throughout the south and west.

While nineteenth century missionaries often evangelized at the expense of native American culture, contemporary native American Catholics are engaged in a vibrant process of incarnating Catholicism in traditional native cultures.

*Evangelization as the Conversion of America: Isaac Hecker and Walter Elliott*

For most immigrant Catholics, church-state separation meant that, in a predominantly Protestant environment, they would be free to worship publicly and practice their religion without state interference. But Yankee Catholics raised an alternative voice in the immigrant church. For them church-state separation meant a providential opportunity to transform American society voluntarily by conversion to Catholicism. As the chief advocate of this approach, Isaac Hecker was an "evangelical Catholic."

Whether invoking or impugning his name, contemporary commentators often focus on Hecker's effort to adapt Catholicism to the American environment of political freedom. Such a focus ignores his spiritual depth and his genuine commitment to the transformation of American culture. In Hecker's view, church and state could be legally separated and religious freedom guaranteed. Religion and culture, however, could only be separated at the peril of a just and humane society. Religion and culture had to be joined voluntarily by free individuals in association. Only shared religious faith could ground true social reform.

In "On Evangelization in the Modern World," Pope Paul VI decried "the separation between the gospel and culture." He spoke of evangelizing culture "from within." The church evangelizes when she "seeks to convert, solely through the divine power of the message she proclaims, both the personal and collective consciences of people, the activities in which they engage, and the lives and concrete milieu which are theirs" (n. 18).

One could hardly find a better description of Hecker's life project of converting America.

> America presents to the mind, at the present epoch, one of the most interesting questions . . . whether the Catholic Church will succeed in Christianizing the American people as she has Christianized all European nations . . . ?
>
> We say the question is fraught with great interest for the future of humanity. Our people are young, fresh, and filled with the idea of great enterprises; the people who, of all others, if once Catholic, can give a new, noble and glorious realization to Christianity; a development which will go even beyond the past in achievements of zeal, in the abundance of saints, as well as in art, science and material greatness.

The Catholic Church alone is able to give unity to a people, composed of such conflicting elements as ours, and to form them into a great nation.[8]

Founder of the Missionary Society of St. Paul the Apostle (the Paulist Fathers), Hecker spent a lifetime evangelizing American culture. He sought to awaken to the divine presence within them the baptized in his own communion who were already seriously living the Christian life. To those outside Catholicism, he presented conversion not as a radical denial of their Christian pasts, but as a fulfillment and completion of gifts already received. Although many who followed him in the Americanist tradition lost his emphasis on gospel transformation and trusted instead in their ability as political power brokers, Hecker never lost hope in the cultural transformation that his belief in America's mission presupposed.

In a pre-ecumenical environment, one of the chief means Hecker had hoped to use in evangelizing America was his lectures to non-Catholics. Walter Elliott (1842–1928) inherited Hecker's dream of America's conversion. With its expansive optimism about America's prospects and its sense that Protestant culture was coming apart, the 1890s offered the perfect moment for Elliott to take up Hecker's convert apostolate. He was convinced that God willed America's conversion and that the Paulists' primary vocation was to work for it.

In 1893, two years after publishing his soon to be controversial *The Life of Father Hecker,* Elliott plunged full-time into non-Catholic missions. Beginning in rural Sand Creek, Michigan, he spoke in the town hall without a collar. His format consisted of a hymn, the question box, and a talk. His method was expository, persuasive and polite. As Hecker had, he presented the truths of Catholicism as the fulfillment of the deepest human needs and desires. After twenty missions in the Detroit diocese, he went to Cleveland where he received episcopal permission to form a mission band of three diocesan priests. The best of these was Stephen Kress who worked on the non-Catholic missions until 1917 and later joined Maryknoll in 1920. Between 1893 and 1895, Elliott published accounts of his mission experience in the columns of the *Catholic World.*

In 1896 Elliott and fellow Paulist Alexander Doyle founded the Catholic Missionary Union and its organ *The Missionary* to promote the convert apostolate. Elliott's Apostolic Mission House on the campus of Catholic University offered a one-year program to train priests for the non-Catholic missions. Critics faulted the convert apostolate for failure to produce results. There were converts—Kress reported sixteen hundred in the first thirteen years of the Cleveland mission—but not in

sufficient numbers to suggest America's imminent conversion. Still Elliott defended the work:

> The claim we here make is not that we shall convert America because
> our people will listen to us, though that is a valid claim. But we insist
> that if Protestants will listen to us, we are bound in conscience to
> address them. . . . As to converts, there are sure to be a few brought in
> almost immediately; the conversion of large numbers is a work of time
> and patience. . . .[9]

The irenic method, it has been argued, robbed the missions of evangelical urgency and defeated the goal of mass conversions. By 1908, in
any case, it was clear that Elliott and Doyle could not gain sufficient
support to sustain their work on a large scale. In that year, Francis C.
Kelley (1870–1948) organized in Chicago what he billed as the First
American Catholic Missionary Congress. In his talk at the congress,
Doyle would point out in vain that there had been three previous missionary congresses sponsored by the Catholic Missionary Union. It was
clear that leadership in Catholic evangelization was passing from east to
midwest, from the Paulists to the Catholic Church Extension Society
founded by Kelley in 1905.

The 1890s had offered a unique opportunity. The cultural consensus on America was breaking down before the advance of what fundamentalists would later call modernism. Elliott and the Americanists
sensed the religious vacuum and rushed to fill it. By 1908 their moment
had passed. American Catholicism had begun the process of consolidating into a formidable subculture. The heirs of nineteenth century evangelical Protestantism were building their own fundamentalist subculture. The resulting secular-pluralist approach to church-state separation
made anything like evangelization as transformation of culture difficult
to imagine. The public religious vacuum was filled but by something like
what Robert Bellah and Will Herberg have called respectively the American Civil Religion and the Religion of the American Way of Life. In the
Catholic subculture, evangelization meant home and foreign missions,
and the primary metaphor used to talk about it was "church extension."

## THE IMMIGRANT CHURCH CONSOLIDATED, 1908–VATICAN II

*Evangelization as Church Extension: Francis C. Kelley*

Both Elliott and Kelley wanted to convert America. Both would have
joined Pope Paul VI in decrying the separation of gospel and culture.
Elliott responded to the breakup of the dominant Protestant culture in

the U.S. by trying to make American culture Catholic. Kelley by contrast sought to reinforce the separation by strengthening and extending the Catholic subculture.

Though he came from the Canadian Maritimes, Kelley was a midwestern populist who viewed urban America as corrupt and godless. A country pastor in the diocese of Detroit, he lectured on the waning lyceum circuit in order to raise funds to build a parish church. In his travels, he saw the "real America . . . the America of small towns, villages and countryside." He found rural Catholics without pastors and churches. To extend the urban church into the rural south and west, he conceived the idea for Church Extension. "Thinking men know," he said in 1908, "that the country boy is the future ruler of the city."[10]

Kelley's idea caught on. Through *Extension* magazine, he reached Catholic America and raised money to build chapels and schools and educate priests for rural missions. Hispanic Catholics in the southwest often received less than their fair share. As the church in the U.S. emerged from its mission status, Kelley challenged "missionless" American Catholics to stop thinking like a mission country. No single person did more than Kelley to raise Catholic evangelization consciousness in the early twentieth century.

Despite his disdain for urban corruption, Kelley remained the ecclesiastical promoter and impresario. The aging Archbishop Keane found Kelley's plush Chicago offices too much like a bank. Like his populist fundamentalist counterparts, Kelley was not above using "modern" means. He borrowed the term "extension" from the world of commerce. In addition to his fund-raising genius and his use of the mails, he introduced railroad "chapel cars" into Catholic evangelization. He borrowed that idea from the American Baptist Publication Society. Specially designed for Kelley by the general manager of the Pullman Company, the chapel cars were named for St. Anthony, St. Peter and St. Paul. On the wheels of these Pullman cars, the Catholic Church Extension Society rode into the imaginations and hearts of American Catholics.

By the time Kelley left in 1928 to become bishop of Oklahoma, Extension was well on its feet. When he first started it in 1905, such unified national action was suspect and difficult. Kelley argued that mission awareness would help overcome the nationality differences among American Catholics. The rise of Extension coincided with the formation of a national Catholic consciousness, best typified by the National Catholic War Council, which evolved into the present National Conference of Catholic Bishops (NCCB). It was a time of confident optimism and national expansion. Corporations, labor unions and government were consolidating. National mission organizations proliferated. Extension continued to flourish as a national mission clearinghouse. It succeeded because it fit well with the way most Catholics felt about the church and its relationship to American culture. In a period of building and consolidating America, Extension's success could be measured by the number of chapels and schools it built rather than by the number of converts.

*Evangelization as Overseas Convert Making: Foreign Missions*

Removal of their own mission status in 1908 brought greater mission awareness to American Catholics. In 1911 James A. Walsh (1867–1936) and Thomas F. Price (1860–1919) founded the Catholic Foreign Mission Society of America, or Maryknoll. Price was a veteran of the convert apostolate in North Carolina and he and Walsh had met through Elliott's Catholic Missionary Union. In 1918 Maryknoll sent the first of many departure groups to China. The next year Price died in Hong Kong, a truly exemplary American Catholic evangelist. Walsh's magazine *Field Afar* became *Maryknoll* magazine and through its stories and pictures brought the foreign missions into countless American Catholic homes.

During most of the twentieth century, Catholics supported the foreign missions generously with both money and vocations. Mission magazines, visiting missionaries, and international organizations such as the Society for the Propagation of the Faith and the Association of the Holy Childhood fostered awareness of and interest in the foreign missions. With communists in control of China after 1949, foreign missions often became associated with American anti-communism. A generation of American Catholic school children lionized Bishop James E. Walsh and other heroic Maryknollers imprisoned in China. They took their places in the American Catholic imagination next to Father Damien of Molokai and the Jesuit martyrs of North America.

*Evangelization as Public Witness: Lay Catholic Evangelism*

Having a cloistered Carmelite nun, St. Thérèse of Lisieux (1873–1897), as patron of the missions reminded Catholics of the need to pray for the missions. Various mission societies such as Extension made people aware of the missions' financial needs. Members of organizations such as the Missionary Association of Catholic Women, founded in 1916, made vestments and altar linens for the missions. But some Catholic laity felt called to a deeper participation in the church's missionary task.

Already in 1909, Vincentian mission preacher Thomas A. Judge (1868–1933) founded in Brooklyn, New York one of the first U.S. lay apostolate organizations, the Missionary Cenacle Apostolate. He envisioned "a highly spiritualized laity" and inaugurated a program of spiritual formation designed to support lay missionaries in more direct apostolic works such as home visiting, catechetics, and hospital and prison ministries. From the original group of lay missionaries, two religious communities eventually branched off. The Missionary Servants of the Most Blessed Trinity (women) and the Missionary Servants of the Most Holy Trinity (men) have contributed significantly to home and foreign missions.

New York governor Alfred E. Smith's defeat in the 1928 presidential campaign shook the confidence built up by Catholics after World War I. The election revealed anti-Catholicism as a potent force in American society. In response to this situation, various forms of more active lay evangelism emerged in the 1930s.

The Catholic Evidence Guild had been founded in England in 1918 to train lay men and women for outdoor speaking on Catholic doctrine. Frank Sheed and Maisie Ward are its best known English members. Between 1931 and 1935, Catholic Evidence Guild branches sprang up in Baltimore, Washington, Detroit, Oklahoma City, Philadelphia and Buffalo. All but the New York branch included women speakers. In response to her exclusion, Rosalie Marie Levy, a convert from Judaism, founded the Catholic Lay Apostle Guild in 1935 and worked in the outdoor ministry until 1948.

Karl Rogers, a Pennsylvania businessman shocked by the anti-Catholicism of the 1928 election, got together with some fellow parishioners and founded the Catholic Information Society of Narberth, Pennsylvania. They used newspaper advertising and pocket-sized, direct mail tracts to make a clear presentation of Catholic beliefs to Americans. Like the Evidence Guild lecturers, Rogers aimed primarily at exposition.

The 1930s also saw the urban Catholic Evidence Guild concept combine with Kelley's rural extension idea. Spurred by a campus lecture by Maisie Ward, the Rosary College (Illinois) Evidence Guild sent college students as "women missionaries" into rural towns in Kelley's Oklahoma diocese, North Carolina and Louisiana. Working from a pickup truck, they billed their presentations as revivals and themselves as "street preachers." A newspaper account of their 1940 summer commented:

> The work was unique inasmuch as meetings were conducted entirely by the girls. They gave the two talks on each evening's program, conducted the question and answer forum, provided the music and singing, ran the public address system, and drove the pickup.[11]

Perhaps the most colorful street preacher of this period was a Catholic convert from Judaism, David Goldstein (1870–1958). Goldstein began his long career as an evangelist under the tutelage of Martha Moore Avery (1851–1929). Both came to Catholicism from socialism and carried its forthright activist spirit into the church. They lived in Boston and eventually gained the confidence of Cardinal William O'Connell (1859–1944). In 1917, with revivalist Billy Sunday at the peak of his popularity, Avery and Goldstein started the Catholic Truth Guild. Goldstein envisioned it as "a sort of a Catholic salvation army made up of action workers only—those who would speak, would sing, would write for the press, or sell literature."[12] The Guild's trademark was its custombuilt, yellow and white (for the colors of the papal flag) sound car.[13] After Avery's death, Goldstein took to the road in response to the same needs that had given rise to the Evidence branches. He changed the name of his ministry to Catholic Campaigners for Christ. In 1941 at the age of seventy-one, he retired.

### Evangelization of Culture: Catholic Action

Relatively few Catholics were street preachers, but significant numbers wanted to do more to share their faith than pray for and contribute to the missions. During the middle decades of this century, the term "Catholic Action" was applied to their activities. Pope Pius XI used the term in 1922 to designate the laity's participation in the apostolate of the church's hierarchy. Through Catholic Action, as applied in subsequent decades to the American context, many Catholics came to attribute an "apostolic" or "missionary" dimension to their participation in such organizations as the Christian Family Movement and the Catholic Interracial Council. Catholic Action promoted the idea of the laity as a leaven in society and thus a certain intensification of evangelization consciousness. This trend increased with the general revival of religion that followed World War II.

### Evangelization as the Conversion of America Revisited: Home Missions

A 1936 article in the *Ecclesiastical Review* proposed "A Plan for an American Society of Catholic Home Missions to Operate in the Rural Sections of the United States." This society would work for nothing less than the "conversion of America to the church of Jesus Christ." Convert making and church extension and the conversion of America had come together in the person of William Howard Bishop (1885–1953), a diocesan priest in rural Clarksville, Maryland.

Like Kelley in the previous generation, Bishop was, in the troubled economy of the 1930s, a ruralist. He found Bishop Edwin O'Hara's Catholic Rural Life Conference "purely defensive." Like Kelley he saw rural America as the country's hope, but also as "a field of offensive missionary enterprise." His article presented a well-conceived plan to evangelize rural America. In 1939 Archbishop John T. McNicholas (1877–1950) of Cincinnati invited him to come to Ohio and begin. The result was the Home Missioners of America, or Glenmary. Bishop began his open-air campaign in rural Adams County, Ohio. The same Dayton, Ohio businessman who had donated two of Kelley's chapel cars gave Bishop a trailer chapel and a tow car in 1941. He later abandoned it for tent preaching.

Bishop's entry into the imaginations of his supporters came through his map of "No-Priest Land," a map of the United States with the one thousand priestless counties (nearly one-half) colored in. Though Bishop never abandoned the goal of converting America he had enunciated in 1936, Glenmary's progress could be charted by erasing another shaded county on the map rather than by counting converts. In the decade prior to Vatican II, he articulated his understanding of evangelization in these terms:

> The work of making converts is the missioner's prime object, and I do not in the least desire to weaken his efforts for this purpose. It is in perfect accord with the Savior's injunction to "teach and baptize," and it must ever be our chief objective.
>
> But I am convinced that side by side with the great convert-making process, there is another objective for us to cherish in our work. The objective is to lift up and improve the moral lives of the people around us, regardless of their beliefs or lack of beliefs; regardless, even, whether they will ever accept the faith or not.[14]

### Concluding Reflections: Toward an Evangelical Catholicism

As this brief survey illustrates, the state of contemporary scholarship on evangelization is limited. The history of Catholic evangelization in the U.S. remains unwritten. Evangelization in the comprehensive sense proposed by "On Evangelization in the Modern World" is new to American Catholics. What resources does our history have to offer today's new Catholic evangelization? How might contemporary agents of evangelization profit from knowing they are part of a history?

As the complexity of evangelization might lead us to expect, our survey yields up at least five models of evangelization. Until 1908 the focus was on evangelization as nurturing the faithful. With Hecker, an increasing secondary emphasis on evangelization as convert-making blossomed into evangelization as the conversion of America, understood as involving deep inculturation or cultural transformation. The twentieth century's consolidated immigrant church brought evangelization as church extension. Though its prime emphasis was on extending the Catholic subculture, Catholic Action, with its move toward evangelizing culture, provided a corrective. With the lay evangelists came evangelization as explicit public witness. The example of the Negro and Indian missions and the Hispanic Catholics annexed to the U.S. along with Mexican territories shows that none of the models of evangelization were sufficiently respectful of the need for inculturation.

The most comprehensive model and the one most congenial to the vision of "On Evangelization in the Modern World" (transforming every sphere of human life) is that of evangelization as the conversion of America. It must be understood in a contemporary setting where the quest for Christian unity supersedes convert-making among Protestants, religious liberty remains a theological given, and church-state separation a constitutional one. In presenting Isaac Hecker as an "evangelical Catholic," David O'Brien argues persuasively that the more deeply one understands the voluntary character of religion in modern society, the more evangelical one must become.[15]

The greatest obstacle to Catholics becoming more evangelical is their general acceptance of American religious pluralism as a kind of ideal natural state in which people are best left alone with their beliefs. This secular-pluralist approach to church-state separation dates to the beginning of our century and ignores the need for public discussion about the deepest shared basis for this culture. In such a view, imagining effective ways to share faith life with inactive Catholics or the unchurched appears as somehow in poor taste, an impolite invasion of privacy or even un-American. Catholics who are really serious about evangelization as transformation of culture from within must learn to behave more as fired-up evangelicals than as civil republicans or pugnacious immigrants.

## NOTES

1.  James Hennesey, "First American Foreign Missionary: Leonard Neale in Guyana," *Records of the American Catholic Historical Society of Philadelphia* 83 (1972), 82–86.

2.  On Thayer see Christine M. Bochen, *The Journey to Rome, Conversion Literature by Nineteenth-Century American Catholics* (New York and London: Garland Publishing, Inc., 1988), 124–39.

3.  Ann Taves, *The Household of Faith: Roman Catholic Devotions in Mid-Nineteenth-Century America* (Notre Dame: University of Notre Dame Press, 1986).

4. Jay Dolan, *Catholic Revivalism, The American Experience 1830–1900* (Notre Dame: University of Notre Dame Press, 1978).

5. William L. Portier, "John R. Slattery's Vision for the Evangelization of American Blacks," *U.S. Catholic Historian* 5 (1986), 19–44; Stephen J. Ochs, *Desegregating the Altar: The Josephites and the Struggle for Black Priests 1871–1960* (Baton Rouge and London: Louisiana State University Press, 1990).

6. James Hennesey, "Supplement to American Catholic Bibliography 1970–1982," *Cushwa Center Working Papers Series* 14/1 (Fall 1983), 11; see also Christopher Vecsey, "Sun Dances, Corn Pollen, and the Cross, Native American Catholics Today," *Commonweal* 114 (June 5, 1987), 345–51.

7. James Hennesey, *American Catholics* (New York: Oxford University Press, 1981), 192.

8. I. T. Hecker, *Questions of the Soul* (New York: D. Appleton & Company, 1855), 292–93.

9. Cited from Elliott's *Non-Catholic Missions* by Thomas J. Jonas, *The Divided Mind, American Catholic Evangelists in the 1890s* (New York and London: Garland Publishing, Inc., 1988), 236. My treatment of Elliott relies on Jonas' excellent study.

10. Francis C. Kelley, "Church Extension" in Francis C. Kelley, ed. *The First American Catholic Missionary Congress* (Chicago: J.S. Hyland & Company, 1909), 100. This talk presents a good view of Kelley's program. See also Kelley's *The Bishop Jots It Down* (New York and London: Harper & Brothers Publishers, 1939), 84–85, 114, 153–54.

11. Cited by Debra Campbell in "Part-Time Female Evangelists of the Thirties and Forties: The Rosary College Catholic Evidence Guild," *U.S. Catholic Historian* 5 (1986), 371–83, 377.

12. Goldstein to Avery, April 21, 1917, as cited in Debra Campbell, "A Catholic Salvation Army: David Goldstein, Pioneer Lay Evangelist," *Church History* 52 (1983), 322–32, 323 n. 4. My treatment of lay evangelism relies almost entirely on Campbell.

13. See Goldstein's description of the "autovan" in David Goldstein, "Lay Street Preaching," in John A. O'Brien, ed., *The White Harvest: A Symposium on Methods of Convert Making* (New York: Longmans, Green & Co., 1927), 209–38, 216–17.

14. Cited by Herman W. Santen, *Father Bishop, Founder of the Glenmary Home Missioners* (Milwaukee: Bruce Publishing Co., 1961), 100. For Bishop's proposal, see *The Ecclesiastical Review* 94 (April 1936), 337–47.

15. David O'Brien, "An Evangelical Imperative: Isaac Hecker, Catholicism, and Modern Society" in John Farina, ed., *Hecker Studies* (New York/Ramsey: Paulist Press, 1983), 87–132. O'Brien applies to Hecker the phrase "evangelical Catholic" on p. 94.

## DISCUSSION QUESTIONS

1. How are the various models of evangelization in American Catholic history related to the needs and influences of their times? Is your understanding of evangelization appropriate to our time?

2. Past Catholic evangelists have advocated America's conversion. How does this strike you? Is American religious pluralism an ideal natural state?

3. What would it take to make you an "evangelical Catholic"?

4. Which of the past American Catholic evangelists do you find most inspiring and why?

## FOR FURTHER READING

Debra Campbell. "Catholic Lay Evangelization in the 1930s: Four Models." *Records of the American Catholic Historical Society of Philadelphia* 95 (1984), 5–14.

Debra Campbell. " 'I Can't Imagine Our Lady on an Outdoor Platform': Women in the Catholic Street Propaganda Movement." *U.S. Catholic Historian* 3 (1983–84), 103–14.

Cyprian Davis, OSB. "Evangelization in the United States Since Vatican Council II." In *Catholic Evangelization Today*, ed. Kenneth Boyack, CSP, 22–37. New York/Mahwah: Paulist Press, 1987.

David O'Brien. *Public Catholicism*. New York: Macmillan Publishing Company, 1989.

Peter Schineller. *A Handbook on Inculturation*. New York/Mahwah: Paulist Press, 1990.

# EVANGELIZING AMERICAN CULTURE
## Most Rev. Francis E. George, OMI

"Everybody's doing it" has long been a refrain of youngsters who want to persuade their parents to permit something which family rules do not allow. It is also a phrase that shows how culture, like faith, shapes our lives. Both culture and faith tell us how to behave and what to believe. Both give us norms for acting and thinking and loving. Bringing people to know and love and accept Christ is easier or harder depending on what their culture tells them is good to know and love and accept. Recognizing the importance of culture's interaction with faith, Pope Paul VI wrote that the split between gospel and culture is the drama of our times. He added, however, that it was the drama of other ages as well. The dialogue between faith and culture is as old as the history of God's self-revelation and the human response to it in faith.

### INCULTURATING THE FAITH AND
### EVANGELIZING THE CULTURE

The dialogue between faith and culture is called "inculturation of the faith" when a particular culture's symbols, institutions and values become vehicles for expressing the universal faith. Missiologists invented the term "inculturation" because it recalls the mystery of the incarnation. Somewhat as the word of God became man, the faith of the church becomes Nigerian, Chinese or American as Nigerians, Chinese and Americans come to know, love and accept Christ. *In* you, Pope John Paul II tells the citizens of China, Christ has become Chinese; so *in* us, Christ has become American.

How does this happen? Between a transcendent gift, the faith, and an immanent construction, a culture, there will almost always be some tension. Sometimes a given culture will not possess the resources for expressing the faith in its fullness. A culture might be unable to make sense of God's self-revelation, unable to understand a merciful Father, an obedient Son, a self-effacing Spirit.

Beyond the inevitable tensions which arise when a culture is stretched to express Catholic faith, more positive resistance might develop. A culture can resist the faith as a sinner resists grace. The culture might enshrine customs opposed to evangelical life: polygamy, ritual murder, sexual promiscuity, abortion, exploitative business practices. When believers recognize demonic elements in their culture and work to diminish or eradicate them, the dialogue between faith and culture turns into "evangelization of culture."

To form gospel-shaped people, the church must work to create gospel-friendly cultures. A faith which demands that culture change is sometimes called "counter-cultural." The adjective is unfortunate if it leads believers to see themselves on one side and their culture on another. Our culture is as much in us as we are in it. Religious critics of a culture can imagine a bad system opposed by good people, but the distinction is too easy. If our social system and culture are, at least in part, evangelically deficient or even corrupt, so are we all. The evangelizer begins by taking responsibility for the culture to be evangelized.

## CATHOLIC CONCERN FOR CULTURE: LOVING WHAT YOU EVANGELIZE

Separating good from bad in a culture's values and way of life, its institutional patterns, goals and accomplishments, demands a principle of discernment. When the Catholic evangelizer looks for such a principle, he or she reaches for the gospel as interpreted by the church.

The church tells us that our culture, despite its deficiencies and the positive obstacles it might place to belief, is lovable. The Catholic Church teaches that grace builds on nature, for human nature, while wounded by sin, is not hopelessly corrupt. As grace builds on nature, so faith builds on culture, which is second nature. Culture is damaged by human sinfulness, but it is not hopelessly corrupt. A culture is a field which offers plants from native seeds for grafting onto the tree of faith.

Are there such seeds in American culture? Pope John Paul II, speaking in Chicago on October 5, 1979, found a seed of God's word in the history of different peoples coming to the United States to form a new union. Our bringing many rich cultural heritages together to create a new people reminded the pope of St. Paul's description of the church: "We, though many, are one people in Christ" (Rom 12:5). The church is enriched by the diversity of her members, who make up the one body of Christ. All are united in one apostolic faith; all live through the action of one Spirit. Thus united, the church can be active in evangelizing, much as a nation's strength and ability to act depend on its internal unity. United States history and American efforts to form a nation are, in some sense, an analogue of the unity which is given believers in the church. American evangelizers can build on our collective experience to form here an indigenous Roman Catholic Church. Like the pope, we can search for *semina verbi*, seeds of God's word, in American history and cultural patterns.

More than any previous pope, John Paul II has moved culture to the center of evangelization. Perhaps his own experience as a bishop in communist Poland convinced him that culture is more important than institutions in preserving and spreading the faith. In his country, as in other Marxist lands, the church lost almost all her public institutions; but even as the schools, newspapers and social organizations were taken over by a hostile state, the faith remained strong in the hearts of many Poles because their culture had been shaped by the Catholic faith.

In an evangelized culture, turns of phrase and cherished customs, habitual attitudes and daily activities serve to remind people of the gospel. Pope John Paul II has said many times that faith must "become culture." A faith which does not become culture, the pope explains, is not fully received, not entirely thought through, not faithfully lived. Faith is not true to its nature unless it transforms everything human.

Faith becomes culture, however, as culture is opened to the ultimate truth about human nature and destiny. While the church in the United States enjoys a certain institutional freedom, she exists in a culture which, in often surprising ways, resists Catholicism. Are there clues to this American pattern of resistance to Catholic faith?

## AWARENESS OF AMERICAN CULTURE: KNOWING WHAT TO EVANGELIZE

Perhaps Americans have greater difficulty than others in understanding their own culture. The United States, while too small to be the world, is big enough to be a world. Unlike the people of Denmark or Zimbabwe or Uruguay, Americans can interpret what happens elsewhere in terms of their own experience. Since American popular culture influences the world, we can be led into thinking that all peoples are more like us than they really are. Further, to safeguard a national unity forged across great distances from peoples of different races, national origins, religions and cultures, Americans often relegate differences to the private sphere, explaining that all peoples are really alike, at least under the skin. Awareness of American cultural peculiarity is suppressed by American culture itself.

In any society, however, the evangelizer is hard put to analyze his or her own culture. Culture is so all-inclusive that hundreds of definitions have been crafted to capture it. Pope John Paul II offers one of the broadest: culture is the realm of the human as such. Father Avery Dulles, SJ gives more details:

> By a culture we normally understand a system of meanings and values, historically transmitted, embodied in symbols, and instilled into the members of a sociological group so that they are spontaneously inclined to feel, think, judge and behave in certain characteristic ways.[1]

Cultural analysis includes, therefore, a way of uncovering the meanings and values which are implicit in a people's behavior; a sense of the historical influences in a society; and a notion of how cultures interact, develop and are transmitted.

*Anthropology*

From cultural anthropology, the evangelizer learns methods of questioning which tease out meanings and values hidden in collective behavior.[2] Take, for example, a family picnic on the Fourth of July. A cultural anthropologist preparing to evangelize American picnickers begins by asking *who* they are (people related by blood and marriage), *what* they are doing (eating hot dogs, playing a ball game, talking), *when* they are doing it (on a summer day), *where* they are doing it (in the open air), *how* they are doing it (some cooking, some cleaning, some organizing games, but all cooperating), and *what kind* of activity this picnic really is (a family coming together to relax in the context of a larger civic holiday).

Each of these questions enables the evangelizer to know the forms by which a culture organizes itself, but the more important question remains to be asked: *Why* is the family celebrating? On one level, "why" is answered functionally: the family eats hot dogs in order to satisfy their hunger without preparing an elaborate meal; the family plays games in order to exercise; the family spends time together because they love each other. If the evangelizer continues to question why a whole nation engages in this kind of behavior on the fourth day of the month of July each year, a deeper level of meaning unfolds. A story of the fourth of July in the year 1776 is told; bits of multi-colored bunting are displayed and the evangelizer recognizes the flag of the country; hot dogs are not just energy sources but "typical" food of the country; the ball game turns out to be the country's national pastime. Participating in the event is a way of reaffirming values—national independence and personal freedom— and the event itself is a symbol of the family's participation in the life and purposes of the nation. The family picnic, in short, displays meanings and values which define the cultural context. Questions should continue to be pressed until the evangelizer recognizes an order of importance among the meanings and values discovered. This hierarchy explains a culture's distinctive character and will indicate how the evangelizer might foster the culture's dialogue with faith.

*History*

Observation and questioning uncover meanings and values, but study of a group's history explains why a culture transmits only certain meanings and cherishes particular values more than others. In the case of the United States, our culture's historical roots are traced to the pilgrims and English Puritan dissenters; to the Deists of the American enlightenment; to the founders of the republic, who created the forms of American democracy; and to the activists and pragmatists of the last three and a half centuries, whose work generated economic growth and the cult of successful results. Each of these strains, sometimes existing in the same historical personage, has interacted with the others to create the distinctive system of values and meanings which is American culture.

No matter what our culture's roots, we live now in a society no longer integrated by religious faith. Most Americans might believe in some sort of God, but faith is compartmentalized, set apart, unrelated to much of contemporary experience and life. Of the historical shapers of culture in this country, Puritanism would seem to have most clearly lost ground. Yet attitudes and values can perdure even when separated from the historical movements which gave them birth. America is different from other modern, secularized societies because it is a secularized Puritan society rather than a culture which has replaced the Puritan ethos with something else.[3]

To speak of Puritan attitudes and habits, meanings and values surviving in a modern society may seem strange, but the conflict can hide a deeper continuity. The Puritan conversion narratives of colonial Massachusetts show a pattern of behavior which remains familiar today.[4] In Puritan New England, proof of internal conversion to Christ was required to be admitted to church membership, so the candidate testified before the local congregation's representatives to the workings of grace in his or her soul. The congregation, for its part, had to listen carefully and respectfully to this recital of personal experience. Attention to feelings was of particular importance in establishing one's right to belong to the local church. Personal experience and the public recital of it thus became the rhetoric of American identity. Americans claim a right to belong by reason of a personal experience which they choose to disclose and which demands the respect of others. Phenomena as diverse as civil rights and client-centered therapies find legitimation in this cultural pattern.

Beyond a local congregation, Puritans belonged to the New Israel, the kingdom of God in America. The Puritan sabbath was a symbol of Christ's entry into his Father's kingdom after the work of redemption; and weekly sabbath observance made the American Puritan community the church in new and purified form, without the baggage of Catholic history which encumbered even Protestant lands in once-Catholic Europe. The United States has no medieval memories; America was a new dispensation. Here the kingdom of God was at hand, and its coming was presaged in a series of revivals, beginning with the great awakening of the 1740s and renewed periodically to this day.

When the nation's purpose became the spread of democracy rather than the spread of the gospel, Americans still thought of their land as a light to other nations and themselves as people with a mission. American public discourse remains millennialist. Puritan eschatology is echoed in predictions of nuclear holocaust or ecological disaster. The end is always near, and we must change our ways. Even if we no longer believe in an angry God, a wounded earth will punish us.

The secularization of Puritan rhetoric and behavior began early. Alexis de Tocqueville, who visited the United States early in the nineteenth century to see how democratic political structures influenced character development, noted that Americans were "individualists."[5] Is this a help or hindrance to the Catholic evangelizer? Like many cultural phenomena, it is evangelically ambiguous. To the extent it means that each person is regarded as unique and even sacred, individualism is fertile soil for planting the faith. To the extent it means that persons are valuable because they have experienced justification, whether by grace of the Puritan God or, more recently, by declaring themselves estimable, individualism is an unreliable base for Catholic ecclesial communion, whatever merits it might possess as a foundation for civic life.[6]

De Tocqueville's complement to individualism was something else he discovered in America: the voluntary association. This bridged the gap between self and society. American individuals do not isolate themselves. They form and join groups for social purposes, just as Puritan believers, individually converted, joined the local congregation. Voluntary associations conform also to the enlightenment vision of rational individuals forming a social contract which respects the rights of each while providing common security and the means for all to advance economically and politically. Americans belong: to the Red Cross, Greenpeace, the Moose and the Elks, the ACLU, Holy Name Societies, mutual funds, Gay Pride movements, the volunteer army. Americans have a right to belong, provided only that they want to and that they have had the experience which the rules demand for membership. Once in, of course, members have the right to change the rules.

*The Catholic Church in America*

This deeply ingrained pattern of individualism and voluntary association is an inadequate analogue for the Catholic Church's self-understanding as an hierarchical and participatory communion. American culture understands two ways of being religious: liberal and evangelical. How do these differ? To oversimplify to the point of distortion, liberal religion treats God as an ideal, a goal expressing all that is best in human experience, while the real agents of change in the world are human persons. Religious language is important poetry, agnostic about who God is but expressive of our experience of wholeness. The traditional sacraments are signs of our own interior dispositions and intentions. Worship might be structured, but, at its heart, religion is ethical and the social agenda central.

By contrast, and again to indulge in gross simplification, evangelicals have a keen sense of God's agency. God is real, independent, powerful, active. They know God in their emotional experience at prayer and from the reading of God's word. Religious language, at least among fundamentalists, is literal, and the Bible is read much like a newspaper. Sacraments are signs of the interior faith given us before we receive them. The social agenda tends to be peripheral, because God will change things at the beginning of the millennium or at the apocalyptic rapture or at some other moment we can only wait for.

This split in the American Calvinist religious heritage occurred in the last century, during the controversies over Darwin's theory of the evolution of species and the legitimacy of historical-critical approaches to Bible study. Some denominational lines were redrawn on the basis of liberal and evangelical tendencies. Left out of each is the Catholic sense of the church as mediator of God's life and teacher of God's truth, the church as a body one is joined to in order to be converted.

American Catholics who no longer belong to subcultures which buttressed Catholic identity while permitting interaction with society in general now have to discover and foster in American culture itself the resources they need to express their faith. If these resources are only ambiguously there, American Catholics who have remained somewhat distant from the dominant culture naturally hesitate over their relationship to it.

### Minorities as Subcultures

Among the most visible minority groups in the United States today, four are founded on a relationship to faith different from that found in the dominant culture. How these groups relate to both culture and church might offer insights to American Catholics intent on evangelizing American culture.

## Hispanics

U.S. Hispanics inherit a culture formed in dialogue with the Catholic faith on the Iberian Peninsula and re-formed in Latin America during the past five hundred years. The Hispanic Catholic bishops have described their people's cultural uniqueness as a second *mestiza* tradition. The original mixture of Spanish and Indian cultures is now a mixture of Hispanic and U.S. values. The values mentioned by the bishops, however, are fairly universal: love of family and community, love for life itself, and respect for each person. These values are integrated through Catholic faith and, especially, through love for the Blessed Virgin Mary. Lists of values evoke cultural loyalties, but the integration presents the distinctive pattern of values and meanings in which the genius of a culture becomes clear.

Hispanics have developed pastoral plans from national *Encuentros* in 1972, 1977 and 1985. With sure pastoral insight, the U.S. Hispanic bishops have placed the faith-culture dialogue at the center of reevangelization. They have pointed out groups among Hispanic Americans in need of pastoral attention: young people, those susceptible to pressure from religious sects, those exploited by unjust conditions of employment and immigration difficulties. The development of vocations to church leadership is a priority, and the traditional devotions of Hispanic Catholicism must now be complemented by love of scripture in a country whose believing Protestants have shown us all what it means to reverence the Bible. The emphasis in the pastoral plans is on preserving and deepening the faith of a people traditionally Catholic; there is little on how Hispanic Catholics might evangelize U.S. culture.

## Blacks

African-American and other black Americans are also, for the most part, baptized Christians. Their original African cultures have been enriched here by Protestant faith. Black Catholics, through the National Office for Black Catholics (NOBC) and the letters of the African-American Catholic bishops, are continuing a series of reflections on their experience begun with Negro Catholic Congresses from 1889 to 1894 and meetings of the Federated Colored Catholics from 1914 to 1935. Both the Secretariat for Black Catholics in Washington and the NOBC responded to the 1974 Roman Synod on evangelization by reminding American Catholics that the church is the object of evangelization as well as the subject evangelizing, since the U.S. church has not been free of the racism which afflicts the general culture. Where Hispanics talk of the church, blacks more often talk of the gospel; the goal of evangelization is a fusion of gospel truth and black cultural experience.

Like Hispanics, African-American and other black Catholics want to see Catholic leaders from their ranks and want responsibility for the church's mission shared with lay people. Catholic schools in African-American neighborhoods are both means of advancement and a way to deepen Catholic identification with black culture. This culture's relation to Protestantism, analogous to Hispanic culture's relation to Catholicism, leads some African-American Catholics to ask that styles of worship and preaching incorporate elements from the black Protestant heritage. Finally, no program for evangelizing among African-Americans fails to mention the paramount importance of the church's continuing aid in the struggle for racial justice in the United States.

### Asians

Americans of Asian background are, with the exception of Filipinos, culturally non-Christian. Their traditional cultures developed in relation to Buddhism, Confucianism, Shintoism, Hinduism or Islam. Those who are now Catholic in faith are also Buddhist or Hindu or Confucian in culture, living in a secularized society rooted in Calvinist Christianity. What insights for evangelizing culture might the complex faith-culture dialogue which is their inner life offer other Catholics? This is still to be discovered, since little has been written about evangelization among Asians in this country. American interfaith dialogue has been mostly with Jewish believers rather than with the Hindus, Buddhists and Muslims engaged by Catholic bishops in Asia itself. A point of entry for the church into Asian-American experience is, of course, concern for social justice.

### Native Peoples

Concern for social justice is also a way into the experience of the first Asian peoples to settle here, the North American Indians or native pre-Americans. While few in number and culturally diverse among themselves, the native peoples make unique collective claims on all Americans. Their cultures express a religious relationship to the land from which they have now been largely dispossessed. The current rise of ecological consciousness among the U.S. cultural elite makes American Indian religion fashionable; but among non-Indians there is little evidence of submission to religious demands which developed in a still untamed natural environment.

Catholics among American native peoples ask for religious leaders from their number. They are also incorporating into Catholic liturgy elements from pre-Christian worship; and every document from the annual Tekakwitha Conferences and other pastoral meetings speaks of restoring their collective self-respect with the cooperation of the church.


## WHAT IS TO BE DONE?

When American Catholics consider the church in their society, they usually speak of tensions between faith and culture as problems in constitutional law or as clashes of values in a pluralistic society. When U.S. bishops speak of American culture, they sometimes list values which Americans believe are particularly their own: equality, freedom, openness, participation in decision making, communication. These are values of a popular liberal culture, and defenders of American culture point out that the United States has played a providential role in the history of human liberty. It is unfair to reduce American culture to consumerism and hedonism, selfish individualism, and the history of oppression of minority groups. These vices, like American virtues, are also part of larger historical developments. Tabulating collective strengths and weaknesses, virtues and vices, successes and failures can, however, distract from the more fundamental question: Does this culture now provide a sound context for human life or does it stifle the human spirit?

In a talk to U.S. religious in San Francisco during his 1987 visit, Pope John Paul II said that an evangelizer of culture brings out evils only to show the power of God's word to heal and uplift, to unify and bind with love. A program for evangelizing American culture, therefore, begins, continues and ends with love for the people and their culture. The people whom God calls to form Christ's body in a way that respects the best in their heritage are constantly in an evangelizer's prayers. Prayer itself, an activity with no immediately productive goal, evangelizes culture by introducing a rhythm which opens daily life to the transcendent.

In a society often driven by short-term goals, the inner discipline needed to live prayerfully creates an alternative sense of time.

Second, the evangelizer of culture will look for the places where significant conversations take place. A culture is a communications network; the gospel is a message. The evangelizer needs to be present in those places where the messages which form the culture are created and transmitted.

Third, American Catholics need to enlarge their culture's appreciation of human reason. Reason is diminished when it is reduced to calculating means for achieving individual ends. A shriveled intellect cannot insist on truthfulness in public life and fails to recognize its natural ability to seek a transcendent God.

Fourth, because the dominant culture in the U.S. privileges voluntary relationships to the detriment of others, the evangelizer works to strengthen relations which are given rather than chosen: family, race, linguistic group, the land and nation itself as our home rather than willed messianic project. Within the context of these relationships, the church as gift, as ecclesial communion with her source of life in the love of Father, Son and Spirit, becomes culturally possible. American culture reduces the church to a voluntary association and treats the nation itself the same way. American cultural myths, by reason of our history, are inevitably voluntaristic. We are a people of choice rather than of blood. One can choose to become American in a way that one cannot become Japanese, Navajo or Arab. The melting pot myth has enabled the United States to welcome almost anyone and everyone, at least in principle; and its inclusivity can serve the gospel's universalism, as Pope John Paul II has pointed out. It cannot, however, be allowed to destroy the public legitimacy of non-voluntary relationships and communities. The Catholic evangelizer in the United States will cherish and strengthen the relationships that faith tells us we have no right to "un-choose."

Fifth, evangelizing American culture means purifying our sense of mission. Catholics believe that groups play roles in salvation history; but a collective vocation within God's call to everyone is different from the Puritans' notion of their covenant with the Lord. Transforming our national purpose in the light of God's plan for all peoples means listening to a source of truth not limited by American experience. Here again, our cultural resources fail us.

We have, in American culture, resources for reexpressing evangelical freedom. Freedom is our major cultural value, and even the church can talk about what it should mean. We have resources, too, for reexpressing evangelical justice, because justice is another cultural value. Even when we recognize the deficiencies of our theories of justice and our failure to practice it, justice remains a public imperative. The church can figure in conversations around it and help change institutions and structures. But there are no public resources in our culture for reexpressing evangelical truth, because religious truth is no longer a public virtue. Any truth not immediately verifiable in observation or through the methodologies of the hard sciences becomes private opinion. It enters the public realm under the rubric of personal expression, a value which is the subject of arbitration but not of intellectual research. The public authority, the government, while it must protect freedom and foster justice, cannot teach. But the church can; and this claim to teach the truth is truly counter-cultural. It explains why anti-Catholicism is a socially and intellectually respectable prejudice among much of the cultural elite in this country. Since the culture is too narrow for gospel truth, Catholic evangelizers want to enlarge it.

## A CIVILIZATION OF LOVE

Pope Paul VI preached a civilization of love, and Pope John Paul II speaks of a new Christian humanism. The popes are not calling for a "Catholic state" of any sort but for the creation of a culture which will be rich enough to provide means for expressing the Catholic faith in culturally distinctive fashion and resourceful enough to support the relationships of universal and local Catholic ecclesial communion. An evangelized culture will offer no special favors to the Catholic Church; but it will privilege the human person in ways that American culture presently cannot.

Creating a culture which provides a more evangelically authentic environment for daily life in the United States is less a program with clearly defined stages than a movement of gradual growth. Cultural change is slow; but it can be steady if our purpose is clear and our nerves are strong. Evangelizers need a broad vision and strength for the long haul. Evangelizing culture relies on deep insight into the mysteries of our faith and keen vision for understanding the bases of our culture. Evangelizing culture is, finally, a contemplative activity. The dialogue between Catholic faith and American culture takes place in the media, in the schools and the marketplace, and in the public square; but it begins in the heart of every American Catholic who loves both faith and country.

## NOTES

1.  Avery Dulles, SJ, *The Catholicity of the Church* (Oxford, 1958), 175.
2.  Louis J. Luzbetak, SVD, *The Church and Cultures: New Perspectives in Missiological Anthropology* (Maryknoll: Orbis, 1988), 223–91.
3.  Marcello de Carvalho Azevedo, SJ, *Inculturation and the Challenges of Modernity* (Rome: Gregorian University Press, 1982). Father Azevedo, a Brazilian Jesuit, explores the relations between Catholic faith and modern culture. While American modernity is influenced by our Puritan heritage, it is also the product of the dynamics of capitalist economic development. A capitalist economy can flourish in different political systems, but it has natural affinity for the social contract theories associated with classical liberalism. In this situation, which is the case in the United States, the model for all relations easily becomes the commercial contract.
4.  William A. Dyrness, *How Does America Hear the Gospel?* (Grand Rapids: Eerdmans, 1989), 62–64 and 84–86.
5.  Alexis de Tocqueville's *Democracy in America* is the starting point for an influential cultural critique by a group under the direction of sociologist Robert N. Bellah, *Habits of the Heart: Individualism and Commitment in American Life* (Harper and Row, 1986).
6.  While this article traces individualism back to Puritan religious experience, its civil counterpart is usually attributed to the political theories of English philosopher John Locke (1632–1704). Locke retained a sense of natural law which the American founders used to justify their rejection of the social contract with the British Crown. As our legal system becomes more positivistic and our society more pluralistic, Locke's defense of the natural rights of individuals becomes less influential and the philosophy of Thomas Hobbes (1588–1677) more so. Hobbes taught that rights are reducible to force and government acts primarily as a referee among competing interests.

## DISCUSSION QUESTIONS

1. In a society once influenced by Christian faith, whether Protestant or Catholic, remnants of religiosity sometimes innoculate against accepting and living the faith now. How do you present the gospel anew to people who reject its prior forms of expression?

2. What or who are the most important agents of cultural change in the United States today, and how might they be influenced by the gospel?

3. When American Catholics think of themselves as church, what images come to mind? Do they picture themselves as body, family, bride, living temple, or as organization, association, religious club?

4.  How can the Catholic Church in the U.S. become a true home for minority groups?


## FOR FURTHER READING

Hervé Carrier, SJ. *Gospel Message and Human Cultures from Leo XIII to John Paul II.* Pittsburgh: Duquesne University Press, 1989. A systematic arrangement and explanation of the modern papacy's teaching on the dialogue between culture and faith.

William A. Dyrness. *How Does America Hear the Gospel?* Grand Rapids: Eerdmans, 1989. A superb analysis of American culture and a critique of its contemporary religiosity from the standpoint of evangelical Christian faith.

Louis J. Luzbetak, SVD. *The Church and Cultures: New Perspectives in Missiological Anthropology.* Maryknoll: Orbis, 1988. A history of Christian missions and mission theology which uses insights from cultural anthropology to suggest methods for evangelizing.

Peter Schineller, SJ. *A Handbook on Inculturation.* Mahwah: Paulist Press, 1990. The author is a missionary in Africa who presents the central ideas on inculturation in clear and short chapters. He takes evangelical justice as the standard for judging the progress of evangelization.

# THE NEW CATHOLIC APOLOGETIC
## Frank DeSiano, CSP

My first formal introduction to apologetics occurred at the age of eighteen. It was a college course for freshmen. I remember the textbook: about one and a half inches thick with a heavy green cloth cover. The type was very neat: crisp, clean letters formed into sentences of bolder and lighter print.

The bolder print carried the argument; the lighter print, in an extended paragraph form, carried all the supporting information that backed up the argument.

There it was, page by page, all in one handy book: a way to "prove" the truth of the Catholic faith.

I hardly remember the contents of the book, but I remember the gist. How religion was based on truth. How truth was connected to God. How God backed up truth with divine authority. How this divine authority had become revealed in history, then in Jesus, then in the apostles. Of course, the apostles left writings which could be proved to be authentic, honest and trustworthy, and a church which could authentically and honestly interpret those writings, gaining for itself a divine trustworthiness.

I doubt I was the only college freshman being exposed to this form of religious certainty and verification. I'm sure thousands of other Catholics were similarly exposed. This has begotten, for sure, in many people a mind-set about religion (and true religion) and a longing for the neat certainties that apologetics spawned in young, restless minds. At the same time, it surely begot an opposite mind-set of suspicion and doubt. For if the mind could be employed to "prove," could it not also be employed to "disprove"? Could not one person's argument be another person's empty rationality? Could not someone's decisive syllogism be, for someone else, a crafty trick?

## USES OF APOLOGETICS

It would do us well to be aware, at the outset, of the many uses to which "apologetics" has been put, because it is not one thing, nor even one set of attitudes. Rather, the term "apologetics" has covered a variety of religious thinking and strategies. This variety stands us modern Catholics in good stead: it helps us know that new directions and approaches are always possible.

One obvious use of apologetics has been the defense of faith or, more particularly, of the church. To show that the faith or the Christian community has been unjustly attacked or portrayed is to defend it from false innuendo and outright slander.

Another use of apologetics is the exposition of the weakness of another opposing position. St. Iraeneus served as an effective apologist against different kinds of Gnostic groups. He could ridicule their positions; he could show the absurdities of their thinking in sometimes humorous passages.

Yet another use of apologetics is to deal with another's position as a reason to expose the cogency of Catholic faith. A master at this was St. Thomas Aquinas whose *Summa Contra Gentiles* exposed several lines of then current Moslem thought, all the while magisterially exposing the lines of Catholic thought. It might be difficult to distinguish this apologetical task from other tasks that theology undertakes.

Apologetics can also be the way new thought is absorbed by Christians. The second century Origen, the thirteenth century Aquinas, the seventeenth century Pascal, and the twentieth century Küng were all, in their apologetics, doing the Christian church a great favor by showing how new ways of thinking could have a place in Christian life and even further it.

Finally, apologetics can be the way people are invited to consider faith. Because apologetics makes use of human reasoning and human longing, it can seek to evoke from the experience of people (from their thinking and longing) a way of considering the Christian life. John Henry Newman's work not only defends the faith but subtly moves people from their positions to consideration of the Catholic faith.

## A CLEAR CHOICE

This simplified list of the various uses of apologetics is sufficient to bring out some of the complex dynamics that lie behind this religious activity. For much of Christian history, apologetics has been a way to protect the Christian from the meanness, anger, deceit and onslaught of the enemy. Apologetics was the way Christians constructed the bulwarks lest its own purity be contaminated by some infidel or other. It was defensive. It denounced. It protected.

Yet, curiously, apologetics could also be the way in which Christian thought was opened up. Just knowing what the enemy was thinking at least got Christian thinkers to read something different. We are changed by the opponents we choose. But often it went beyond that: Christians were able to find sympathetic lines in the thought or attitudes of others. Those sympathetic lines created an openness, perhaps even a bonding, with the non-Christian. Apologetics, instead of defending and denouncing, could also dialogue.

In recent years we have not seen much apologetical material in Catholic or Christian circles. The word itself has had a bad reputation, carrying the stigma of a closed kind of defensiveness. Indeed, some people see apologetics as returning to forms of thought that defend and prove faith as in the "good old days." Reprint houses find gems from pre-Vatican II times and sell them to a populace that still thinks in pre-Vatican II terms. Catholics, attacked by certain Protestant groups, write tracts that prove and defend Catholic positions against these attackers.

This means that any contemporary apologist faces a clear choice: whether to construct bulwarks or to open windows. Whether to defend or to dialogue.

Of course, there are ways in which both functions can exist, in different ways, at the same time. One can smile as one defends; one can define as one dialogues. But the *fundamental* framework of apologetics today calls for a choice. If there will be any kind of new apologetics, what will be its purpose?

If the last quarter century of our experience has any validity, that purpose can only be to dialogue, to open windows, to invite and to share. That said, what would be elements of a new Catholic apologetic?

## A NEW APOLOGETIC

The very appearance in a book of a chapter titled "The New Catholic Apologetic" begs its own argument. I clearly presume that apologetics is an important religious function and that it is time for some new things to begin appearing under the aegis of this function. To renounce apologetics is to renounce, at the same time, the existence of others who do not accept our faith and the opportunities to begin sharing with them.

But if apologetics is a dimension of Christian life and if we should undertake it again, what would it be like? What would be new about it?

The remainder of this chapter deals with the question of "The New Catholic Apologetic" in three sections: (1) its uses; (2) its qualities; (3) an exploration.


## ITS USES

For all the centuries apologists have been defending the faith and attacking its enemies, it is probably a sobering question to ask: Who has been listening?

Do enemies of the church read the attacks of churchmen? I think Celsus was dead before Origen wrote against him! Do atheists, agnostics or other kinds of self-asserting infidels run out to Christian bookstores to buy books by believers? Do the heathen listen to arguments on Christian radio or seek correction by watching Christian television?

One of the main uses of apologetics traditionally has been to strengthen the faith of believers. And this is a major objective of the new Catholic apologetic.

Ask Catholics why they are Catholic. One will invariably see an open mouth, puzzled eyes, shrugged shoulders. "I was born that way," people will answer, as if it was a handicap or genetic limitation.

Modern Catholics have a complex legacy from the Second Vatican Council and a huge piece of that legacy was self-criticism and self-doubt. The church reformed itself. It looked at itself with complete thoroughness. It raised questions. It posed uncomfortable issues. It laid everything out on the table. And, in a real way, it is still doing that today.

The price of this, however, is high. It makes people pause. It makes them think twice before answering. It makes an answer go through a dozen qualifications and a dozen more generalizations. One sees so many sides to an argument, one ends up not seeing anything clearly or firmly.

Yet Catholics have even more reason to be proud of and celebrate their faith since the Second Vatican Council. The council clarified so much, put so much in context and perspective, and affirmed so broadly the heart of Catholic life that it's hard to realize the enormity of its contribution.

But Catholics have not absorbed this contribution in direct and personal ways. It has not become part of their conscious self-expression. They remember the clarity of the Baltimore Catechism and think that unless their faith is put in that kind of package, it must be weak and watered down.

A new apologetic would help Catholics say what their own contemporary faith experience is and the values that earn their daily adherence. A new apologetic would help Catholics rediscover what they already know: the reason for their faith. A new apologetic would help reap, in new pastoral ways, the fruits of an epochal historical period.

The second use of the new apologetic would be to dialogue with others in earnest. The new apologetic would choose the open, dynamic side of our apologetical tradition and exploit it for the purpose of sharing. This would also be the fruit of the Second Vatican Council, affirming its openness to modern culture even as it affirmed its difference from it.

Religion is always easier when there are enemies. Enemies help give us a clarity about our own faith. But the specter of powerful enemies can also give us the illusion of more certainty than we actually need. How much energy has gone into denouncing others rather than looking into our own hearts?

We Catholics know this because we are considered enemies by some. How do we feel when we are portrayed as worshipers of idols? Perpetrators of superstition? Part of an international political conspiracy? "Absurd," we say, "that anyone should believe this about us"? In fact, people believe this about us because it makes them feel more certain in their own position, just as we, in our centuries-long denunciation of Protestants, felt more secure in our positions.

Yet the list of enemies, after the Second Vatican Council, is much shorter. Acknowledging our differences with others, we no longer take those differences as a warrant to mistrust, attack, ridicule or undermine the sincere faith of others. We have identified ourselves as fellow pilgrims with Protestant and Orthodox Christians, as inheriters of a rich legacy from Judaism, as co-seekers of God with people of other faiths, and as brothers and sisters with all humanity in its quest for peace and justice.

So whom are we against? And what if we are *against* no one? Certainly there will be positions that Catholic Christians will always oppose and seek to correct. Even so, one of the clear legacies of the Second Vatican Council is to try to think and live our faith on the basis of its own integrity more than on the basis of its opposition to others. It's knowing what we are *for* that is far more essential than knowing whom we are *against*. It is learning to think out our faith in a pluralistic world that will contain Protestants, people of other religions and humanists—who certainly will not be disposed to hear from Catholics if the terms of that hearing are their own denunciation.

So the second use of apologetics, in addition to fortifying the faith of Catholics, is to foster dialogue with others, particularly with non-believers. To do this, it must seek a common language of the human heart and a public language of the marketplace. To do this, it must persuade by dialogue more than by decree.

The Second Vatican Council, along with the major development of theology in the twentieth century, has given Catholics wonderful tools to understand their faith and to offer that faith to others. The new Catholic apologetic would not only recognize this but utilize this as much as it could.

## ITS QUALITIES

If a new Catholic apologetic will emerge, it will have qualities that are of the same cloth as the religious revolution that was the Second Vatican Council as well as the whole global transformation that has marked the second half of the twentieth century. I propose the following as an initial list:

1. *The new Catholic apologetic will seek to communicate.*

A new apologetic must claim its rightful place. It is not dogma, not a special catechism, not systematic theology or liturgy. If it benefits those who are church members, it does so because it is *addressed to those who are not members.* Because of this, its purpose will not be to elaborate technical dogmas but to explicate basic positions in cogent, clear ways. So often we are sharing our inner, dogmatic language with people—and are surprised when these same people think that is all we are about. The new apologetic will be a form of communication with others, primarily concerned with what in their lives will enable them to take on our Catholic vision.

If it communicates, it will use many media. The days of the pamphlet are over! The world has become mostly literate; at the same time, the world is passing beyond literacy into a comfort with visual, aural and social forms that frequently pass on what words cannot. This may seem frightening to those who think of apologetics as a quest for dogmatic purity which carries a nuance that only many words can balance. Once apologetics is seen as a species distinct from dogma, however, one can begin to think of special ways this might happen: television, radio, computers, home gatherings, mass rallies, telephone, and so on.

If it communicates, it will communicate first things first. The Second Vatican Council has given us the concept of a hierarchy of truth.

Formerly, apologetics was concerned with defending what seemed distinct about Catholicism: Mary, the rosary, purgatory, the pope, indulgences, etc. This, in turn, overloaded those elements because we were trying to say what we were all about through them. As a result, it never got clearly said that we were a scriptural church, that Jesus was the center and source of our life, that the Holy Spirit empowers every religious moment, that our sharing at the Lord's table was crucial to our gathering. We never got to say what was most *important* about us clearly because we were so busy defending what was so *different* about us.

But now we can deal with first things first, laying out the rich heart of our faith so that people have a basic context for understanding us. From that context, they can begin to grasp what seems different, if not outlandish, to them.

### 2. *The new Catholic apologetic will be consistent.*

Once it is clear that we want to communicate what is at the heart of our faith with others, then the meaning of that faith will have to be seen at every step of our church's life.

This may seem like a tall order—who *really* can live the faith consistently? But reflection on our church, its teaching, its organization, its charity, its moral vision and fidelity yields a remarkable picture of just how much *we do* live consistently with our beliefs. The new Catholic apologetic will have to be attentive to this consistency and intolerant of its absence.

Once it is clear that we do want to deal with people authentically, any inauthenticity will obscure that goal. We cannot be saying one thing about ourselves to a wider public and signaling quite opposite things in our institutions, educational structures or theological journals.

If we would speak, that word must be coherent from our highest institutions to our smallest parishes, from our most elevated prelates to our humblest parishioners.

This means that our desire to dialogue with others entails an ongoing dialogue within ourselves. Dialogue, discussion, sharing, cherishing: if we would speak with one consistent voice, we must continue living one Catholic way of life. The desire to talk with others will force us to be more clearly disciples with and to each other, because, without this, consistency is impossible. Without this, we have little to say that will be ultimately convincing.

### 3. *The new Catholic apologetic will be cast in provisional terms.*

Catholic life has endured so long that we often confuse that endurance with the structures through which it has endured, particularly thought structures. Once something has been said, it seems like common sense to say it again, and again, and again.

But Catholic life is, as the Vatican Council has reiterated, pilgrim life. That means it is provisional life, with passing glances along the highway and bold dreams of a direction. When our image of ourselves was that of a "perfect society" (an image that was popularly misunderstood by many Catholics), we could imagine perfect statements coming out, honed in elegant Latin or shaped by a noble metaphysic.

But a pilgrim society, perfect or imperfect, keeps moving, keeps looking, keeps adjusting. This, indeed, is the only way we can live honestly in the modern world which seems capable of regularly rewriting itself.

If we seek to dialogue, then those to whom we speak become an inevitable part of the conversation. Their needs, questions, insights and frustrations force a constant readjustment of what we are trying to say. We should not be surprised about this; the New Testament is a marvelous record of just such adjustment, as Christians moved out from Jerusalem into a Gentile world.

Apologetics need not come up with perfect formulations and timeless phrases. Apologetics need only attend to the one to whom one is speaking.

### 4. *The new Catholic apologetic will be multi-layered.*

Part of dialoguing consistently, using modern forms of media, will call for new ways of communicating at every human level.

The personal experiences of Catholics, through which their faith has been appropriated, will be in some cases more "apologetic" than the most exquisitely drawn paragraph. Individual Catholics will have to learn to witness; tools will have to be created to help Catholics understand and express their own rich experience.

Parishes, and their smaller components, will be part of the apologetic venture. What happens in small groups in the homes of Catholics may communicate the faith in ways more open and accepting than the Information Centers of the past. How a community celebrates (welcomes, includes, praises, prays and commissions) may say more than the cleverest tome.

Dioceses, most of whom have organs of communication to facilitate the bishops' teaching role, will have to expand and diversify those organs if they want to communicate faith to people in a public and open way. Bishops will be as conscious about the implicit messages they give as they are about the wording of the explicit messages they disseminate through official letters. They will be challenged to speak freely, openly and directly. What would bishops sound like if they didn't speak the "ecclesiologese" they usually have to speak?

Diocesan conferences and larger church groupings, so conscious of the modern world, will need to develop ways to effectively share the core Catholic experience with that modern world.

5. *The new Catholic apologetic will use a public idiom.*

The last quality, implicit in all that has been outlined here, is that of public language or idiom. It needs to be developed and, given our Catholic heritage, there is no reason why it cannot be expertly developed.

The Catholic legacy is one of constantly matching our religious experience with the experiences of "secular" people. As a great church (and not a small sect), Catholicism has addressed cultures, one by one, through its history, absorbing the insights and phrasings of these cultures, employing their syntax and vocabulary.

To speak a public idiom is to risk entering the public arena with one's most precious treasures. It is to leave behind our "stained glass" versions of reality to accept the terms of those with whom we speak, struggling to see the divine in their lives and inviting them to see the divine in their own experience. And that *is* risky.

But apologetics has always been something of a dangerous kind of work (I'm not just thinking of Hans Küng). The apologist is straining Catholic categories even as he or she works, seeing new possibilities of explaining and persuading, opening new directions of exploration. Yet such risks have gained for the church its achievement: the vitality of faith in ever new forms.


AN EXPLORATION


The best kind of concluding section for this article would be an exploration of what a new apologetic might sound like. It will take the form of a letter to a friend. Much of it might not sound new—it shouldn't! Our problem in recent decades has been that we've been talking to ourselves, and talking better, but not talking as effectively to others. If we could begin the process of sharing our riches with others, how much more would we appreciate those riches ourselves?

Dear Tom,
    I know you think I'm crazy to be a believer, but I'm not so sure you aren't one yourself! No, I'm not patronizing you, good friend, but really describing you—the way you instinctually think of everyone else before yourself, the way you evaluate your decisions, the way you

speak what is in your heart with striking openness, the way you've supported me in my most difficult moments.

I know you'll call this "being good natured," but, really, why do you do it? Millions of people survive quite nicely without such good natures; human nature, which might be transformed marvelously if everyone were like you, seems to sustain the most wretched kinds of people in every generation.

You are the way you are, Tom, because of the values you hold: the importance of every human life, the absoluteness of love and justice, the crucial quality of our human dreams. You call that "humanism"—I call it more! I call it faith, Tom, because, if you peel away all your ideas, if you try to get right at the rock bottom of your heart, you will find there a ground so solid, so undeniable, that it is nothing less than *something absolute*. Something real, that always is, that always has been, that calls and challenges, that bestows values, that says "love" comes before "hate" and "truth" before lies. That's in your heart, Tom, and that's very close to God.

At least it's close to the God I believe in—not that there is more than one! You'll say that I've been contaminated by my Catholic upbringing through coming to see everything in terms of Jesus. You'll say: "What about the millions that don't know Jesus, the good people of other religions—Jewish people, Hindus, Buddhists and, of course, humanists?" And I'll say that I'm no more contaminated by being Catholic than you are by your fear of being Catholic or religious! I won't take anyone's experience away, Tom, whatever his or her culture or background. But don't take away mine or ours.

I'm not talking dogma here, Tom. But I *am* talking about experience, starting with the experience of Jesus, this prophet who walked ancient Israel with such a clarity of vision, such intensity, such honesty that every word of his seems to illumine life. Really, Tom, can you read the New Testament and not be moved by the sheer spiritual vision of this man? It's impossible *not* to be contaminated—that's why he's so compelling.

But never more so than in his death and resurrection. I don't know about you, Tom, but unless someone deals with death I don't think he or she has much to say. But no one has dealt with death as has Jesus: he takes it for real, he knows the emptiness at the center of our souls, and he cries the cries I'm afraid to cry.

Is it silly to believe he has risen? You've been in love, Tom, and you know how you want love to endure forever. Why is eternal life so puzzling to you?

Or are you afraid of something more immediate than eternal life? Are you—sorry if I'm getting a bit brutal here—afraid of the witness of this present life, the witness of believers? People who have given their lives for others without flinching. Thinkers who have looked into the gravest questions with trust. Searchers who have opened their souls to the deepest experiences of the heart. Prophets who have denounced social evils without anything to gain for themselves.

I'm a Catholic, Tom, because the church has begotten people like this in every generation. And from every walk of life. And every economic bracket.

I don't like "tribal" religion any more than you; and I know Catholics can seem tribal at times—am I less ashamed of our programs and prejudices than you? But in our heart, in our gut, in our very spirituality, from Jesus himself, we are all one, all humanity, called to unite, to be at peace, to experience justice, to be what Jesus called "the kingdom" forever. And maybe we'll have to wait for a future age for this to be accomplished. But I see it happening all the time, Tom, in parishes, discussion groups, prayer groups, in ordinary people. People I know at work or people I know at the club.

Tom, I'm going to stop now because you'll feel I'm persecuting you again. But write me, write me back; I want to hear from you! You make me think better and help me understand myself. I'm not going to hound you. I just have this feeling that, if I give you enough time, you'll see why I believe and you'll ask to join the church yourself. And if you do, it won't get in the way of our friendship at all! I think we'll be better friends, even if we don't have religion to toss back and forth.

Tom, my regards to your family and to Mary, who, I presume, is still your favorite girl! I'm always praying for you and I know that you, in your way, are praying too.

Your friend . . .

## DISCUSSION QUESTIONS

1. What practical uses do you see for apologetics?

2. What are situations in which you have had to explain or defend your faith?

3. Would a new apologetic help you invite people to the Catholic Church?

4. When people ask you why you believe, what do you say?

## FOR FURTHER READING

Avery Dulles. *A History of Apologetics*. New York: Corpus, 1971.
Hans Küng. *On Being a Christian*. New York: Image, 1976.
———. *Does God Exist?* New York: Vantage, 1981.
Richard Rohr and Joseph Martos. *Why Be Catholic?* Cincinnati: St. Anthony Messenger Press, 1989.

# II

# New Strategies

# THE EMERGING ROLE OF THE LAITY
Peter Coughlan

## OPEN THE DOORS TO CHRIST!

"Do not be afraid! Open, indeed, open wide the doors to Christ!"

With that impassioned cry to all peoples and nations, Pope John Paul II inaugurated his pastoral ministry as supreme shepherd of the church. From the top of the steps in St. Peter's Square, the words of the newly installed successor of Peter the apostle were carried by radio and television around the world. "Open to Christ's saving power the confines of states and systems political and economic, as well as the vast fields of culture, civilization and development. . . . With humility and trust I beg and implore you, allow Christ to speak to the person in you. Only he has the words of life, yes, eternal life."

Those words constitute an ever-recurring theme of John Paul II's pontificate. They express its heart: the missionary, the evangelizing energy that pulses constantly through it and which is seen most clearly of all in the apostolic journeys that characterize his papacy.

The exact same words lie at the center of the longest document to date to have been published by John Paul, namely "Christifideles Laici," the apostolic exhortation written to implement the 1987 synod on the vocation and mission of the Christian faithful. Before, however, considering the relation of that document to evangelization—the main focus of this essay—let us look back for a moment at the events upon which it builds.

## WHAT'S IN A NAME?

John Paul was the name chosen by both Albino Luciano of Venice and Karol Wojtyla of Krakow on their election to the papacy. Their choice was a commitment and a program.

Pope John XXIII had called the Second Vatican Council and set it on its way with the first session in 1962. Paul VI saw it through three more important sessions before presiding over its conclusion in 1965. He then dedicated the rest of his life to implementing its constitutions, decrees and declarations. The choice of the name John Paul by their successors was a clear declaration of intent. It was a commitment to continue in the spirit of the council and to make its implementation their program.

## THE COUNCIL AND MISSION

The Second Vatican Council decided to begin its most important document, the "Dogmatic Constitution on the Church," by contemplating the church as mystery. This was of the utmost importance. If it had begun by considering the external, visible aspect—the church as institution—there would have been the danger of seeing mission as something peripheral, rather than central. "The missions" are often thought of as far away and the same can happen to the notion of mission itself.

In its first chapter, however, the council document places the church in the context of the mystery of "the utterly free and mysterious decree of the eternal Father's wisdom and goodness" by which he created all that is and destined men and women to "a participation in his own divine life." The mission of the Son and the sending of the Spirit are seen as the events by which the church is born and given life. She is seen as "the universal sacrament of salvation." At the end of chapter 2 on the church as people of God we find a clear proclamation of mission as central to the life of the community inaugurated by Christ: "Just as the Son was sent by the Father, so too he sent the apostles . . . the obligation of spreading the faith is imposed on every disciple of Christ, according to his or her ability."

It was on this basis that the council's "Decree on the Church's Missionary Activity" firmly asserted: "The pilgrim church is missionary by her very nature. For it is from the mission of the Son and the mission of the Holy Spirit that she takes her origin, in accordance with the decree of God the Father." It was that insight that later was constitutive of one of the greatest documents of Paul VI's pontificate, "On Evangelization in the Modern World" (EMW), the text that the present volume recalls and celebrates. Given the focus of this essay, it is above all the fact that this mission belongs to all the baptized, to all the church, that I wish to signal.

## THE SYNOD ON EVANGELIZATION

In choosing the name of the apostle to the Gentiles, Paul VI deliberately gave a strongly missionary imprint to his future service of the universal church. In his first encyclical letter he spoke of "the clear awareness of a mission which transcends the church, of a message to be spread. It is the duty of evangelization. It is the missionary mandate. It is the apostolic commission."

Note the reference to "evangelization" here. A phenomenon of the post-conciliar years is the rapidity with which the word evangelization has come to be understood as a synonym for the mission of the church itself. In this regard the 1974 synod on evangelization and the apostolic exhortation that followed it had a decisive effect.

The 1974 synod opened with two major sections, the first a sharing of experiences introduced by five bishops from the various continents, the second a theological reflection that sought to relate and integrate these different experiences. The person asked by Paul VI to present this second part was Cardinal Wojtyla of Krakow. In the lengthy text of the Polish cardinal one can recognize themes he was to stress once he became pope.

As a point of historical interest, the first speaker to follow that presentation was Bishop, now Cardinal, Tomasek of Czechoslovakia. Who could have guessed on that October day of 1974 that sixteen years later, with the Berlin Wall down and possible doors to Christ opening up across eastern Europe, these same two would be able to stand side by side in Prague and call openly, in a country where repression of the church had been particularly severe, for a new evangelization of Europe, east and west?

## TOWARD THE YEAR 2000

In Lent 1976, a matter of months after the publication of "On Evangelization in the Modern World," Paul VI asked Cardinal Wojtyla to give the annual retreat at the Vatican. "Coinciding with the end of the 1975 Holy Year," said the cardinal in his retreat, "we have entered into the last twenty-five years of the second millennium after Christ, a new advent of the church and of humanity." Faced with the challenges and temptations of this moment in history, "We have been given a sign precisely for this time: Christ, a 'sign of contradiction' (Lk 2:34) and the woman clothed with the sun: 'A great sign in the heavens' (Rev 12:1)."

A decade later, John Paul II inaugurated the second universal Marian Year in the history of the church as an Advent pilgrimage—to use the words of his encyclical "Redemptoris Mater" ("Mother of the Redeemer")—toward the Great Jubilee or Holy Year of the two thousand years since the incarnation of the Son of God. As John Paul II emphasized in his encyclical on the Holy Spirit, "Dominum et vivificantem," what was accomplished by the power of the Holy Spirit "in the fullness of time" can only through the Spirit's power now emerge from the memory of the church and be made present in the new phase of human history on earth: the year 2000 from the birth of Christ.

The contemplation of this date brings John Paul II repeatedly to stress the urgency of evangelization and of reevangelization. In an important address to a group of bishops from the United States in the course of their "ad limina" visit in 1988, the pope declared: "What I wish to do today is to leave with you and with the whole church in America a vision of the millennium as a pastoral initiative, an ecclesial event, a response of faith to the God who 'so loved the world that he gave his only Son' (Jn 3:16). This vision must be captured by the whole church in the United States and expressed in each diocese, each parish, each community. All the institutions in the church must be challenged by this spiritual event. The church's fidelity to Christ is at stake in the way she will proclaim the incarnation and the redemption, in the way she will celebrate, interiorly and publicly, the most important anniversary that humanity has ever known."

The essence of the pope's concern, as expressed in his encyclical on the Holy Spirit, is that the church's entire life—"as will appear in the great Jubilee"—means going to meet the invisible God, the hidden God: a meeting with the Spirit "who gives life." As the year 2000 since the birth of Christ draws near, he wrote, it is a question of ensuring that an ever greater number of people may fully find themselves through a sincere gift of self.


## A NEW EVANGELIZATION

In 1983, speaking to a group of Latin American bishops gathered in Port au Prince, Haiti, the pope called for a new evangelization, an "evangelization new in its ardor, in its methods and in its expression." In his address in Santo Domingo a year later, John Paul declared: "I want to inaugurate this great novena of years [in preparation for the fifth cen-

tenary of the first evangelization of the Americas] to be a new evangelization, an extensive mission for Latin America, an intense spiritual mobili-
zation." He added that this included an ever more aware sacramental
practice, oriented toward mobilizing the sanctifying and apostolic
dynamism which is proper to baptism—an implicit reference to the
dynamic role of the laity in this evangelization. Since 1984 the various
aspects of this call to a new evangelization, involving all the baptized,
has been a constant refrain in his apostolic journeys throughout the
Americas.

In Europe, too, the call for a new or renewed evangelization has
been central. In October 1985, the sixth symposium of European bishops took as its theme "Secularization and Evangelization in Europe Today." Many of the themes so prominent in the exhortation on evangelization were evident at that symposium ten years later. There were,
however, particular emphases reflecting the needs of the moment and
the place. For example, many stressed the primacy of the witness of
Christian life: Before we evangelize by what we say, we evangelize by what
we are. "The signs which accompany the word," observed Cardinal
Hume, president at that time of the Council of European Episcopal
Conferences, "are often the key to effective evangelization." In the continent which contributed so much to disunity among Christians, it was
recognized that European Christians should take a lead in the recovery
of Christian unity. This unity is of vital importance if Christians are to be
able to evangelize effectively.

In his address at the conclusion of the 1985 symposium, the pope
emphasized two points that are important in our consideration of the
"new evangelization."

He stated firmly that the most secure reference point for all contemporary evangelization must remain the Second Vatican Council: "The
Spirit of God has spoken to the church today and his voice echoed in the
Second Vatican Council." He added that the council remains the foundation and inspiration for the gigantic task of bringing the gospel to the
world of today.

Secondly, in urging that the church must always strive to "give soul
to modern society," not by imposing itself from the outside and from
above but by inserting itself and growing outward from within, the pope
offered a challenge to each and every one of the baptized: "We need
heralds of the gospel who are experts in humanity, who know the depths
of the human heart, who can share the joys and the hopes, the agonies
and distress of people today but who are at the same time contemplatives
who have fallen in love with God. For this we need the saints of today."

## GOD CALLS EACH BY NAME

The profound and beautiful words just quoted take us directly into the themes of the apostolic exhortation that followed the synod on the lay faithful. Each and every one of the baptized, as "Christifideles Laici" (CFL) emphasizes, is called to be a herald of the gospel.

I can think of no other papal document, or even any council document for that matter, where the personal and individual call by God to each of the baptized is so vividly and repeatedly underlined as in "Christifideles Laici." "From eternity God has thought of us and loved us as individuals. Every one of us he calls by name . . ." (CFL, n. 58). The text adds that this eternal plan of God is revealed to us in a concrete way through the moments and events of our personal life-story.

One of the key images of "Christifideles Laici" is the vineyard parable of the gospel of Matthew, chapter 20. This same image is intimately connected with the evangelization theme that runs throughout the document. The world is seen as an immense vineyard that must be transformed according to the plan of God in view of the definitive coming of the kingdom of God. The words of the parable, "you go into my vineyard too," are seen as the call of the Lord Jesus to all Christians, both men and women, to go and work in this vineyard.

## CALLED TO HOLINESS

A distinctive feature of "Christifideles Laici" is its emphasis that this call from God is a call to holiness, a holiness that was described by the council as "the perfection of charity." More forcefully than any other document since the council, this apostolic exhortation recalls our attention to the importance of chapter 5 of Vatican II's Constitution on the Church, namely, the "universal call to holiness."

This call to holiness is an essential and inseparable element of the new life of baptism. It is also intimately connected to mission and to the responsibility entrusted to the lay faithful in the church and in the world. "Holiness," declares "Christifideles Laici," "must be called a fundamental presupposition and an irreplaceable condition for everyone in fulfilling the mission of salvation."

The fruitfulness of the church's missionary effort is entirely dependent on her union with Christ, a principle that applies to each member of the church. The second key image of "Christifideles Laici," and in fact the image around which the document is structured, is that of the vine and the branches in John's gospel. Whatever is said regarding evangelization, we must never forget these words: "As the branch cannot bear fruit by itself, unless it abides in the vine, neither can you, unless you abide in me. I am the vine, you are the branches. Those who abide in me, and I in them, bear much fruit. Apart from me you can do nothing" (Jn 15:4–5).

As Paul VI stated in another context: "The most perfect preparation of the evangelizer has no effect without the Holy Spirit" (EMW, n. 75). Recalling what was said above about the primacy of witness in evangelization and that "for this we need the saints of today," we are yet again confronted with this truth: Only those evangelizers who are themselves evangelized by constant conversion and renewal are able to evangelize with credibility (cf. EMW, n. 15). No effort or program of evangelization will be credible without the witness of lived experience.

In a remarkable passage "Christifideles Laici" moves from this broad outline to look "with the eyes of faith" at the countless number of lay Christian men and women, busy at work in their daily life and activity. For the most part, these people are far from the spotlight or the headlines, but "they are looked upon in love by the Father, for they are the untiring laborers who work in the Lord's vineyard. Confident and steadfast through the power of God's grace, these are the humble yet great builders of the kingdom of God in history" (CFL, n. 17).

## A CALL TO COMMUNION

The call that lies at the heart of Christian life is a call to communion. It is a call to share with all the baptized in communion with Jesus Christ, a communion that is the reflection of, and participation in, the mystery of the intimate life of love in God as Trinity—Father, Son and Holy Spirit.

This communion with God through Jesus Christ in the Holy Spirit is not something incidental; it is the very purpose of human life. The church, the community of the baptized, is a real expression of this communion. But it is at this point only a partial expression. It is also a pilgrim church making its way along the paths of history to the fullness of that communion. Because this communion is in Jesus Christ who came that all may have life, the Christian community seeks to share this communion—the pearl without price—with everyone: "The Church feels it owes to all humanity and to each person the gift received from the Spirit who pours into the hearts of believers the love of Jesus Christ, a prodigious force of internal cohesion and at the same time of external expansion" (CFL, n. 32).

## A MISSIONARY COMMUNION

Paul VI wrote that the whole church receives the mission to evangelize (EMW, n. 15) and that "evangelizing is the grace and vocation proper to the church, her deepest identity" (EMW, n. 14). In n. 32 of "Christifideles Laici" John Paul II develops this and shows the inner dynamism linking and uniting the call to communion and the call to mission. He emphasizes that communion with others is the most magnificent fruit that the "branches in the vine" can give. It is the gift of Christ and of his Spirit, a gift to the church, a gift destined for all people.

In a passage that offers a profound insight into the meaning of evangelization, the pope declares: communion generates communion! It becomes a missionary communion. This is the heart of the evangelization that reveals the true identity of the church, her deepest vocation. "Communion and mission are profoundly connected with each other. They interpenetrate and mutually imply each other, to the point that communion represents both the source and the fruit of mission: communion gives rise to mission and mission is accomplished in communion" (CFL, n. 32).

In this reflection upon communion and mission we are able to see more clearly the way in which three great documents of the Second Vatican Council are profoundly and indissolubly linked together: the "Dogmatic Constitution on the Church," the "Pastoral Constitution on the Church in the Modern World," and the "Decree on the Church's Missionary Activity."

## UNITY OF THE CHRISTIAN VOCATION

We are also able to see the inner unity of the Christian vocation. The call to build up living Christian communities—dioceses, parishes, small faith communities, families—is not something separate from Jesus' command to "go and preach the gospel." The work put into catechesis and Christian education, the effort to build up faith communities that are nourished by the word of God and the celebration of the sacraments, is in itself evangelizing. Living Christian communities are in themselves a sign for the world and a force that draws people to believe in Christ. Moreover, as has just been stated, if these communities really live their communion in Christ there will be an irresistible force within them to seek to share this life with others, to see others and to love others as Christ sees them and loves them and goes out toward them, offering them God's own gift of life.

## THE URGENCY OF EVANGELIZATION

A major concern of "Christifideles Laici" is to draw out the consequences of these insights insofar as concerns the vocation and mission of lay Christians in their daily life in the world. What strikes one, however, after reading and rereading that document side by side with "On Evangelization in the Modern World" is the strong note of *urgency* in John Paul's exhortation.

The present state of affairs "calls with a particular urgency for the action of the lay faithful," he declares, and "if lack of commitment is always unacceptable, the present time renders it even more so" (CFL, n. 3). He states plainly that this applies both to the reevangelization of lands where Christianity has flourished in the past and to the evangelization of the millions and millions of men and women who as yet do not know Christ the redeemer of humanity (CFL, n. 35). "The church today ought to take a giant step forward in her evangelization effort," declares the pope, "and enter into a new stage of history in her missionary dynamism" (CFL, n. 35). In exploring why John Paul II has this overwhelming sense of urgency we are taken back to a theme already mentioned, namely, the significance of the year 2000. Lay Christians are called to take part "in the mission of the church *in this great moment in history,* made especially dramatic by occurring on the threshold of the third millennium" (CFL, n. 3).

## TRANSFORMING THE WORLD IN THE LOVE OF CHRIST

The drama of evangelization unfolds, in the words of John Paul II, on "the frontiers of history": the family, culture, the world of work, economic goods, politics, science, technology, social communications; the great problems of life, of solidarity, of peace, of professional ethics, of human rights, of education and religious freedom. It is here that all the baptized, but in particular the lay Christians who pass the greater part of their lives in these fields, live the gospel by serving the human person and society.

The Christian call to discipleship within the world is a call to service, a call to transform the world through the love poured out in our hearts by the Holy Spirit. "Christifideles Laici," in its reflections on the vocation and mission of lay Christians, considers key areas for their evangelizing presence and action. It reminds us that the future of humanity passes by way of the family. It adds that charity toward one's neighbor, through contemporary forms of the traditional spiritual and corporal works of mercy, represents the most immediate, ordinary and habitual way in which the lay faithful contribute to the Christian animation of the temporal order.

Particular stress is laid in "Christifideles Laici" on responsible participation in public life, namely, the many different economic, social, legislative, administrative and cultural areas which are intended to promote the common good in an organic and institutional way. There is careful attention, likewise, to the mission of the lay faithful in the world of economy and work, in the fields of education, of health care, and of the mass media. For example, speaking of the press, cinema, radio and television, the pope states explicitly: "There too the gospel of salvation must be proclaimed" (CFL, n. 44).


## COMMUNITY AND FORMATION

I would like to make two brief points regarding the evangelizing presence of lay Christians.

The first concerns the crucial importance of Christian community. We have already spoken of the church as a missionary communion and observed that the life of ecclesial communion is in itself a sign for the world. It is also true, however, that in the midst of a deeply secularized society it is extremely difficult for most individual Christians—impossible for many perhaps—to live out their call to evangelization unless they are sustained and nourished by a living and worshiping faith community. I have heard this again and again from lay Christians in different parts of the world. It is, quite simply, a fact! This means that local communities need to be constantly aware of this fact. They must consciously seek for ways to encourage and support the individual members of the community according to the needs of time and place.

The second point concerns the vital importance of formation. As the synod of 1987 stated: "The formation of the lay faithful must be placed among the priorities of a diocese" (CFL, n. 57). At the 1990 synod on the formation of priests the same point was affirmed repeatedly, with special emphasis on the intimate relationship between the formation of lay Christians and the formation of priests. What I want to stress here is the need for a formation for lay Christians that takes fully into account their daily life, their workplace, with all the stresses and strains and challenges that they encounter.

"Christifideles Laici" pointed out that there cannot be two parallel lives in the existence of lay Christians, the so-called "spiritual life" on the one hand and the so-called "secular life" on the other. What is required is formation in an approach, in a spirituality, that enables people to live as members of the church and citizens of human society in a profound unity of life. As the *Letter to Diognetus* observed as far back as the second century, Christians will never cease to experience the tension of their twofold belonging to the church and to the world. It is there, however, in living out that tension as disciples of Christ and members of his mystical body that they will be sanctified and the world will be evangelized.

## EVERYONE IS AN EVANGELIZER

While we must make every effort to carry forward the task of evangelization as the "grace and vocation proper to the church," the effectiveness of evangelization can never be fully measured in terms of human productivity. When speaking of the vocation and mission of the sick and the suffering, "Christifideles Laici" addresses them, saying: "We need you to teach the whole world what love is" (CFL, n. 53). It reminds us forcefully that the church was born in the mystery of redemption in the cross of Christ and that God's ways are so often not the way we—in our wisdom!—would have chosen.

The sick, those who have handicaps, the suffering, must not be considered simply as the object of love and service of the church but must be seen to be "active and responsible participants in the work of evangelization and salvation" (CFL, n. 54). Elsewhere in the document the pope repeats this in relation to the aged, to children and indeed to all.

The whole church is missionary, declared Paul VI, and every one of the baptized is called to be an evangelizer, echoes John Paul II. God calls each by name and he calls us in Jesus Christ to communion with him and to communion with one another. The church is the sacrament of this communion, a communion that by its very nature seeks to be shared . . . a missionary communion. We are thus able to see *why* "evangelizing is the grace and vocation proper to the church, her deepest identity."

## DISCUSSION QUESTIONS

1. Why is baptism into Christ and into Christ's church the foundation for a lay evangelizing spirituality?

2. In what ways is each baptized Catholic an evangelizer?

3. What are the areas in which laity are especially called upon to evangelize today? How is this evangelization best accomplished?

## FOR FURTHER READING

Bishops' Committee on the Laity, National Conference of Catholic Bishops. *Gifts Unfolding: The Lay Vocation Today with Questions for Tomorrow*. Washington, DC: USCC Office of Publishing and Promotion Services, 1990.

Coughlan, Peter. *The Hour of the Laity*. Philadelphia: E. J. Dwyer Pty Ltd., 1989.

John Paul II. *The Vocation and the Mission of the Lay Faithful in the Church and in the World [Christifideles Laici]*. Washington, DC: USCC Office of Publishing and Promotion Services, 1988.

Kinast, Robert L. *Caring for Society: A Theological Interpretation of Lay Ministry*. Chicago: Thomas More Press, 1985.

# STRATEGIES FOR AN EVANGELIZING PARISH

## Patrick J. Brennan

In what I intend to be a pastorally practical offering, I would like to begin by mentioning three documents that have recently struck me as we in Chicago strive to improve our evangelization efforts. The first is the "National Plan for Hispanic Ministry,"[1] which I think has great wisdom for all of us in evangelization and pastoral ministry, whether or not we are working with Hispanics. The document suggests the following:

1. Ministries in a parish or institution are often compartmentalized and fragmented. There needs to be a new coordination of ministries, a convergence as many of us have said for years, around the central mission of evangelization.

2. The anonymous large congregation must be transformed from a *place* to a *home*. This can best be done by the multiplication and proliferation of small groups, or basic Christian communities, ideally in homes.

3. In an attitude shift, in a spirit of missionary zeal, we must move from *pews* to *shoes* in bringing the good news to the marketplace, neighborhoods and the world.

4. More of the above will happen. In fact, evangelization will remain only *good will* if we do not take serious steps toward planning, goal setting and equipping people with skills.

The National Plan makes three specific recommendations for renewed evangelization strategies: (1) help existing ministries, governance bodies, and organizations to reimagine themselves as converging for a common mission; (2) realize that small groups are proving to be among the most effective strategies for evangelizing active, inactive and unchurched—largely through their informal, relational reach-out style; (3) move away from maintenance ministries to a realization that mission

81

territories or target populations are largely under our noses and not in far-distant lands.

Perhaps the greatest challenge, though, is found in the word *planning*—setting goals, prioritizing, saying yes to some things and no to others which are either no longer needed or ineffective. Planning means engaging in timelining, training people (a deeply spiritual activity, the unleashing of gifts of the Holy Spirit), and articulating *indicators* of what successful strategies for evangelization look like. Planning enables us to look back and evaluate whether our efforts were successful or in need of reshaping. Note: Success, however, is not always found in numbers, but in investing time, energy, funds and charisma in areas of genuine need and toward creating a climate wherein conversion and transformation of life may genuinely occur.

## INDICATORS

The National Plan mentioned several indicators of good evangelizing. Let us move on to two other of the three documents that I think are beneficial in the strategies that they advocate and the indicators that they suggest.

First of all, recently the bishops of Alta Baja, California, released a pastoral statement titled *Dimensions of a Response to Proselytism.*[2] The bishops' focus was to study why many Catholics in their area are gravitating away from their Catholic Church of origin to proselytizing churches. Their findings are simple and helpful. First, they say the Catholic Church as it exists in America today has inadequate structures for effective evangelization. They go on to define what adequate structures would look like and in so doing they almost define what good evangelization strategies must include: *personalized attention to people.* Good evangelization involves much more *personalized attention* than current parish structures involve. The bishops then further refine what personalized attention looks like. First, divide parishes into sectors or sections which deacons, deaconal couples or trained laity would pastor. Then further subdivide sections or sectors into small Christian communities, in which even more qualitative pastoring is done by the leaders of the small groups. Finally, the bishops suggest that parishes begin pro-active, yet non-proselytizing, home visits, which keep the community bond with the churched, unchurched and inactive.

The third document that speaks to me regarding indicators and strategies for evangelization are the recommendations made by the Diocesan Synod of the Diocese of Joliet, Illinois, in spring 1990.[3] The synod—a gathering of ordained, religious and laity—named evangelization as the diocese's number one priority. Then the synod leaders gave very clear indicators on how to actualize that priority:

- many and varied outreach processes that touch those in personal and spiritual need;
- processes of reentry for those "away," who want to return to the church;
- better welcoming processes for new parishioners;
- more concentration on adolescent and young adult evangelization;
- a reconfiguring of the process of catechetical formation for confirmation for adolescents and young adults that is modeled on the RCIA process;
- better implementation of the RCIA, with ongoing pre-catechumenate throughout the year;
- a reimagining of traditional religious education efforts to include and evangelize families;
- an inbuing of all sacramental processes with principles and dynamics of the RCIA;
- continued diocesan support for multiplication of small faith sharing groups, or basic Christian communities;
- a greater sensitivity to the dynamics of effective inculturation, that is, allowing the gospel to grow in and via native culture (a healthy syncretism), especially in ministering to Asians, African-Americans and Hispanics.

Fr. Allan Figueroa Deck writes incisively on this last indicator in his book *The Second Wave: Hispanic Ministry and the Evangelization of Cultures.*[4] He reminds us that evangelization is never totally privatistic, concerned with personal salvation. He reechoes the wisdom of Paul VI, who speaks of evangelizing as "transforming humanity" with the power of the gospel.[5] The evangelization of *cultures* is another important indicator or strategy for evangelizing. It involves the paradoxical double movement of allowing the gospel to express itself in culture, while simultaneously teaching people skills for critical reflection in the dominant culture, which is steeped in consumerism.

## CREATIVE CHAOS

The age we are in reflects some of the chaos on the day of the first Pentecost. Out of the chaos, however, something new and exciting can be born. Vincent Donovan, in his excellent book *The Church in the Midst of Creation*,[6] says we are witnessing the death of the industrial revolution parish. The metaphor of "industrial revolution" says a lot. Donovan is suggesting that heretofore American parishes have been run like factories, with centralized control: whole groups of people going through religious experiences at the same time, in synchronized fashion; concern for organization; emphasis on specialization in ministries; and concern for dealing with hordes of anonymous people at one time. These "industrial revolution" attitudes and values expressed themselves in traditional parish schools, CCD programs and parish organizations.

In the 1960s, 1970s and 1980s "factory" attitudes and values were still present, only now in lay ministries and renewal-type programs. Donovan believes that as the "factory" parish dies, a new style of church is emerging, one congruent with the church of Pentecost day and following.

The Acts of the Apostles, chapter 2, describes the infant church as living under the powerful sway of the Holy Spirit, with clear evangelization taking place as well as genuine conversion expressing itself in ritual, namely, baptism. The early Pentecost church valued not only large assembly in temples but also gathering in each other's homes for the Lord's supper, prayer and instruction. These ecclesial groups were invested in the transformation of society into the reign of God, a just society. Day by day the Lord added to their number, we are told. In other words, the very community itself became a magnet, or the evangelizer attracting people. Acts 2 tells us that a vibrant, evangelizing community was "the strategy" for evangelization in the first days of the church. Personal contacts, small groups in homes, and works of mercy were all pieces of the overall communal motif.

## SUCCESS STORIES

Let us focus on some pastoral settings where people are making serious attempts at strategies for evangelization. I apologize for the Chicago emphasis in the examples, but that is where I spend most of my time.

1. In the Bridgeport area of the city of Chicago, eleven parishes converged to do training for home visits. The visits had a purpose: to invite actives, inactives and the unchurched to an area-wide mission, or week of renewal. The mission was held in four different parishes for the English-speaking, two parish sites for Hispanics and another site for youth. The mission was held in neighborhood sites for four nights. The

fifth night was held at Holy Name Cathedral, to emphasize the Bridge-port area's connectedness with the rest of the church in Chicago. The calling also surfaced many pastoral needs for which new ministries have begun.

2. At St. Denis Parish on the southwest side of Chicago, over one hundred and fifty people were trained to be neighborhood ministers. Fifteen to twenty households are assigned to each minister; I stay in contact with as many of these households as possible. All efforts are toward better pastoring of the people of God.

3. A similar model is being implemented at St. Joseph's Parish in Cockeysville, Maryland. In addition to home visitation, the neighborhood minister tries to organize at least one neighborhood event per year.

4. At St. Michael's in Orland Park, Illinois, they found that terminology was important. Trying to implement a neighborhood calling program, the leaders first referred to the ministry as "neighborhood ministry." The term scared people off, and few came forward for training. In a second attempt to get people involved, they simply renamed the ministry "neighborhood block captains." People seemed less threatened, and they now have many more ministers.

5. At St. Odilo's in Berwyn, Illinois, about thirty-five people have been trained to visit the homes of people who have recently registered in the parish and formally welcome them.

6. At St. Thomas the Apostle in Naperville, Illinois, people have been trained for a more extensive welcoming effort. In addition to visiting newcomers, callers also bring the parish mission statement, a loaf of bread and bottle of non-alcoholic wine to stress the centrality of the eucharist in Catholic life, a brochure of parish ministries and how to get involved in them, and even a three-minute video on the parish.

7. The late Father Jimmy Nolan initiated a movement in Dublin, Ireland, called Christian Friends. People were trained to visit the families of children celebrating sacraments in the coming year. To use RCIA language, these people were in effect trained to sponsor these families, with a special eye toward those who were not active in church attendance.

8. Church of the Holy Spirit, in Schaumburg, Illinois, purchased

the names, addresses and phone numbers of every resident within the geographical boundaries of the parish. Phone lines were installed in the church, which can be turned on and off for phone call campaigns. In their first campaign, over one hundred "telephone evangelists" called nine thousand of the eleven thousand residences. Of the nine thousand called, over nine hundred expressed a strong interest in getting more information about the parish, joining the Catholic Church, or returning to the church. About one hundred and fifty showed up for the pre-catechumenate after the calls. The parish has also begun an eight-week mini-series for returning Catholics called *Once a Catholic*.

9. St. Thomas the Apostle in the Hyde Park area of Chicago has broken out of the fall-to-spring model of RCIA, and now does year-round pre-catechumenate. A team is trained to serve as "a catcher in the rye," accepting people into the inquiry process whenever they express an intent.

10. Nationally, the North American Forum on the Catechumenate sponsors training in Re-Membering Church, an RCIA-Order of Peni-tents process for those alienated from the church through hurt, sin or some sort of addiction.

11. The archdiocese of Chicago has adapted Re-Membering Church into a process suited to our local church. We call it "The Recon-ciling Parish." The nature of the process, plus some model faith forma-tion sessions for the process, are contained in my book *The Reconciling Parish*.[7]

12. Msgr. Thomas Cahalane from Tuscon, Arizona, has a six-week process that he offers at least twice a year titled "Alienated Catholics Anonymous." Though catechetical in nature, Cahalane has a very pas-toral approach that motivates many to return to the next series and actually minister in it.

13. The archdiocese of Chicago's Young Adult Ministry Office sponsors a summer series in dozens of parish sites throughout the arch-diocese titled "Theology on Tap." Thousands of young adults (ages twenty through early forties) are offered meaningful talks and opportuni-ties for sharing. In cooperation with the Office for Evangelization, the office has also begun Young Adult Missions, specifically focusing on the human-spiritual needs of the young adult.

14. Nicholas van Dyke, president of Religion in American Life in Princeton, New Jersey, has spearheaded an effort titled "Invite a Friend." Through informal but personal contacts, people are encouraged to not proselytize for their own church, but rather to encourage friends to return to their church of origin, whatever it may have been.

15. Clusters of parishes in the diocese of Joliet and Chicago are doing peer-to-peer ministry, trying to support each other in the reshaping of parish life into a network of small groups, or basic Christian communities. The parishes actually teach each other through the sharing of successes and failures in the reimagining of parish life around small groups. These parishes are convinced that small groups are the natural way to do evangelization, and through them evangelization is not confined to an occasional or terminal program.

## THREE ROADBLOCKS TO EFFECTIVE EVANGELIZATION STRATEGIES

In my book *Re-Imagining the Parish*,[8] I hint at what is, or can be, one roadblock for a parish or any organization in establishing effective evangelization efforts. It is the syndrome of "process addiction," that is, "holding on" to largely ineffective or even life-robbing strategies, simply because "we've always done it this way." A church (global, universal) or a parish in process addiction is more concerned with maintaining the status quo than it is in adopting, removing itself to accomplish its original mission.

Stephen Covey, in his excellent book *The Seven Habits of Highly Effective People*,[9] writes about the characteristics of truly effective people and organizations. Among those characteristics, he says, are: (1) a habit of being *pro active,* not waiting for life to do something for you, but rather using will, choice and imagination to grapple with and shape life; (2) a sense of mission, a statement of purpose; (3) the ability to set priorities, i.e., knowing when to say yes and when to say no; (4) *synergy,* or learning that interdependence rather than independence is the key to both effectiveness and maturity; in other words, many people can harness their gifts and energies to work cooperatively toward a common mission and set of goals; (5) a discipline of renewal—of mind, body, spirit and relationships—to "sharpen the saw" or keep fresh.

Process-addicted churches and parishes violate most of the above five characteristics and the rest of the wisdom in Covey's book. The most frightening problem with addicted organizations is that they have lost the original mission of the organization and are preoccupied with the ministries of maintenance. An example of this happened recently in a large archdiocese where I serve as consultant. After months of self-scrutiny and discernment using highly credible consulting firms, the archdiocese had to begrudgingly admit that it had no clarity as to what its central mission was or is. Without this mission statement, from which flow goals, priorities, roles and ministries, it is easy for a church or parish to become "busyness" addicted. To sum up, dioceses or parishes often are not fed up enough to recognize strategies for evangelization because they are "stuck," unable to articulate life-giving yes's and no's as to priorities.

A second roadblock to effective evangelization strategies is the culture in which we live. George Gallup alerted us to this in *The Unchurched American* (1988).[10] In that study Gallup found a crisis in most mainline churches today of "believing vs. belonging." Many people, said Gallup, claim to believe in and have a relationship with God; but in both attitude and behavior, they do not seem to value *belonging* to or connecting with a body, a community of believers. Gallup's antidotes to this dilemma sound almost like the bishops of Alta/Baja. He recommended in 1988: (1) that churches start processes of reach-out to the inactive and unchurched; (2) that greater experimentation be given to family evangelization over the shell models of religious education; (3) that small groups within the parish be supported and facilitated; (4) that institutional models of church be stressed less, so that religious experience can be encouraged more—inviting people to a relationship of love with God, in community. Gallup is saying that besides intramural issues that occasionally hinder us in our mission, the very call to community will be culturally resisted.

A third roadblock to successful evangelization strategizing is the American preoccupation with the pre-packaged, and inevitably terminal program. I see parishes running from one evangelization program to the next. As an archdiocesan and national consultant on evangelization, I refuse to push programs. We need to be into the work of evangelization "for the long haul." Therefore, local parishes and clusters of parishes need to grow their own strategies, timeline them, evaluate them, shape them for improvement. In other words, rather than implementing someone else's program, a parish would do better to develop, gradually, its own internal discipline for evangelization. I always tell parishes, relative to evangelization strategies, "I can't give you programs; I can help you organically grow your own strategies."

## MULTI-ETHNIC EVANGELIZATION AND INCULTURATION

We already discussed briefly the issue of inculturation. This needs some special attention in the analysis of strategies. Especially in urban areas, parishes are becoming a conglomerate of many different ethnic groups and races. A strategy that I would like to propose for such parishes is a vague one, but an important one. Such parishes should not be looked on as melting pots; rather, the parish needs to be reimagined as having under one church building several different parishes—perhaps Mexican, Puerto Rican, Vietnamese, African-American. These different parishes must be allowed their separate identities, as well as styles of worship and formation, while simultaneously being called to communion with all the other sub-groups in the parish. This tension between inculturation, or allowing the gospel to express itself in unique cultures, and then connecting these groups in worship and socialization is one of the key challenges for evangelization strategies in the future.

## COLLABORATIVE MINISTRY:
## PREREQUISITE FOR EVANGELIZATION

In trying to improve evangelization strategies, we need as a church to pray and study more around the issue of collaborative ministry. Collaborative ministry refers to the unleashing of the charisms and gifts of all the baptized for evangelization and ministry. Evangelization strategies must be rooted in the conviction that all the baptized share in the one mission of evangelization, no matter what their gifts or charisms may be. Until we break out of the mindset that ordained or volunteer specialists do evangelization while the rest of the congregation looks on as an audience, our strategies will be anemic and impoverished.

One possible move toward collaborative ministry is to model it on the diocesan level. So many dioceses still operate out of the compartmentalized model, with each agency or office doing its own thing, its own programming, while simultaneously protecting its own turf. The diocese of Erie, Pennsylvania, is one place trying to break out of that paradigm. Over the course of two years, the diocese has formed a secretariat for evangelization. Under that umbrella are all the offices that used to constitute separate, independent agencies. While admitting to his or her own expertise, gifts and interests, each of those former "agency directors" now sees himself or herself more as a "generalist" working on the

Pastoral Service Team of the diocese. Using his or her own training and gifts, each member of the team plays a role in consulting with parishes, keeping them to "grow their own" evangelization strategies. The folks in Erie hope that such a collaborative model, with people forgetting their turf and using their gifts for the common mission, will spark similar styles of ministry on the parish level.

Crucial to developing collaborative, synergistic and interdependent evangelization strategies is learning the skills of discernment. Discernment involves both listening to the promptings of the Spirit in one's own life and looking for the Spirit's gifts, as revealed to me by others. Lots of burnout, "rust out," and non-accountability for the mission of evangelization could be avoided if greater efforts were made at discernment of charisms.

## CONFRONTING SACRED COWS

Nowhere is collaborative ministry needed more than in the relationship between people doing evangelization (pastoral ministry) and those doing religious education (catechesis). A needless, non-helpful dichotomy has been made between these groups of people. As one charged with the mission of evangelical renewal of parishes, I cannot do my job effectively if I cannot speak about the status of catechesis in a parish and how it is done. I need to dialogue with the people responsible for this ministry, and to work with them in devising new and creative forms of evangelizing catechesis.

Certain sacred cows—the typical parochial school, parish religious education programs, and programs for sacramental preparation—seem to continue untouched and uncritiqued relative to their mission. All three of these mainline ministries touch most of the people we seek to evangelize; however, many of them, despite the ministries, remain in some degree of inactivity relative to church life. Evangelization, catechesis and sacramental formation need to be reimagined as interlocking pieces of a process, a tapestry. Ministers need to work collaboratively in these areas, with the main thrust being the mission of evangelization. And all such efforts can no longer focus on children. Each of the three pieces needs to be reimagined as a key time to evangelize, not just an individual child, but the child and his or her social context or primary relationships. Some would call this evangelization with a family consciousness. In these three areas we need to cease doing merely private education in parochial schools, babysitting in CCD programs, and distributing holy things or cultural milestones when it comes to sacraments.

We do not have to "blow up the bridge" to accomplish better evangelization in these three efforts. We simply need to fine-tune such efforts to include more family involvement. Children in faith formation processes who return to essentially non-practicing homes are receiving a louder message at home than they are in the parish context.

## CONCLUSION

Talk of strategies really should come fairly late in a planning process. We begin to strategize only after there has been an awareness of a need, and then a conviction that a mission is crucial, namely, the mission of evangelization. We have talked a good game about evangelization being the church's central mission since the release of the apostolic exhortation "On Evangelization in the Modern World" in 1975. Despite all the rhetoric, we still invest most of our time in the maintenance of the "industrial revolution parish," a process-addicted organization with amnesia regarding its own central mission.

As a priest friend of mine said recently, "If we don't do something with this ship (church) soon, we're going to wake up and find that we no longer have passengers."

## NOTES

1.  National Conference of Catholic Bishops, "National Pastoral Plan for Hispanic Ministry" (Washington, D.C.: United States Catholic Conference, 1987), 11–16.

2.  See Bishops of Alta/Baja, Cal.: Episcopal Commission of Alta/Baja (February 28, 1990).

3.  "Synod '89," *New Catholic Explorer* (Joliet, Catholic Explorer, March 23, 1980), 12A.

4.  Allen Figueroa Deck, SJ, *The Second Wave* (Mahwah: Paulist Press, 1989).

5.  Pope Paul VI, "On Evangelization in the Modern World" (Washington, D.C.: United States Catholic Conference, 1976), n. 18.

6.  Vincent Donovan, *The Church in the Midst of Creation* (Maryknoll: Orbis Books, 1989).

7.  Patrick J. Brennan, *The Reconciling Parish* (Allen: Tabor Publishing, 1990).

8.  Patrick J. Brennan, *Re-Imagining the Parish* (New York: Crossroad/Continuum, 1990).

9.  Stephen Covey, *The Seven Habits of Highly Effective People* (New York: Simon and Schuster, 1989).

10. The Gallup Organization, *The Unchurched American* (Princeton: Gallup Organization, 1988).

## DISCUSSION QUESTIONS

1. What are the blockages in Catholic life that get in the way of effective evangelization strategies?

2. How can we get strategies or structures that better fit our mission?

3. How would a parish change if it were to make evangelization its true central priority?

## FOR FURTHER READING

Patrick J. Brennan. *The Evangelizing Parish*. Allen: Tabor Publishing, 1987.
———. *The Reconciling Parish*. Allen: Tabor Publishing, 1990.
———. *Re-Imagining the Parish*. New York: Crossroad/Continuum, 1990.
Patrick Brennan & Dawn Mayer. *Reaching Out*. Cincinnati: St. Anthony Messenger Press, 1990.
Ann Wilson & Diane Fassel. *The Addictive Organization*. San Francisco: Harper & Row, 1988.

# FAMILY POWER: AWAKEN AND ANNOUNCE GOD'S LOVE AS REAL

David M. Thomas

Whenever the subject of evangelization is discussed, before long the role of the family must be examined. To overlook the family would be like building a house without a solid foundation—and Jesus himself warned of such short-sightedness.

Sometimes we fail to see clearly when the object to be viewed is just too close at hand. We might attend to the needs of those distant from us and fail to even notice the needs of close family and friends. We need to develop an awareness of those around us, and we seem to need reminders, both as individuals and as a church.

Sometimes we open our eyes in times of crisis—when someone close dies or suffers a serious financial loss.

And sometimes we see with new eyes when something is happening within—a new awareness of vitality or limitation, a religious conversion, a forgotten dream—and we need to reformulate everything.

Something like all this happened to the Catholic Church twenty-five years ago when changes on the outside ("the signs of the times") and changes on the inside (a new awareness of the church as the people of God on pilgrimage) brought about what some consider an unprecedented amount of change in the life of the church. The Second Vatican Council was a launching pad for change, vitality, newness and experimentation.

Among the council's more profound changes was an appreciation of the role of the laity as active participants in the total life of the church. My own interests (and those of this essay) concern changes which have affected our understanding and appreciation of the place of the family within the church.

Vatican II referred to the family as "the domestic church."[1] Pope Paul VI, in addressing the many aspects of evangelization, built upon this idea in reminding us that within the family we will find the essential features of church life.[2] This fundamental insight into the meaning of the Christian life of the home has created a new set of blessings and responsibilities for the family. Related to our interests here, we may speak with enthusiasm about the role of the family in the process of evangelization and catechesis. This new (or old but recently remembered) task of the family comes at precisely the right time. Why? Because the church (and its families) are now submerged in a vast secular milieu which no longer contains in explicit form a religious sensitivity or worldview. We have effectively separated church from state, or, more significantly, religion from culture in today's world.

Because of pervasive secularity, I believe that it now falls to the more basic units of society, especially the family, to "carry the ball" in restoring, maintaining and perfecting a religious climate, a set of values which point to our Godly existence.

To accomplish this, a new strategy is needed for Christian families, and for the wider church, to assist ordinary families in fulfilling their God-given task and responsibility.


## FOUNDATIONS FOR FAMILY-BASED EVANGELIZATION

To articulate the foundations for this new strategy of family-based evangelization, I will divide my comments into seven points. Seven, you may recall, is an important Catholic number. We are gifted by God's Spirit with seven empowering gifts, and we celebrate our faith sacramentally in seven distinctive and enriching ways.

Further, while certainly important for me, I will not draw any major theological conclusion from the fact that my wife and I have been blessed with five children, thus making us a family of seven. Yet perhaps this point is important because as both a family person and a theologian, I willingly allow my personal experience of family life to season my theological reflections.

So without further preamble, reflect with me on how evangelization, the process of living and sharing God's word of life and love, occurs within the family. We will also note how the family itself is a powerful, although sometimes undervalued, source of evangelical vitality for the whole church.

1. *The family as context for communicating Christian values.*
    Look at any survey of those values and ideals which touch deeply the

sentiments and feelings of adults, particularly if they are parents, and you will find at the top of the list the desire to communicate healthy and enriching values to children. We want to make their lives happy, safe and holy. We want to pass on to them what we have learned which is of value, and perhaps even of eternal value.

To accomplish this, many parents are willing to expend vast amounts of energy and precious time with the hope that their children will be enriched in body and spirit. I realize that this may appear idealistic, perhaps even naive, but I am convinced that many Catholics believe in the value of "generativity," as described by the psychologist Erik Erikson, i.e., the passing on to the next generation that which is most valuable in one's own.

Every healthy and loving person desires to share whatever one has with others. Our desire to share is even more intense if we believe that what we have was earlier given to us. And in our later days, if we actually witness to its presence in those we have cared for, no greater satisfaction is possible. We not only live in the memory of having lived a good life, but, deeper, that our life was shared, a small measure of it passed on into the lives of others. We rejoice that, in some small way, their lives are better because we gave a part of ourselves.

I begin with this reflection to challenge those who claim that our era is exclusively one of outright individualism, hedonism and self-centeredness. This is not my experience. Like everyone else, I recognize some of the twisted values in our midst, particularly in the public world of entertainment, big business and politics.

But my world, and the world of most Catholics, is constituted more by the world of the home, the neighborhood and the local parish. Here, the values of generosity, commitment and genuine care and concern for others, while challenged every day, still remain dominant. And it is from this base of strong communal concern that there are countless people who care and who will express heroic generosity if invited to do so. I personally believe there is a vast reservoir of generosity in the common person. Yet part of the tragedy of modern life, and of so many of our contemporary organizational systems, is that we fail to tap into the riches latent within people.

Related to the topic of the evangelical role of the family, I believe that most families would joyfully and enthusiastically embrace the challenge of evangelization within the family if it were offered to them in realistic family terms and in a familiar language. In fact, I would add that many families are already doing it with uncommon effort, yet without an awareness of their exalted activity. It would be wonderful if they possessed an adequate language of evangelization relating to the ordinary relationships and events of daily family life. This would make their efforts all the more meaningful and effective.

And this is very sad because within so many family relational events, we find heroic concern, forgiveness and honest love. "Ubi caritas, Deus ibi est": Where there is charity, there also is God. Or in the profound words of the wonderful music of "Les Miserables": "to touch another person is to see the face of God."

2.  *The family as Christian community.*

As I mentioned, I am a family person. My wife and I have been married for twenty-four years, and have more or less survived the delight and drudgery of rearing five teenagers. At the present time my wife's mom lives with us, along with a one-year-old foster child we have been caring for since her birth. The experience of family fills a good part of my life. And it is much the same in the lives of so many others.

While family structures have been undergoing rather dramatic changes in the last two decades, the family remains a primary setting for so much of our human and Christian life. It forms the context of many, if not most, of our relational experiences. And if our church experience is to be one of community—a major theme of the post-Vatican II church —then I would argue that much of this experience happens in the family. I should also mention that I interpret Pope John Paul II as having a similar approach, but I will say more about that under my next point. Here I simply suggest that family life can be a rich setting for living the Christian faith and for communicating its riches to others. Let me share two examples from our own family.

A few years ago during dinner one day, our youngest son, who was then a five year old, announced to us between passing the mashed potatoes and peas that he no longer thought that there was a God. Now you have to remember that I, the "father almighty" in our family, possess a Ph.D. in systematic theology from the prestigious Catholic university Notre Dame. Surely I would be able to adequately respond to my son's declaration of atheism, and by the time of dessert he would be successfully restored to the fold.

But wisdom prevailed and I kept my mouth shut, except to ask our other children what they thought of Timothy's statement. I wished we had recorded the event for later generations of scholars. During the next ten minutes I heard from the mouths of his older brothers and sister (we have four sons and one daughter) distant although recognizable versions of Thomas Aquinas' five proofs for the existence of God. I can only recall now their first response which went something like, "Timmy, you idiot, how in the heck do you think you got here? Nobody creates themselves!"

As you might expect, Timothy probably wished he hadn't brought up the subject of his personal religious convictions, but he did, and it was a wonderful moment of family evangelization for us all. What remains most memorable for me is that my wife and I were silent during the debate. We let it all flow from "the mouths of babes."

A second family example is not so much a single event but rather a long series of happenings related to our experience of foster care. The New Testament contains many references to family life although the family context is often overlooked. For example, one of the primary indicators of the authenticity of the early Christian communities was their care for widows and orphans, along with their willingness to offer hospitality to the traveler or stranger. What's happening in those texts, I believe, is a recognition that genuine Christian witness often involves the sharing of what one possesses with others, particularly those in special need. And I would assume that this also meant sharing one's home with them.

That's part of why our family decided to accept the invitation of our diocese to become a foster family. It's our own small way of making our home a place for those in need. Other families help the needy in different ways, but whatever they do, it shows that the family is not simply a place to escape from the big, bad world or just a place where you store your stuff—two images of the modern secular family—but is a community where life and love are shared. There is an essential link, I would argue, between evangelization and hospitality.

3. *The family as "domestic church."*

Some of these religious dimensions of family life have been captured in recent church teaching. We see a simple, although most important beginning of this "family perspective" in the documents of Vatican II when they describe the various embodiments of church—and I refer you to paragraph 11 of the "Dogmatic Constitution on the Church" where we first encounter that phrase "domestic church" in reference to the family's ecclesial identity.

Paul VI picked up on this phrase in his writing on evangelization in making two very important additions to the teaching. First, he noted that within the family you will find all the essential features of church life, and, second, not only do parents evangelize their children, but children evangelize their parents.

I once gave a retreat to parents on this latter point, and it was wonderful. Daily, children remind us parents of the freshness of creation. They keep alive the questions which are part of life's everyday events. Children relate to their parents in wondrous, paradoxical ways;

they keep us young and age us quickly at the same time. Facing the mystery of life in all its harshness and comfort is always part of the family agenda. This is a climate receptive to the gospel message.

Finally, I have followed the thought of John Paul II, with one of the major themes of his pontificate being the importance of family life. He seems to take two approaches. One is based on his concern that the dignity of the person be preserved in a world that is increasingly manipulative and impersonal. He notes that the family has the primary role of preserving human dignity. And, second, he holds that the family is a source of much of the evangelical vitality of the rest of the church. In his communications associated with the world synod on family a decade ago, he described the family as the primary subject, not object, of evangelization. I interpret this as an underscoring of the foundational character of the family as a source or reservoir for much of the life of the church.

In his writing on the family, John Paul II invites the rest of the church to take on a more familial spirit.[3] And where will that come from if not from the family itself? I, of course, concur with these developments. My experience tells me they are true. So do some of the exciting developments in our understanding of human development, and it is to these that I now turn.

4. *The family as foundation for healthy spiritual development.*

In your estimation what is the most important year of life from a developmental perspective? You might answer that it is the last year lived. After all, we know that as each year passes, our lives become more rich and complex.

Recently, I have changed my thinking about this matter, as I have become aware of the singular importance of the first year of life.

In the last few years, much attention has focused on what is called "attachment theory."[4] Summarizing volumes of discourse and debate, I share with you this simple fact: During that most vulnerable first year of life, a foundation of awareness and relationality is established which influences all subsequent events during one's lifetime.

During year one we are attached to another person (or persons), which causes us to arrive at a very rudimentary awareness that we possess a self. This identity "flowers" as we learn that we are someone valued, appreciated and accepted. If this kind of "in-formation" is not communicated effectively, one's formation as a healthy human person is threatened. This process takes place deep within the little one and can be easily overlooked to the untrained eye.

When healthy attachment occurs, one feels secure. And if one is secure with one's "being in this world," one will possess the necessary foundation for taking risks later on, risks which influence one's autonomy, one's maturity as a person.

To put it another way, unless we are first connected, we cannot be free to seek and form that unique and special identity which God intended for each of us. Attachment, I would argue, is a fundamental religious issue and is tied to one's capacity to eventually hear the word of God that one is loved and will risk sharing this "good news" with others. And attachment takes place primarily in the family.

A second area of research and concern relates to what is being termed "the wounded child" situation. In brief, I refer to the work of John Bradshaw.[5] He notes that within many adults "lives" a child, a vestige of childhood, a child who was not treasured but abused or neglected, a child who retains many unmet needs, and who seeks to meet those needs in the body of an adult.

From his research and therapy practice he concludes that the unfulfilled needs of the child resurface in adult life and cause many adults to become addictive or compulsive. Even a quick review of the literature describing life today will show that addictive behaviors are at the root of many of our societal ills. They can also, I suspect, create serious problems for the life of the church.

The task of accomplishing healthy human development for infants and children is primarily a family matter. It is related to spiritual development too, as our core attitudes and beliefs come from our families.

What comes from this brief description of human development processes is a confirmation that family life is central to the spiritual life as it prepares the human and religious foundation for lifelong development. John Paul II notes that parents are the first to proclaim the gospel to their children.[6] And how soon would you suggest that this begins? I believe that it is sooner than most realize. In fact, there is no time before it begins.

5. *The evolution of smaller, more personal structures.*

As we move to the end of this century, there is widespread consensus that many of our major institutions have failed to deliver what we had hoped. Big business, big government, big education and big church are not the answer.

For many, the next century will call for a return to the basics of human life, to small communities of friendship and the sharing of life, and to family where one experiences that which we all deeply desire, the constant flow of recognition, support and care.

Of course, there is a good and bad news side to this growing conviction. It is the old insight of Pogo: We have met the enemy and it is us.

Maintaining vitality on a small scale establishes accountability for all. We may have different roles but we all have roles. We may encounter different responsibilities, but we are all responsible.

I foresee, and look forward to, a shift to the smaller dimensions of life. When Jesus described life in the kingdom, he said that it only took two or three. That's not very large, but it is very significant. I anticipate that the church will slowly evolve into more concentrated, more personal structures. This is what so many Catholic Christians are already calling for.

Like any basic and perhaps new insight, it will take a while for an idea to be turned into structure. It seems to be happening quickly in the third world, however, where Christianity is undergoing a vitality we in the first world will do well to concelebrate—and learn from.

6. *Evangelization as relational event.*

Christianity is fundamentally relational. It mirrors God's communal life within the Trinity, which is a revelation of the meaning of life as God intends because it is the life that God lives.

So too with us. Attracting others to our faith will depend in part on how they observe our life, particularly our life together. Wasn't there some reference to this type of evangelical strategy mentioned at the last supper?

7. *Renewed partnership between home and parish.*

Finally, the Catholic Church in the United States has recently issued a document on family life called "A Family Perspective in Church and Society."[7] This document invites the church to examine all that it does, particularly at the parish level, and assess the impact of its programs on family life. Does the religious education program really assist family solidarity? Do our RCIA programs involve the whole family? And so forth.

What's called for is a renewed partnership between the church of the home and the church of the parish. Each is important and demands ongoing support. These are the churches at the local level, the level that is closest to people both within and outside the church. Health in both will keep membership strong and will help attract new members.

Evangelization can appear as a complicated task reserved for only a few. But that is not the intent of the church. It is a task for all. I believe that if it is understood and lived within the family, it will extend to other settings. But unless evangelization is rooted in those relationships closest to home, it will lack the credibility needed by a skeptical public, and it will lack the depth needed by those who hunger for the knowledge of God's personal love.

In one of his few public addresses as pope, John Paul I said that the church should do everything it can to assist family life.[8] For those committed to the evangelical life of the church, this deserves repeating.

The door of a home may appear welcoming and hospitable or it can give the message to stay away. The same can be said of the church, whatever its structure. It can open up and reach out to the alienated and to the stranger, or it can give the impression that it is not really interested in outsiders. For that reason, I am deeply moved when a parish—or a family for that matter—selects as an evangelizing motto, "Welcome home!" In those two simple words, I believe, you will find the core of the gospel.

## STRATEGIES FOR EVANGELIZATION

As I conclude this reflection, I want to briefly suggest some specific strategies for evangelization which relate to the seven points already mentioned. Appropriate strategies always require local sensitivity based on the maxim of the Music Man: "You've got to know the territory."

I offer these suggestions to church leadership with the idea that it is as important to examine the spirit of evangelization as it is to test its practice. We must always be honest and authentic, virtues easily identified within family life although sometimes "faked" in the more public arena.

1. *Train families to be evangelizers.*

With family being a major value for almost everyone, evangelization programs should build on that priority. Train whole families to be evangelizers, but do so in a manner which builds upon their fundamental family spirit. Show ways to reach out within the family itself to relatives both near and far. Show how to be inviting rather than judgmental.

2. *Practice invitation and hospitality.*

A key virtue of the Christian family is hospitality. The range of that hospitality ought to be broad. Look for today's widows and orphans, who are those without family. So many people today live alone, particularly the elderly. They might be invited to become active evangelizers themselves. Family problems in the past might have been a cause for their leaving the church. We need to make room in our hearts to invite them to return. And don't overlook families with single parents. Often they feel inadequate and may need a special invitation to participate in the evangelical life of the church.

3. *Use familiar language.*

Faith begins at home. We need a new language, a new awareness of what vital and dynamic faith looks like when lived in an ordinary family. But use family terms, familiar expressions.

4. *Heal the brokenhearted.*

Are there barriers to hearing and appreciating God's invitation because of inadequate bonding or lack of joy in childhood? Do we view evangelization as being for those who are emotionally and socially healthy? Jesus came for everyone. In fact, did he not single out those who were weakened or victimized by hurts in earlier days of life? Today thousands of groups throughout the country deal with all types of addictions. These groups could be special settings where God's healing word can be heard with relief and gratitude.

5. *Keep it small, personal and inviting.*

Think of evangelization as a small operation. It involves lots of groups of two or three. Make it personal, inviting and intimate.

6. *Love one another.*

What will invite others to join us is their being "turned on" by our witness to love. This approach is as old as the words of Jesus at the last supper.

7. *Consider the impact of programs on families.*

As we create programs, particularly within the parish, remember that both the design and implementation of whatever we do should consider the impact our programs will have on families. People draw strength from relationships of intimacy; the same rule applies to our Christian life.


CONCLUSION

It is time to consider the close and pervasive connection between common family life and the life of the church. And with so much of healthy church life involving the sharing of faith and with so much of Christian family life involving the sharing of life, we might discover that in the end we are not describing two radically different events, but one in the same viewed through different lenses. If I may add to this image, when we look with both eyes, we see life in the dimension of depth.

## NOTES

1.  See *Vatican Council II,* Austin Flannery, OP, ed., "Dogmatic Constitution on the Church," n. 11.
2.  Pope Paul VI, "On Evangelization in the Modern World" (Washington, D.C.: United States Catholic Conference, 1975), n. 72.
3.  Pope John Paul II, "On the Family," (Washington, D.C.: United States Catholic Conference, 1982), n. 64.
4.  See Robert Karen, "Becoming Attached," *The Atlantic Monthly,* February 1990, 35–70.
5.  John Bradshaw, *Homecoming* (New York: Bantam, 1990).
6.  Pope John Paul II, "On the Family," n. 52.
7.  "A Family Perspective on Church and Society" (Washington, D.C.: United States Catholic Conference, Dept. of Education, 1989).
8.  Pope John Paul I, "Address to Bishops from the United States on the Occasion of Their Ad Limina Visit," September 1978.

## DISCUSSION QUESTIONS

1.  Out of our renewed awareness of the ecclesial identity of the family, what resources do families possess to help them communicate the good news of Jesus effectively?

2.  Has the family been challenged in realistic ways to share faith with others?

3.  What does it mean to say that faith begins at home, and how can Catholic parents convey this to their children?

4.  How can the family model help us to share God's good news of love to those who are *not* emotionally and socially healthy?

## FOR FURTHER READING

Ernest Boyer. *A Way in the World: Family Life as Spiritual Discipline.* Scranton: Harper & Row Publishers, Inc., 1984.

Betsy Caprio & Thomas Hedberg. *Coming Home: A Handbook for Exploring the Sanctuary Within.* Mahwah: Paulist Press, 1986.

Pope John Paul II. "On the Family." Washington, D.C.: United States Catholic Conference, 1982.

Wendy Wright. *Sacred Dwelling: A Spirituality of Family Life.* New York: Crossroad/Continuum, 1990.

# WORK AND EVANGELIZATION
## John C. Haughey, SJ

Human behavior is of itself witness-bearing. One's interiority inevitably stands forth and is made manifest in one's actions (or omissions). Bearing witness to one's values and to what one takes to be meaningful (or meaningless) is as much a part of human behavior as walking, thinking, eating. The exterior points to the ingredients operating in the interior. When one of those interior ingredients is faith, faith in God and in Jesus Christ, his Son, one's external behavior will inevitably reveal this unless one intends to keep it hidden. Therefore, even before evangelization becomes a matter of intentionality it is already part of our anthropology.

Evangelization is usually looked at in terms of a conscious, intentional activity. It can also be looked at in terms of interiority made manifest. Although there is no way of proving it, my suspicion is that the most effective evangelization is done by those who are not conscious of impacting others. Their impact is due to their interior faith. By acting in faith they inevitably evangelize.

Going to church, for example, would be an act of evangelization, though this would be far from the minds of the participants. Saying grace in connection with the act of eating or drinking could also be an act of evangelization. Refraining from sexual intercourse with a partner outside of marriage because it goes against one's faith-informed conscience would be an act of evangelization. Showing a special sensitivity to a person in trouble could be an act of evangelization, as would giving thanks to God for a display of nature's beauty.

This book is interested in making evangelization more intentional, more formal, more knowledgeable, more frequent. It wants to have that which happens with anthropological inevitability come to be more consciously undertaken so that the faith ingredient in one's interiority is named. In this essay I would like to make a connection between evangelization and the most frequent activity in the lives of all of us, namely, our daily work.

## SOME ASSERTIONS

For the reader to anticipate the line of thinking pursued in this essay, it would be helpful to state some assertions.

1. Work is one of the most effective environments within which evangelization can and does take place.
2. The most effective evangelization ordinarily takes place when it is not part of the intention of the person who is its instrument.
3. The ability to give to one's work colleagues a faith account of matters of common concern or interest, the ability to name the faith factor in matters that touch both parties, can have a conversional effect without evangelization in the formal sense entering the situation.
4. The quality of one's life creates a context or an atmosphere of credibility or non-credibility wherein the faith factor will be credible or non-credible to one's fellow workers.
5. A notable differentiation between the lifestyle or worldview of the evangelizer and those of one's work colleagues will create an atmosphere of curiosity at least within which an opportunity for faith sharing can develop.
6. By consciously developing an understanding of the faith dimension of one's daily work, one will have more than enough matter for religious discourse with one's work colleagues.
7. Seeking to find God in one's work situation is the best direction to pursue if one is desirous of evangelizing one's colleagues.
8. Finding God regularly in one's work situation supplies the worker with communicable matter for sharing his or her faith.
9. The consolation that accompanies the finding of God at work in one's everyday work situation is upbuilding for oneself and also invaluable for one's colleagues.

It should be obvious from the above contentions that I am somewhat guarded about evangelization and, therefore, wary of would-be evangelizers. I know that this wariness comes in part from my own experience of would-be evangelizers who have been notable for their incompetence in either the curricular things expected of them at work or in their knowledge of the faith they are attempting to convey. I'm sure there is no certain connection between these two things but non-competence either in technical or professional knowledge or in catechesis makes evangelization ineffective, even at times ludicrous.

## THEOLOGICAL REFLECTION

Aside from personal experience and its already confessed bias, theological reflection on the motivation for evangelization is invaluable. What is the worldview of the evangelizer that is prompting him or her to evangelize? Presumably, hopefully, love of God and of the world God made and so loved that the Son was sent into it. If someone is world-despising, their evangelization motivation is built on falsehood. The world-despising is seldom explicit. More often it lurks behind a facile dichotomizing of the natural and the "supernatural," as it used to be called, so that all esteem for natural, human, everyday things suffers. As long as the supernatural is cordoned off from the natural, the natural isn't usually given its due, nor is its potential for mediating the divine appreciated.

If the world and all that is in it isn't filled with the goodness of God, then it can be seen as being in dire need of what it doesn't have. Or, as often, there must be flight from this worldly world. When someone has such a dichotomized worldview, he or she will be sure that evangelization is called for, demanded, urgent. While I believe that evangelization is an essential part of the work of the church, its raison d'être should not be inspired by some deprecation of the world through some worn-out worldview. To be even more specific, many Christians are guilty of a religiously constructed deprecation of the world of work. They do not see their everyday work in the world as having any relationship to the kingdom of God unless it is "church work."

One of the contributions of Vatican II to theological reflection was its insight into culture. Its treatment of culture is a good example of a worldview that is more sophisticated than one which dichotomizes the natural and the supernatural. The council recognized the autonomy of human cultures, their distinctiveness and special qualities. It saw the role of Christians vis-à-vis their cultures not as extraneous to them but intrinsic to them. It called on Christians to perfect, preserve, heal, strengthen or restore their respective cultures, depending on the moral condition of the culture. The council saw the faith of Christ's followers as able to permeate and transform them. It did not apply these conciliar insights into the work culture or the culture of corporations but they are certainly applicable.

Another subject touched on by the council was what it called "the seeds of the word" contained in the national and religious traditions of non-Christians.[1] Before these religions were treated in this nuanced way, the motivation for evangelization of non-Christians was often a lot simpler: namely, one who did not come to belief in Christ and in his church was likely to suffer for all eternity. What a clear reason for the evangelization of non-Christians! The council was commenting on the world religions and did not have in mind the many belief systems embraced by people in today's world. The work world is the place where plural belief systems, those that are formally religious and those that are not, are most likely to be communicated. The would-be evangelizer has to be a reverent listener with respect to the plural belief systems that are operative in every work situation in order to go about the task of evangelization the way Jesus did.

## JESUS' WAY OF WORKING

As with any other activity, Jesus' own way of doing evangelization is the way we should seek to do it. His kind of evangelizing was not world-despising, obviously. In this he was like his Father who so loved the world that he sent his only Son into the world that it might be saved. In all creatures great and small, in the "natural," Jesus saw God at work. As he saw it, the wildflowers were clothed by this good, hard-working God he preached. The birds of the air were fed from the same principle of divine activity. But he saw God at work even more clearly in people. He even reverenced the faith displayed by those who weren't Jewish, seeing God as its author. For example, he is not depicted in the gospels as trying to dissuade from their respective belief systems the Canaanite woman (Mt 15:28) and the centurion (Mt 8:10). In fact, he lauded both of them for their faith. It isn't clear what their faiths were, only that they believed in God and that their God could work through Jesus. (They weren't disappointed.) Jesus, on the other hand, often expressed disappointment with the lack of faith of those who claimed belief in Yahweh, whom Jesus proclaimed.

He saw himself and other people, plus their day-to-day activities, in terms of an imminent, in-breaking fullness that he, like his forebears, called the kingdom of God. The contents, so to speak, of his evangelization in the synoptic gospels were framed by this symbol of the in-breaking kingdom. The reign of the working God was not wholly future, but was already operating, extending out far beyond Jesus. It anteceded and anticipated him. Jesus' ministry was constituted by discerning and naming this reign and work of God as he saw it unfold before his very eyes in people, things and circumstances. He was able to state that the fields were white for the harvest. These "fields" were begging to be harvested by those who could discern their actual religious condition.

The God of many Christians is too small, and their Jesus is too

Christified. In fact, one could ask whether Jesus had evangelization, as it is usually practiced today, as part of his agenda. As I have already observed, it's not even clear that he sought to bring his hearers into a faith other than the ones they had already embraced. He was certainly not trying to make his Jewish hearers disengage from their Jewish faith and become Christians. What he did seek was to purify their understandings and hearts about the God they had believed in and whose mercy and goodness and love they had undoubtedly heard about but whom they hadn't come to wholly trust. Jesus exhorted them to a degree of trust and love of God that they had not previously even imagined.

He seemed much more of an experiential aposteriorist about his ministry than a theoretical apriorist. By this I mean that Jesus seemed to take his cues about what his work was to be on a given day from what he discovered God already doing in those people and circumstances in which he found himself. For example, he healed the man who was lying sick on his mat for thirty-eight years on the sabbath because he found the compassion of God speaking to him that day through the man and he acted on it, since "my Father is at work until now, [and] I am at work as well" (Jn 5:17). There is no indication that he had gone to the pool at Bethesda with that particular work of healing in mind. It was prompted by what he discerned. "I solemnly assure you, the Son cannot do anything by himself—he can do only what he sees the Father doing. For whatever the Father does, the Son does likewise" (Jn 5:19).

The gospel of John does not make much use of the symbol of the kingdom of God. Instead, it highlights the relationship between Jesus and his Father to describe the in-breaking future. In the fourth gospel the Son has become the way this definitive future will come about. In the synoptics Jesus announces the kingdom of God. But in John he inaugurates it and becomes the contents of that reign, in a manner of speaking. Jesus begins the gospels announcing the good news and ends up becoming the good news.

Jesus' way of going about evangelizing is important to understand and imitate. Apriori evangelization knows too much about what the other or others ought to believe and too little about what they actually do believe. Aposteriori evangelization is a more reverent way of proceeding. It begins by listening, not by speech. And it doesn't speak words about God or theological ideas. It speaks words that have already been eaten by the speaker, words that God has enabled the speaker to taste and digest, words that come from experiencing God actually at work in a given situation and person (Ez 3:1–4).

Jesus' experience with the Samaritan woman is a case in point. In this seemingly chance encounter by Jacob's well he discovers and uncovers "everything I ever did" (Jn 4:29) and everything God had done and was doing to keep her from destroying herself by pursuing her unquenched and unquenchable thirsts. (She was in a tryst with her sixth "husband.") Jesus is not described by John as having preached to her, only as having probed her, unearthing the things in herself she did not wish to look at, the graces she had declined, the sins she had committed.

She becomes a messenger to her townspeople, convincing them that here was someone so special they had to come and see for themselves. Subsequently, many came out to see him and succeeded in having him stay with them for the next two days. From what he taught them they came to believe "that this really is the savior of the world" (Jn 4:42).

Still another aspect of Jesus' aposteriori way of "evangelizing" people—his opening them up to God's in-breaking reign—looks at what was going on in the evangelizer himself during the dialogue with the Samaritan woman. We know that he stopped at the well because he was thirsty and that the apostles went off to get food because he and they were hungry. When they returned with the desired victuals he indicated that he had become indifferent to their food because "I had food to eat of which you do not know" (Jn 4:32). His food was the joy of finding God at work in her soul. While he was "evangelizing her," stripping away all the defenses she had put up between herself and God, he found joy in the Lord, whose working in her he was able to uncover.

## IGNATIUS OF LOYOLA

I am indebted to Ignatius Loyola for these ways of looking at Jesus. Ignatius in his *Spiritual Exercises* does not have the retreatant focus on evangelization of others but on their spiritual condition vis-à-vis God and their use of created reality. He saw all things as so many ways of finding and glorifying God. In the last meditation of the month-long Exercises he recommends that the person praying "consider how God works and labors for me in all creatures . . . conducting himself as one who labors."[2] By having "an intimate knowledge of the many blessings" God continually bestows, one "may in all things love and serve the Divine Majesty."[3]

This insight into God and God's manner of being in the world supersedes the insight which was in the calm possession of the church before Ignatius, namely, that God indwelt creatures. Indwelling was God's perceived mode of presence. But Ignatius' own mystical experi ences enabled him to see more deeply. He saw a working God, a God who "conducts himself as one who works."

He goes on to invite the retreatants to see that God has a specific motive for so "conducting himself," namely, God is working "for me," out of love.[4] Lest this sound narcissistic, Ignatius' comment was not intended to communicate an elitist or exclusivist divine myopia but, rather, something that all can discover about God who is at work not just for them but for everyone through everyday things, ordinary circumstances and people. Awareness of this is a grace to be prayed for, not a philosophical achievement to be striven for.

I would like to add to his paradigm something that Ignatius did not have in mind. The God one finds at work "at work" (or anywhere else for that matter) can, in turn, be made known to one's colleagues. But this would make that which is matter for personal growth and consolation also serve as matter for evangelization. This broadens the material, so to speak, with which one can evangelize. And since this material comes out of the situation one has in common with those with whom one works, it has a naturalness about it. It comes to us and our co-workers horizontally rather than down from above.

Those who discern God in everyday work occurrences and in one's associates (as well as in oneself) can then evangelize those who do not see or have not seen God at work. But Jesus' insights from his own daily experiences of God at work are exactly what make up the contents of the four gospels. Every gospel situation is replete with Jesus' insight into God at work in it and in the principals who play a part in a given episode. Jesus is functioning constantly as a reaper who discovers what the sower has sown. Not only does he tell others what the sower has sown, but he acts on what he sees the sower wants him to complete. He also encourages his hearers and followers to do the same. "Open your eyes and see! The fields are shining for the harvest! The reaper already collects his wages and gathers a yield for eternal life, that sower and reaper may rejoice together" (Jn 4:35–36).

Finding God at work "at work" is an easy aspiration to entertain but not an easy practice to develop. God will not be blatantly and unmistakably there—as in the heavy winds that crushed rocks or the earthquake or the mighty fire. Rather God will usually be there "in a tiny whispering sound" (1 Kgs 19:12). For Ignatius the discovery was always accompanied by what he called "devotion," an affective movement of awe and love. He measured his own and others' spiritual growth by whether there was a growing experience of devotion or a lessening of it. The affectivity involved in the discovery could be slight or intense. If people developed a facility for discerning God at work in their immediate circumstances, their love of God would strengthen notably. Discerning "the tiny whispering sound" is necessary for devotion to grow.

It would take us too far afield in this brief article to explain in any great detail one of the unique forms of prayer Ignatius recommended for developing a facility for detecting this tiny whispering. He called it the "Examen." This prayer retrospectively goes back over one's day seeking to surface the positive and negative affectivity that surfaced in the course of it. He was sure that God's workings were much more discernible at the level of affect than at the cruder level of accomplishing, planning, implementing, communicating—in a word, working.

Expectation and intention are two keys to finding God at work in one's own immediate work situation. If God isn't expected to be working in humble circumstances (which every circumstance is), the perceiver will have to be hit over the head (it's not beyond God to do so) to discover any divine activity. The intention one takes to one's work is the other important feature that makes success likely. If the overall intention one has for going to work is explicitly directed to God, chances are much better that one will find God in work. Ignatius stressed the need for frequent offering of oneself and one's work to God "so that to some extent at least we may be of service to his Divine Majesty by helping souls for whom he died." Furthermore, "the more one binds oneself to God our Lord and shows oneself more generous toward his Divine Majesty, the more will those who do so find God more generous toward them and the more disposed will they be to receive graces and spiritual gifts which are greater every day."[5]

If one has a clarity that one is going to work with an intentionality directed to God, there is less likelihood that there will be self-seeking or self-interest inimical to God pursued by that work. Purity of intention is the way classical spiritual authors referred to this practice. For example, Ignatius wrote to superiors of young Jesuits, instructing them to frequently exhort those rookies "to seek God our Lord in all things, stripping off from themselves an [autonomous] love of creatures—to the extent that this is possible—in order to turn their love [of them] upon the Creator of them, by loving him in all creatures and all of them in him."[6]

Ignatius did not seem concerned with evangelization as such but with forming people to make themselves totally available to God so that they might be used by God as Jesus was, as a reaper of what the sower had sown. How well his kind of spirituality succeeded in these inner dynamics can be seen by the meteoric evangelization undertaken by someone like St. Francis Xavier after he was formed by Ignatius.


## EXTRINSICIST EVANGELIZATION

In asking myself why Ignatius didn't seem to have evangelization in mind, at least the same way it is ordinarily practiced, I found myself thinking in terms articulated by Maurice Blondel (1861–1949). He was able to surface his complaints about the apologetics of the Roman Catholic Church as that was understood in his day. I find that my own misgivings about evangelization are well expressed in his concepts.

Roman Catholic apologetics misused God's revelation, Blondel contended, because it construed the truths to be communicated to people as coming down from above into finite minds rather than up from below through human experience. He called this misconstrual "extrinsicism" because these truths from heaven were then obeisantly accepted on the basis of the authority of their source irrespective of their relevance to human life and the meanings about life one had already developed.[7] Blondel's caricature of the theology of revelation and the apologetics that accompanied it was that imported truths from an outsider God were added from without and existed like foreign bodies in people's mental processes. These were "supernatural truths" consequently, irrelevant to the majority of potential believers.

He developed an anthropology of action that saw God's revelation latent or implicit in the whole trajectory of willing, choosing and doing that human beings were invariably caught up in. We become who we are through our actions, and these actions begin to reveal truth to us. Our work, of course, is the major portion of these potentially truth-laden actions.

Blondel called for reflection on our action-trajectory by a method of immanence.[8] By applying oneself to a methodical reflection on one's actions, one would realize that we undertake each action in order to be more truly ourselves but that we never arrive at who we sense we really are. The logic of our actions also discloses that no matter how widely we expand our loves, there remains a deep willing at the core of our beings that wants to do more, be more, love more, be more loved. By following the drive intrinsic to all of our actions we come to the point where the very limitations of what are accessible to us thrust us beyond the finite into the undetermined, into that which is without content. If this is not what surfaces in using the method of immanence. Blondel contended, it will probably be because the person has chosen to stay enclosed within his or her own finite options and refused to open out to the undetermined. This refusal usually means that one is investing something finite with infinity. Such an investment will be the actor's undoing because it can't live up to its promise.

Blondel's next step is what he called the apologetics of the threshold.[9] In this step we reflect on the logic of our action pattern. This can lead one to the imperative of faith. We can be brought through our actions to a fundamental option: to either continue pursuing the choosing, willing, doing, working and loving into the beyond into which we are being drawn, or to fall back and settle for something less than our whole being craves. The gospel will begin to have great appeal for those pursuing the first direction and will seem an absurdity to those who choose the latter route. They become settlers for the limited.

If we take into account the existential predicament that our actions bring us to and are in touch with the ongoing dissatisfaction which accompanies them, the gospel will "fit" because it spells out the logic of lovingly surrendering to God and committing ourselves to his Son, Jesus Christ, because there is no other place to go. The gospel is not added on to one's life, then, as if from without, but it serves as a clarification of the dilemma my own humanity and actions have brought me to. Revelation, therefore, in the Blondelean scheme, is woven into the fabric of one's inmost being before it surfaces into consciousness. It will be discovered and released from the lair of the implicit, usually assisted by those who have already yielded to the imperative of the good news.

Inept evangelization, on the other hand, is of the superadditum variety. It requires the listener to ignore his or her reality to entertain the incursion. This is especially awkward in a work environment since work colleagues are convened for quite other reasons and to pursue other purposes. Nonetheless, workplace experiences are no less capable of leading employers and employees to the brink of a fundamental option than any other kind of human experience. Only revelation can supply a raison d'être for life commensurate to the transcendental subjectivity described by the Blondelean method.

## A SPIRITUALITY OF WORK

If would-be evangelizers have no notion of the relationship between their own work plus their firm's work and Christ's mission in the world, or have the idea that theirs is a totally secular undertaking without any religious meaning, their efforts at evangelization will almost certainly do more harm than good, even at times bringing about a resentment or opprobrium on Christianity for being opportunistic. A credible effort at evangelization of one's work colleagues should have as its base a spirituality of work. By this I mean that one should be able to give a faith account of what it is one is doing and experiencing in the workplace. The more people can see the religious meaning of their daily work, the more it becomes an occasion for their own growth in faith as well as in hope in and love of God. A better integration of one's faith with one's work brings many of faith's strengths to bear on the work situation. But with this experience as foundational, evangelization follows naturally and inevitably.

An example would help at this point. One's faith should be able to discern when either of the two extremes in relationship to work are operating. These extremes are underinvestment and overinvestment. Those who are underinvested are likely to be guilty of injustice, of a breach of commutative justice, not doing a day's work for a day's pay. Those who are overinvested in their work are likely to be guilty of workaholism or ambition, often to the neglect of family, spouse, loved ones. Certainly a person who preens himself or herself as religious and yet sees no religious meaning in their daily work is either going to be secularized by that work or is going to be somewhat schizophrenic in their consciousness. A spirituality of work is important for the spiritual and psychological integration of the working religious person.

Although many have developed over time an informal series of insights that would function as a spirituality of work, I have elsewhere mapped out distinct steps for fashioning such a tool. A method like the one suggested here gives one a more focused way of proceeding.[10] These steps can be traversed by an individual or, better yet, by a group. I will cite them here very briefly:

1. *The naming step.* Let the salient components of the work situation be given a chance to panoramically, impressionistically engage your consciousness: e.g., the kinds of jobs being done and the objectives of the whole operation; the roles played by the individuals and their interaction with you and one another; the policies of the firm and its moods; naming your feelings about all this data.

2. *The decoding step.* A deeper reading is given to the items that surfaced in the first step. A coding is an interpretation communicated to you of the component parts of the operation. A decoding is your interpretation of those parts. What must be decoded are the interests of the main parties in the operation as well as your own. Interests are those

reasons for which the parties are working, or what they are getting out of working in the place, or at least trying to get. These are seldom named. Also to be decoded is the ideology with which the place runs. This differs from its mission statement. It is the settled (more or less) ethos: "This is the way things are done around here and we invite you to accept this modus operandi or . . ." Also to be decoded are the structures of power, especially as they differ from the chain of command.

3. *The faith lens.* The data of the first two steps are judged in the light of faith. This can be done in one of two ways, by magnification/discovery or by contemplation/theological reflection. Magnification: a still, small voice is made louder by giving greater attention to it. Something in my workaday world is seen more explicitly in faith terms. It might be a moral issue or a display of virtue that needs to be acknowledged. Discovery: God is found to be at work in the persons with whom one works after the manner noted earlier in this essay. It is also possible that God has been virtually absent from the worksite, at least as far as my consciousness goes. In this case, one has to "mainline" the religious factor by theological reflection on or contemplation of key scripture themes until the horizon of one's mind becomes religiously active. I have in mind such themes as covenant, steward, curse, eucharist, service, vocation, discipleship, the kingdom, justice, etc.

4. *The encoding step.* Once God's connection to the work scene is seen in more explicit terms, a new coding must take place. This reinterpretation is an encoding. One must fit the new angle of vision with the everyday actions and situations. I now begin to see the things that happen every day in a new light. There is also the question of how the actual can be aligned with the possible.

5. *Resolution/praxis.* The different way of proceeding in one's work situation on the basis of one's new angle of vision must be decided and then acted upon. Praxis is action undertaken from a reflective perception of what is called for, in this case, given the insight of faith.

## NOTES

1.   *Ad Gentes* ("Decree on the Church's Missionary Activity"), Vatican Council II, ed. Austin Flannery, OP (Northport: Costello Publishing Co., 1984), n. 11.

2. Ignatius Loyola, *The Spiritual Exercises of St. Ignatius,* trans. Louis Puhl, SJ (Chicago: Loyola University Press, 1951), n. 236.
3. *Ibid.,* n. 233.
4. *Ibid.,* n. 234.
5. Ignatius Loyola, *The Constitutions of the Society of Jesus,* trans. George E. Ganss, SJ (St. Louis: Institute of Jesuit Sources, 1970), Part III of the Constitutions, n. 282.
6. *Ibid.,* n. 288.
7. Maurice Blondel, *The Letter on Apologetics: History and Dogma,* trans. A. Dru and I. Trethowan (London: SPCK, 1964), 19.
8. Maurice Blondel, *Action: Essay on a Critique of Life and a Science of Practice* (South Bend: Notre Dame University Press, 1984), 81.
9. Blondel, *Apologetics,* 70.
10. John C. Haughey, SJ, *Converting 9 to 5: A Spirituality for Daily Work* (New York: Crossroad/Continuum, 1989), chapter 9.

## DISCUSSION QUESTIONS

1. Does your work exercise a secularizing influence on you?

2. Do you find God at work in the people and circumstances in which you work?

3. Have you had any positive experiences about being evangelized or evangelizing in the work site? Negative ones?

4. What "rules" have you developed about evangelization in and through your place of work?

## FOR FURTHER READING

John C. Haughey, SJ. *Converting 9 to 5: A Spirituality for Daily Work.* New York: Crossroad/Continuum, 1989.
———. "Does God Call You at Work?" *US Catholic,* September 1990.
Michael Maccoby. *Why Work? Leading the New Generation.* New York: Simon and Schuster, 1988.
*On Human Work, A Resource Book for John Paul's 3rd Encyclical.* Washington, D.C.: USCC Office of Publishing Services, n. 847.

# A NEW LOOK AT SOCIAL JUSTICE
## Kenneth R. Himes, OFM

When Pope Paul VI wrote that "evangelizing means bringing the good news into all the strata of humanity" ("On Evangelization in the Modern World," n. 18) he included the social dimensions of human existence.[1] Two paragraphs later he noted that "what matters is to evangelize [humanity's] culture" (n. 20). The persons to be evangelized according to the pope are not abstract individuals to be considered apart from their social existence but concrete human beings in all the particularity of their setting. In our case we must consider men and women in the culture of the United States in the 1990s. How will they be evangelized? How will the gospel penetrate all the levels of their human lives?

Like Paul VI, I cannot imagine a strategy for effective evangelization that does not address the question of culture, the social reality in which people live. It is at this point that the linkage of social justice and the task of evangelization must be made. For a commitment to social justice is essential to the effort of evangelizing culture, and an evangelized culture will both facilitate and arise from the evangelization of persons.

In what follows I want to (1) develop the connection between evangelization and social justice and (2) suggest an outline for a strategy whereby the believing community can act upon the commitment to link faith and justice.

## THE CHURCH AS COMMUNITY OF DISCIPLES

Several years ago the Jesuit Avery Dulles suggested a sixth model of the church to add to the five he had explored in his well-known study *Models of the Church*.[2] The sixth model he termed church as "community of disciples."[3] While I will not use the expression exactly as Dulles did, I find it a useful one. Both notions—community and discipleship—require further comment.

In his apostolic exhortation Paul VI noted that one of the elements in the process of evangelization is "entry into the community" (n. 24). This theme is also picked up in the Rite of Christian Initiation of Adults (RCIA) with its renewed appreciation for a catechumenate experience. People cannot simply be preached at or lectured to on Catholic beliefs; rather, they must be brought into a community of believers. Coming to participate in the life of a faith community is a necessary part of the evangelization process.

Thus, the community one enters is not just any gathering of people but a gathering of believers. That suggests it is a group that has a distinctive pattern of behavior, a way of life. In short, it must be a community of disciples. The good news of Jesus cannot be reduced to a matter of correct ideas or formulas (orthodoxy). It must be a word that transforms lives, that affects the way people live (orthopraxy).

This idea of orthopraxy is nothing new, since all of us recognize that Christian faith has implications for human conduct. No one disputes the contention that life in the Christian community demands a code of personal honesty or a disposition to forgive a person's faults. No generation, of course, has ever disregarded completely the moral dimensions of Christian faith, but different eras have been more sensitive to some of those dimensions than other ones. Later on I will suggest that today we are seeing a growing appreciation for the way the gospel calls us to dedicate ourselves to social justice.

In sum, then, evangelization reminds us that we must bring people into an experience of community. Orthopraxy's challenge is that the community must have a way of life. Faith entails more than attitudes or ideas; it requires commitment to a life of discipleship. But to what should the community of disciples be committed? Disciples are to be committed to the teaching and way of life of their master. Thus, the Christian is committed to the words and acts of Jesus.

To pick up the New Testament and read any of the gospels is to read an account of Jesus' total loyalty to the reign of God. In the first chapter of the first gospel we find that Jesus is portrayed as one who goes about the towns of Galilee proclaiming, "This is the time of fulfillment. The reign of God is at hand; reform your lives and believe in the good news" (Mk 1:15). There is little debate among scholars that the reign of God was the central theme of the public ministry of Jesus. Thus, if our ministry as Christians is to be congruent with that of the Lord's ministry we must direct our attention to the reality of the reign of God in human life.

## THE REIGN OF GOD AND THE TASK OF EVANGELIZATION

Without going into an extensive exegetical treatment it can fairly be said that the reign of God is a state of being that is marked by just, peaceful and loving relationships. The reality of God's reign encompasses the Hebrew notion of justice (*sedaqah*). Unlike our modern abstract ideal, justice in the Hebrew world was a term descriptive of concrete relationships. The different relationships we have with ourselves, others, nature and God create a variety of claims upon our behavior. *Sedaqah* refers to the state of these diverse relationships being in right order. It is not stretching a point to say that for the Hebrew mind justice meant being in right relationship with God, self, other persons and all creation.

Another way of putting it is that the reign of God is the experience of being in covenant with God and all God's creation. This is what Jesus was dedicated to in his public ministry, inviting people into the experience of covenant. In this he was faithful to the prophetic tradition of ancient Israel. The prophetic message was a recurring refrain to the Israelite people to return in faith to the covenant, the relationship Yahweh offered them at Sinai. Jesus understood himself to be bringing the prophetic line to its fulfillment since he was the agent of God's reign. In him God was breaking into human existence in a new and powerful way, restoring Israel to the covenant-relationship. Acceptance of Jesus was acceptance of the invitation to once again enter into covenant with God and all of the divine creation.

Now for the modern community of disciples, the church, to be like its Lord, must be a witness to the reign of God. Like Jesus, the church has the mission of incarnating in history the reign of God, a state of relations marked by justice, peace and love. Establishing genuine covenant communities marked by such qualities is central to the church's mission. The appearance of God's reign cannot simply be a matter for the end time. It must be manifested in the present, even if incompletely, through communities faithful to the terms of the covenant.

This is so because Jesus understood himself to be initiating the reign of God. That was the claim, an implicitly messianic one, which put him at odds with the religious leaders of his people. For Jesus the reign of God was breaking into history through his ministry. The call to conversion was an invitation to his listeners to respond appropriately to the fact of God's reign now made manifest.

Today we are aware, of course, that the fullness of God's reign has not come to be in human history. But to focus only on the "not yetness" of the reign of God is to misunderstand a major element of the Christian message: The reign of God is here and now as well as future. Jesus' significance is not just for the future, for he already has become incarnate in history, and so, therefore, must the reign of God be bodied forth in present existence and not just remain a hope for the future.

We cannot give in to a mindless optimism regarding the presence of the divine in history (it is not yet fully realized), but also we must avoid ignoring the here-and-now quality of God's reign (in Jesus it has begun). The reign of God is a reality at work within history and not simply a goal to which history tends. Like Jesus the reign of God must take on flesh and enter into the human drama. That is what the community of disciples must be committed to in its orthodoxy and orthopraxy, the reign of God. The presence of God's reign is the good news which the church must preach and witness.

## EVANGELIZATION AND LIBERATION

Another way of describing the mission of the church is to state that its task is to bring about liberation. This term is one that has been misunderstood and even rejected out of hand by those who equate any talk of liberation with Marxism. Liberation, as the term is used by Catholic theologians, refers to something richer and deeper than Marxist politics. It is a religious vision of the re-creation and total fulfillment of humanity.

Liberation is meant to describe a hope that is religiously grounded. It is similar to the way the Catholic tradition has used the term "salvation." Liberation, however, does not have the otherworldly connotation of salvation and therefore is preferred by many theologians today. Salvation is a perfectly good term but often conjures up a hope that is basically post-history. Attention is focused on the "not yet" dimension of God's reign—salvation in the "sweet bye and bye." Liberation, on the other hand, calls attention to the here and now, the present processes whereby people begin to be extricated from sin and its effects—oppression, violence, racism, sexism, marginalization, poverty, etc.

Today the language of liberation reminds us that the experience traditionally called salvation must be more than a promise for the future. It must mean something for creation here and now. We can experience something, although not the totality, of God's liberation in this world. Such a transformation brought about by God's grace is a religious experience, but it is mediated through historical occurrences. Like the great moment of the exodus in the life of the Jewish people, liberation is a religious event that has political, social and economic consequences.

If evangelization—the proclamation of the reign of God made known in Jesus—is to be effective, then people ought to experience the significance of what the covenant relationship of God's reign means. An experience of being in relationship with God should be transformative of historical existence, or at least call for such transformation. The alternative is to develop a religion that so stresses the future of God's promise that it undercuts the present of God's covenant. That is effectively to deny the incarnate element of the gospel whereby the reign of God takes on flesh, pre-eminently in Jesus of Nazareth, but also in the community of disciples who minister in his name in whatever time and place.

## THE IMPORTANCE OF SOCIAL JUSTICE

In 1891 Pope Leo XIII issued an encyclical which was to become a landmark document in the modern history of Roman Catholicism. In "Rerum Novarum" the pope defended abused workers in the emerging industrial order but opposed socialism as a remedy for the workers' plight.[4] Leo believed that it was the church, drawing upon its tradition of social thought, which could develop a sound teaching about justice for the new era.

When the pope drew upon Catholic tradition, he utilized many of the ideas and themes found in the writing of Thomas Aquinas. The medieval doctor treated justice as a threefold virtue. There was commutative, legal and distributive justice. Commutative justice pertained to those rights, duties and obligations that are involved in one-to-one relations. A person borrows money from another with an agreement to pay it back in one month. The obligation to repay the sum under the terms of the agreement is derived from commutative justice.

Legal justice covered those obligations which arise from citizenship in the community. Payment of taxes, honest voting in elections, defense of the nation are illustrations of a person's duties owing to legal justice. Distributive justice covers the other side of the relationship, namely, what the community owes the individual. Distributive justice specifies the claim that all persons have a right to some share in those goods which are essentially public or social. The fertility of the earth, industrial productivity, communal security are examples of goods which cannot belong in any exclusive sense to one class or group in society. All members of society contribute, indirectly at least, to the preservation of such goods. Distributive justice establishes the equal right of all to share in the goods which are necessary for participation in the community. Thus, Thomas Aquinas' original position.

With the development of modern papal social teaching, beginning with Leo, there has been a further development of the virtue of justice. A fourth area of human life, the institutional patterns of community living, has been scrutinized. These institutional or organizational patterns, which make distributive justice possible, are governed by social justice. In Catholic teaching social justice has a technical meaning: "It refers to the obligations of all citizens to aid in the creation of patterns of societal organization and activity which are essential both for the protection of minimal human rights and for the creation of mutuality and participation by all in social life."[5] Social justice, therefore, has to do with politics, with the way we organize our various social institutions through state action. Those institutions which require attention include the legal, educational and economic systems.

It might be asked: Why this evolution in our understanding of justice? Why a fourth dimension, social justice, in addition to the three traditional forms? The answer is found in the influence of the modern social sciences. Sociology, social psychology, political science, economics, cultural anthropology are all disciplines that have enriched our appreciation for the role of institutions in societal life.

A standard text in the sociology of knowledge, *The Social Construction of Reality,*[5] argues for a dialectical relationship between the human person and society. The authors sum up their viewpoint in a dictum: "Society is a human project. Society is an objective reality. The human person is a social product."[7] This is not a deterministic attitude; the first part states the role of human beings in shaping society. Once social institutions are created, however, they stand over and apart from individuals influencing the person. It is easy to imagine how if we lived in a different era or nation we would be different than we are. That is simply because we are powerfully affected by the society in which we live.

An example might be useful. If human beings are bigoted, that bigotry will be reflected in their society. Racism exists within our hearts. What happens is that such bigotry not only remains within the heart but is given expression in social life. Housing practices are discriminatory, educational opportunities are unequal, cultural standards demean a given race's heritage. To return to the dictum of Berger and Luckmann: Society is a human project. Racist individuals will create a society that institutionalizes racism.

Suppose an individual person is not racist. Would that change the fact that there are many social practices which discriminate against a race? Despite the individual's virtue would a black person be treated fairly in the culture if everything else in society enshrined a racist attitude? Hardly, for the institutions of society have a life of their own. They are more than a single person's view. Once again, our dictum: Society is an objective reality.

Growing up in a society which teaches racism through advertising, folkways, role models, law, media, etc., it is hard not to be affected by the virus of bigotry. We are different people due to our U.S. culture than if we were from another society. For good and for ill we are taught certain beliefs by the culture. We assume a worldview which is not simply of our making but which is inherited. As the third part of the dictum states: The human person is a social product.

Social justice has assumed such importance in Catholic teaching because no understanding of reality is adequate if the central role of societal institutions is ignored. Social justice is the virtue which calls for bringing the values of the gospel to bear on the way we organize communal life, correcting the failures of our social institutions.


## SOCIAL SIN, SOCIAL JUSTICE AND EVANGELIZATION

Once we understand the impact society has upon us, the way is clear for grasping an important theme in contemporary theology, that of social sin. Perhaps no word so captures the opposite of God's reign as sin. If the reign of God is about reconciliation, wholeness and community— the experience of being in right relationship—then sin is brokenness, alienation and disunity.

All of us are familiar with the idea of sin personally and inter-personally. We say "I live in sin" or "I have sinned against my neighbor." Social sin is the term used to describe the presence of sin in a trans-personal sense. "We live in sin," not as a group of separate individuals but as a collective body. We build social structures which are an expression of our personal sin (society is a human project). In so doing we create a sinful reality outside of ourselves (society is an objective reality). That social structure perpetuates and fosters sin beyond my personal case to infect and denigrate human life in that society for generations (the person is a social product).

If liberation, or salvation, is redemption from sin, it must be so at all levels of human existence including the social. Every manifestation of sin must be opposed by the gospel and we are increasingly sensitive to the manifestations of sin which we have come to know as social sin. What is required, then, is not just personal conversion but social transformation. Society's patterns of organization must be changed so that sin can be combated in all its forms. The work of social justice is the effort to overcome social sin and is just as much a part of effective evangelization as efforts to overcome personal sinfulness are. Both share in the same goal: conversion of the created order so that the full truth and beauty of God's word can be known.

The tragedy is that racism is but one illustration of social sin and there is no lack of other examples. The lesson to see, however, is that work to overcome such realities is truly evangelical. Because the work of conversion—social and personal—is linked to the task of evangelization, the community of disciples must be involved in programs to promote social justice. This is what the bishops at the synod of 1971 meant when they wrote:

> Action on behalf of justice and participation in the transformation of the world fully appear to us as a constitutive dimension of the preaching of the gospel, or, in other words, of the church's mission for the redemption of the human race and its liberation from every oppressive situation.[8]

Any plan for evangelization that is not concerned with social conversion through social justice cannot claim to be accurately promoting the message of the gospel.

## A STRATEGY FOR SOCIAL JUSTICE MINISTRY AND EVANGELIZATION

In my remarks so far I have tried to demonstrate that social engagement is an inevitable element in being faithful to the gospel. What remains is to develop a strategy for how church people might act on social justice concerns in a program of evangelization.

Before moving to any specific cause or issue regarding justice, I believe that two preliminary concerns must be treated in any strategy: (1) making the connection between faith and public life, and (2) revitalizing the sense of public life in our nation.

### Faith and Public Life

When relating religion to public life we need to keep in mind that there are two important types of structure in public life, operational and ideological. Operational structures are *patterns of behavior* constituting our social world, e.g., real estate zoning, tax systems, trade agreements, health care delivery, banking policies. Ideological structures are the *patterns of belief,* the configurations of value that make up our social understanding. Operational structures enslave when the ideological structures implicit in them and supportive of them enslave. Ideological structures are enslaving when values other than human dignity become the organizing and dominating value.

For example, arguably the dominant value in American society, at least for some people, is the "good life" understood economically. Mass advertising promotes it, television glamorizes it, our educational system schools people for it. As an affluent lifestyle becomes the priority, other values—justice, excellence in craftsmanship, public welfare, care of the environment, family life and friendship—may be sacrificed. This may be so even if the person formally espouses a value other than economic success. What matters is the value system which drives a person's behavior.

Part of the task in promoting social change is an analysis of the cultural values of a society so as to awaken moral sensibilities and to give voice to new images of human fulfillment. To bring about change on the operational level, there is the need to complement such change by transformation on the ideological level. Therefore, if an ecclesial strategy for justice ministry is to be effective, a dual focus of social operations and social theory which confronts both operational and ideological structures is necessary.

On the whole, church leaders are better skilled at bringing about change at the ideological level. Many are more at home in discussions of value than in detailed debate about public policy. This is a strength to capitalize upon, not lament. Among the chief ways within American society that a church can be linked with public life is through the conscious cultivation of a morally sensitive and informed public opinion.

Public opinion creates an atmosphere within which policy makers operate. By interjecting moral values into public discussion the context within which decision-makers act is enriched. Public opinion does not always determine what a political leader will do but it does set parameters for a public official's use of power. Ethical considerations should be part of what determines the parameters. Failure of the church to contribute to the shaping of public opinion is a serious charge.

Justice ministry by the church should contribute to improving the level of public discourse in the nation. The aim is neither to deny the rightful independence of public officials nor to dominate all discussion. Rather, people who work for justice should sense a duty to bring the moral wisdom of the religious community to bear on the important topics of public life. The goal is to promote deeper understanding of how religion intersects with public life through the formulation and cultivation of morally informed public opinion.

In plotting how we can shape public life at the level of ideological structure we must not forget the role of imagination. Most of us are not so logical that we always use discursive reasoning to come to our viewpoint. Instead, we use logic and reason to defend and explain opinions we come to hold on other grounds. It is frequently the metaphors and images residing in our imaginations that determine our beliefs.

Religion works on the level of imagination through metaphor, parable, ritual and myth. A person raised in a community that tells stories like that of the good Samaritan or holds up role models like Dorothy Day should develop a different understanding of who is my neighbor than a person who is reared on stories of Donald Trump. When reflecting on the meaning of love, the man or woman who meditates on the cross will have different sensibilities than the individual who stares fixedly at rock videos. It may not, therefore, be too much to hope that communities who listen to the gospel and worship at eucharist together will have a more profound sense of social obligation than those who do not. That is the power of metaphor, ritual and symbol—they shape the moral imagination.

## Public Life in Our Nation

If public life in our nation is to be revived, the church will have an important role to play, namely, to resurrect the awareness that citizenship in a democracy entails moral obligations. In speaking about citizenship I am not advocating a servile attitude toward the state or a blind nationalism. What I mean is borrowed from Alexis de Tocqueville's famous study *Democracy in America*.[9] For Tocqueville the genius of American democracy was that the state was not the only institution concerned with public welfare. Many other associations and organizations existed which allowed a person to engage in the life of the community, both local and national. In Tocqueville's mind, active citizenship meant involvement in an associational life. Individuals lack the energy, time and expertise for active involvement in public affairs on a continuous basis. But they can invest some of their time, energy and expertise in concert with others through voluntary associations.

If American Catholicism were to take seriously the duty of active citizenship as part of the moral ideal of the Christian life it would urge all adult Catholics, and not just an elite few, to do what it used to promote in the old strategy of Catholic Action. That is, along with church membership, the Christian citizen of a democracy is called to engagement in the affairs of the republic by joining and participating in at least one association concerned with the public interest.[10]

Today we must face the question of how democratic nations can expand the sense of participation in public life. It is not possible for all citizens to have equal access to decision-making power. In a representative democracy some are charged with the duty of acting for others. Yet too great a distance from social power can foster hostility toward those who hold power or indifference to the public realm due to one's exclusion.

Helping to foster grassroots communities that study, debate and act upon public concerns is an important work of the church in democracy. From Amnesty International to Bread for the World, from credit unions to tenants' associations, there are opportunities for people to establish local voluntary associations that increase their ability to participate meaningfully in American democracy. Justice ministry ought to engage in efforts at providing ongoing support for voluntary associations, for these are an essential element in fostering responsible citizenship.

What if the parish became known for hosting a wide array of such communal organizations? If we made it clear that we are willing to turn on the lights and the heat and unlock the doors so that people could find meeting space? Maybe we could promote such associations by announcements, bulletin board space and membership drives. Parishes might even want to formally sponsor such voluntary associations, to be the local organizers if no local chapters exist.

The point is a simple one. A democratic society such as the United States invites certain means of effecting change. Participatory citizenship is a way of seizing the opportunities for change. Social justice ministry ought to be concerned with the cultivation of citizenship as a moral vocation. In this way the church will (1) help people to see the linkage between faith and their public roles as employer, employee, consumer and citizen, as well as (2) help democratic society to flourish.

Evangelizing the culture requires moving the gospel out of the sanctuary and into the public spaces of our nation. By calling believers to respond to their responsibilities as public persons, American Catholicism can become the leaven in society that the gospel asks us to be. In taking up the tasks of such a strategy, the church will become an agent of evangelization not only in the hearts of individuals but in the culture as well.

## NOTES

1.  Pope Paul VI, "On Evangelization in the Modern World" (Washington, D.C.: United States Catholic Conference, 1976). All references to this work

will appear in the text and refer to the paragraph number according to this edition of the exhortation.

2.  Avery Dulles, SJ, *Models of the Church* (Garden City: Doubleday and Company, 1974).

3.  Avery Dulles, SJ, "Imaging the Church for the 1980s" in *A Church to Believe In* (New York: Crossroad Publishing, 1982), 1–18.

4.  Pope Leo XIII, "Rerum Novarum" ("On the Condition of Labor"). One translation of this letter is found in William Gibbons, *Seven Great Encyclicals* (New York: Paulist Press, 1963), intro.

5.  David Hollenbach, *Justice, Peace and Human Rights* (New York: Crossroad Publishing, 1988), 27. Hollenbach's is a fine work which is richly instructive in the area of Catholic social thought.

6.  Peter Berger and Thomas Luckmann, *The Social Construction of Reality* (Garden City: Doubleday and Company, 1966).

7.  *Ibid.*, 61.

8.  1971 Synod, "Justice in the World" (Washington, D.C.: United States Catholic Conference, 1972), 34.

9.  Alexis de Tocqueville, *Democracy in America*, ed. J.P. Mayer, trans. George Lawrence (Garden City: Doubleday and Company, 1969).

10.  John Coleman, "The Christian as Citizen," *Commonweal* 110 (1983), 457–62.

## DISCUSSION QUESTIONS

1.  How can a parish promote the idea of responsible citizenship?

2.  How can social justice be "mainstreamed" in a parish and not be left to a few people?

3.  What is the role of the individual in combating social sin and promoting gospel values in society?

## FOR FURTHER READING

Parker Palmer. *The Company of Strangers*. New York: Crossroad Publishing, 1986.

John Coleman. "The Christian As Citizen," *Commonweal 110* (1983), 457–62.

David Hollenbach. *Justice, Peace and Human Rights*. New York: Crossroad Publishing, 1988.

# III

# New Methods

# THE EMPOWERING CAPACITY OF
# THE BIBLE FOR EVANGELIZATION

## Lawrence Boadt, CSP

### AMERICAN CATHOLICS AND THE BIBLE

Historically, American Catholics have not been very Bible-centered. Nineteenth century warnings to immigrants included advice that the Protestant Bible was an evil book to be avoided.[1] Catholic devotional practices almost never included Bible reading.[2] Even today, the Notre Dame Study of Catholic Parish Life, begun in 1983 and continuing through the decade, reveals that thirty-three percent of all American Catholics have never read the Bible on their own, and seventy-three percent have never read or discussed the Bible in a group setting.[3] This is changing somewhat as the church puts more emphasis on scripture and parish renewal programs. On the positive side, twenty-five percent of Catholics now read the Bible at least once a month, and thirteen percent are in some type of Bible study group.[4] The study also showed that there was a high correlation between what it terms "evangelical" practices of Bible study and/or faith sharing and active involvement in parish life.[5] Naturally, perhaps, parish leaders are much more likely than the ordinary parishioner to read the Bible regularly;[6] but, overall, there is no factor except the level of college education that is a better predictor of a Catholic's involvement with the parish (and with politics!) than regular Bible reading or study.[7]

Significantly, this renaissance in biblical awareness comes from the renewed emphasis on scripture initiated by the Second Vatican Council in several of its major documents, as the Notre Dame Study itself recognizes.[8] But it was given major impetus by the work of the bishops' synod that met in Rome in 1974 to discuss evangelization. The preparatory commission issued a study document, "The Evangelization of the Mod-

ern World," that called for energetic efforts to evangelize the world with
the good news by proclaiming it and explaining it so as to awaken faith in
non-Christians and nourish it in those already baptized.[9] Shortly after
the synod, Pope Paul VI issued an apostolic exhortation based on the
work of the synod titled "On Evangelization in the Modern World"
("Evangelii Nuntiandi") that is a remarkable document for its biblical
focus and sensitivity.[10] It advocates a very clear link between the mission
of the church to evangelize all peoples and a deep familiarity with biblical
categories such as witness, servant, disciple and the apostle as "one
sent."[11] It also hews closely to New Testament models, found in Jesus
above all but also in Paul as the apostle and evangelizer par excellence.
Although the pope does not go on to say that reading the scriptures
should be the task of every Catholic because of his or her call to be an
evangelizer, it is certainly the implication of the very biblical approach
that he takes throughout.

In order to embody the message of "On Evangelization in the Modern World" in the American church today, three tasks confront us: we
must (1) understand the council's turn to the biblical, (2) develop sound
biblical language and theology while avoiding fundamentalism, and (3)
empower all Catholics to become witnesses, disciples and evangelizers
through their love of and familiarity with scripture.

## THE SECOND VATICAN COUNCIL AND BIBLICAL LANGUAGE

The "Dogmatic Constitution on the Church" ("Lumen Gentium")[12]
of the Second Vatican Council describes the church first in terms of the
mystery of its union with Christ, and follows this in the second chapter
with a complementary definition of the church as the people of God,
called to acknowledge and serve God in holiness everywhere in the world
(n. 9). This people is open to all peoples whom God has created, recognizing the work of God in other faiths, while at the same time making known
to everyone the loving plan of salvation revealed through Christ's life,
death and resurrection (nn. 15–17). The church as the people of God has
a special respect for Jews and Moslems who know the same God and
share many aspects of faith with Christians. It sees itself especially impelled to promote God's glory as the creator and giver of salvation to all
who are caught by the web of sin or are ignorant of a gracious God in
their lives: "Mindful of the command to preach the gospel to every
creature (Mk 16:16), the church painstakingly fosters her missionary
work" (n. 16). Only after this vision of a church which is both mystery

and missionary does the constitution go on in succeeding chapters to address concrete structures of the church.

Two important breakthroughs are emphasized in this view of the church. First, it acknowledges that God's saving plan works outside the church even for those who do not know Christ and never will. And, second, it recognizes a special relationship to Judaism and Islam because they share with Christians at least part of the biblical faith. The church as the people of God, then, is paradoxically both respectful of God's activity beyond its boundaries and deeply conscious of its own mission to make known the New Testament message in every place. These two seemingly opposite characteristics must influence any discussion on the nature of the church that is held today. We will need an ecclesial understanding that is more ecumenical, more missionary and more biblical in its formulation.

The mediating word is *biblical*. To think in biblical categories will put us into contact with the rich mixture of stories, commands and practices from the books of the Old and New Testaments that make apparently opposite insights as each comes alive in its own concrete and original setting or context. Already at the council, a follow-up document, "The Declaration on the Relationship of the Church to Non-Christian Religions" ("Nostra Aetate"),[13] develops the thought of "Lumen Gentium" on these topics in more depth, using largely biblical categories. Still another council document, "The Decree on the Church's Missionary Activity" ("Ad Gentes"),[14] employs biblical language throughout its general introduction to the missionary nature of the church (nn. 1–13). The "Dogmatic Constitution on Divine Revelation" ("Dei Verbum")[15] has strongly supported this recovery of biblical thinking about the church by moving dramatically away from talking about philosophical theories of inspiration toward explaining the scriptural bases of revelation itself. Many Protestant commentators have applauded the council's return to biblical formulations of its missionary role and view it as a major step forward in ecumenical cooperation.[16]

Twenty-five years after the council has closed, we are still faced with the task of making this biblical language an integral part of our consciousness in talking about the church, especially the church as missionary by nature. The task itself can be summed up as the call to *evangelization*, proclaiming the good news inside and out, even though the word itself was rarely used in the council documents.[17] To achieve it, we will not need just more zeal, but an increasingly nuanced and richer familiarity with the biblical text, its role in our spiritual life and its interpretation by modern scripture scholarship. Becoming more biblically-minded will help Catholics in particular not only understand the basis of evangelization, but also see how biblical thought offers a reconciliation that makes possible the missionary outreach of preaching the gospel alongside an ecumenical dialogue of respect with other world religions.

## CATHOLIC RECOVERY OF THE BIBLE FOR EVANGELIZATION

The first and most pressing problem for those who would like to see the Bible as the medium for carrying the gospel message in the community of faith is to get the Bible known. We Catholics have been notably short on both personal familiarity with the biblical text and the development of a biblically-based spirituality. And we have been just as slow as any other Christian group in assimilating and making use of the fruits and insights of modern critical Bible study.[18] Too often Catholics think only of the New Testament as serious scripture, although this is now changing slowly but effectively after the introduction of the Old Testament into the Sunday lectionary. Most Catholics have had some kind of exposure to a pious portrayal of the gospel story which has emphasized the gentleness and kindness of Jesus, and his almost openly divine serenity and foreknowledge of events. It is a cohesive picture built on combining the different gospels into a single story, and is usually understood very literally as a factual account of Jesus' life, i.e., as a biographical report. Since critical biblical study has moved away from this approach and understands most biblical accounts to have a primary function of proclamation and persuasion, and as a consequence to rely for their argumentation much more on both theological reasoning and literary imagination than on specific historical accuracy, Bible study may appear threatening to many Catholics. This is a serious challenge because biblical scholarship may seem to undermine the historical foundations of faith in the church as well as the church's traditionally rather literal use of the Bible in piety and liturgy. While few Catholics seem disturbed when a sermon explains that the six days of creation in Genesis 1 do not necessarily mean six actual days, many express concern over reports in the press that New Testament scholars are voting on whether Jesus really said many of the sayings attributed to him in the gospels.[19] Catholics, indeed most Christians, are probably much more fundamentalistic or literalistic in their reading of the New Testament than of the Old, but in fact scholars would work with most of the same approaches for either Testament.

Two things should therefore be kept in mind in planning to encourage wider Bible study. First, we cannot proceed very far by continuing to feed people a naive, pietistic view of the scriptures as straight history.

Not only are future priests and religious being trained in the insights of modern biblical criticism, but so are the future lay leaders of the church who are enrolled in M.A. or M.Div. programs throughout the country. Moreover, the wealth of new knowledge of the ancient world through document finds, archaeology and the studies of social science supports the critical approach and makes it impossible to view biblical books as simple factual accounts.[20] For better or worse, we understand how ancients thought and must follow where the truth leads.

The second consideration follows from the first. If modern biblical study does involve an effort at critical understanding of the meaning of texts that serve as the normative foundations of faith, then we will need both sound learning and sound pastoral instincts in biblical teachers and facilitators of Bible study groups. Scholars tend to be analytical and questioning of the historicity of texts. But Christians do not read the Bible primarily to improve their grasp of history. Rather they read the Bible because it speaks to them today about how to live now. The church is the medium that links the historical roots of faith with its contemporary relevance for life. And its primary vehicle to achieve this is its proclamation of the Bible that records the foundational story of those roots and yet is read and expressed anew in liturgy, doctrinal declarations, and spirituality for every age.

The centuries of rich tradition of biblical usage in the church include a wide diversity of vocabulary and imagery employed at different times to explain its relevance for people of quite dissimilar cultures. At the same time, biblically inspired devotions to Mary, meditations on the sufferings of Christ, and prayers to the Sacred Heart have entered the living stream of biblical interpretation within the church setting and cannot just be abandoned or dismissed with a scholarly shrug. Even more significantly, the tradition of lectionary selections from the scriptures has shaped the thinking of generations of Catholics who were only exposed to the Bible at the eucharist. Because they contain only selected texts, lectionaries both distort the shape of full biblical books and highlight certain parts. Increased study will need to balance critical scholarship, liturgical awareness and contemporary spiritual applications—a challenging task.

Here again is where the concepts "evangelical" and "evangelization" can help energize the development of widespread Catholic biblical study. One sociological definition of the evangelical spirit is that it (1) respects the normative character of the Bible, (2) inculcates a desire to study the Bible either alone or in groups, and (3) leads to a vigorous prayer life directed to a God who is close and personally companionate.[21] Among Catholics this is not just a quality of the charismatic movement, but has received strong impetus for all members of the church from the council's renewed emphasis on (1) a strong christology at the center of our devotion which will make the Father accessible through the Son, (2) the Holy Spirit that empowers through the word and sacrament, and finally (3) the development of a religiously informed and personally responsible laity. This last point encourages lay lectors who are to read the scriptures in public proclamation at the eucharist.[22] As these aspects emerge in the preaching, teaching and daily life of the church, the evangelical shape of post-Vatican II Catholicism will become more pronounced and lay the foundations for an evangelizing church, i.e., one nourished and empowered to proclaim the gospel to others and to foster a stronger commitment to the gospel in its own witness and growth in spirituality.[23]


## THE MAJOR THEMES OF THE OLD TESTAMENT

How then does the Bible carry the message that the Catholic Church is an evangelizing church? As one becomes more and more familiar with the biblical story, certain themes seem to reappear which give a constant direction and form to its widely divergent types of literature. These themes need to be highlighted so that they begin to imbue the hearer of the sacred word with a vision of the whole scheme or pattern of God's action in the world as Israel and the apostolic church understood it. In the process of searching out such significant themes we must not fall into the trap of thinking there is a master plan for the seventy-two books of scripture which can be put down in some type of clear and simple outline. Its richness defies all attempts at a single theology or single principle that controls the overall message. Nevertheless, there are essential or key elements that should stand forth in any description of what constitutes biblical faith. These in turn can be explored individually so as to throw light on the others and so enrich one another. The core traditions in the Old Testament, which were remembered as occurring early, develop in three stages:

1. Israel itself remembered that the key event of its history was the *special election* of this people by God. It is described in stages from the creation of the world to the fall of Judah, the last remnant of the independent nation, in 587 B.C.E. This is told in narrative form in the core collection from Genesis to 2 Kings. It begins in Genesis 1–11 with a series of vignettes at the beginning of the world in which God gave all humankind blessing and was met by human rebellion and sin. God would punish and then forgive and restore the blessing, only to be met once

more with sin. Having been rebuffed again and again by the whole human community, God narrows the focus to choose and bless one family, that of Abraham, so that it may give witness to the divine love for all of creation. The members of this family are challenged to choose God in return, to identify themselves personally with Yahweh, the God of their ancestors, and to live by trusting faith in the goodness of this God. It is the story of the patriarchs and matriarchs of Genesis 12–50, and of the people liberated from slavery and guided to the promised land, recorded in the book of Exodus. Abraham's life is a model of this faith, but it is fully embodied only in the covenant of permanent loving bondedness between Israel and God at Sinai, and it is concretized in the divine promise of land and in the obedience of the people to the law. This stage is contained in the books of the Pentateuch.

2. The next stage is in the land itself, told in the books of the former prophets, i.e., Joshua through 2 Kings. It centers on rulers, especially David the king, who succeed only when they see themselves as servants to one king, God, and consequently subject their actions to covenant fidelity. The law of Deuteronomy sums up the course of that history in a standard pattern—when the kings and people obey the law of God they prosper, and when they turn from it, they face curse and exile from the land.[24] Connected to this historical interpretation are books such as the Psalms, which emphasize in public prayers the universal kingship of God over the nations, the offer of salvation to all peoples from God's presence on Mount Zion, and God's reconciling and healing love to those who turn back from sin and call out trustingly for help in their anguish.

3. This mega-story has many crucial themes of what we would call evangelization: God's desire to reach all peoples with blessing, the empowerment of a special people to bear witness to that love, the promise of liberation and communion in obedience to the sole king over all creation. But there is a third stage found in the prophetic books that best articulates the model on which the New Testament gospel will build. Four themes in particular are worth examining in detail. These are found throughout the books of the individual prophets, but the salvation message of the Second Isaiah (Isaiah 40–55) accents them most sharply for us, and can be used to illustrate each theme.

*The first is the theme of the divine plan.* The original prophet Isaiah constantly announced that God had a plan to use the nations as instruments of judgment in punishing Israel. In turn, God would subject these foreign powers to punishment for their arrogant usurpation of divine authority (Is 10:5–15; 14:24–27). This message is picked up by a disciple of Isaiah during the Babylonian exile and proclaimed anew as a plan of redemption and deliverance for the exiles by means of Cyrus, king of

Persia, as God's instrument (Is 41:25–29; 44:24–28; 45:1–6). Cyrus does not know Yahweh, but God knows him and will bring about his success. Second Isaiah also emphasizes that God's word never fails but always brings about what it expresses (Is 40:8; 55:8–11). The remnant that will return from exile will be the cornerstone of a new Zion, and their return will be a new exodus fulfilling the ancient plan of God for a permanent community of faithfulness in the land (Is 51:1–6; 51:9–10; 52:1–7).

*The second is the theme of repentance and conversion.* The Hebrew verb *shub* has the sense of returning back to the covenant, not of shifting one's loyalty to something new. But it does have the added dimension of (1) a personal relationship being healed, (2) a spirit of contrition, and (3) a commitment to obedience and love (Ps 51; Jer 31:31; Ez 36:26–27). Second Isaiah makes effective use of the call to return to trust and loyalty in God by framing many of his oracles in the form of trial speeches and disputations in which God conducts a legal case to show that the pagan gods of Babylon are powerless and only Yahweh deserves the people's loyalty (Is 41:21–29; 43:1–13; 44:6–8). As a result, the people are summoned to return to God (Is 44:22; 48:12–19). Then they will know God with an intimacy unlike anything in the past (Is 49:14–18; 55:1–5).

*The third theme is the proclamation of good news.* In the story of Absalom's rebellion against David, messengers bring good news that Absalom has been defeated (2 Sam 18:20, 22), while Jeremiah 20:15 speaks of announcing the good news of the birth of a son. The Hebrew verb used, *basar,* also occurs in the Psalms to refer to proclaiming the joyous announcement of God's salvation and justice (Pss 40:10; 96:2). In this religious sense, the context involves testifying about God's deeds to others. In Second Isaiah, the prophet employs the verb to announce his major theme of God's deliverance from the exile. Is 40:9–10 pictures Jerusalem itself proclaiming the good news that God is in its midst and comes with power to save. The prophet then sums up the message in a ringing passage near the end of his prophecy: "How beautiful on the mountains are the feet of one who brings glad news, announcing peace, proclaiming the good news, declaring salvation, and saying to Zion, 'Your God is king!' " (Is 52:7). A disciple after the return from exile continues this message by extending the promise of good news to the lowly, the brokenhearted, the captive and prisoner and the mourner (Is 61:1–2). Jesus himself will employ this very passage in defining his own mission, at least according to the gospel of Luke (Lk 4:16–30).

*The fourth theme is that of Israel as witness.* The eighth century prophets began to speak regularly of God's lawsuit against Israel for violation of the covenant agreement (Hos 4:1–3; Is 1:2–3). This became the favorite language of the prophetic tradition, found strongly in even late books like Malachi and Third Isaiah (Is 56–66). But never is it used with more power than in Second Isaiah when he confronts the exiles with the claims of Yahweh versus those of pagan gods. God's chief witness is summoned to testify: it is Israel itself! The people are challenged to show that God indeed has always acted on their behalf, has done what was promised and remained faithful (Is 43:8–13; 44:6–9). Even more poignantly, the prophet develops the figure of the suffering servant who alternately speaks or remains silent, but always witnesses to a complete trust in Yahweh. The witness has a well-trained tongue (Is 50:4); it is a sharp-edged sword (Is 49:2). Yet the servant does not cry out, but is tender to the broken reed (Is 42:2–3). Finally, he endures indignity (Is 50:6) and even death for the sake of others (Is 52:13–53:12). The idea of a witness who gives his life contains echoes of the covenant concern that no one be condemned to death unless there are two fully independent and trust-worthy witnesses against him or her (Dt 17:6; 19:15; Num 35:30). For Second Isaiah, the suffering servant is both the prophet testifying and the people Israel testifying against itself. Death was the deserved out-come of their sin, but mercy is what God provides. It is no wonder that for the New Testament, the servant songs explained the death of Jesus better than any other biblical text.

## NEW TESTAMENT DEVELOPMENT OF THE THEMES

This four-pronged message of the prophets provides an essential background for understanding Jesus' proclamation of the kingdom of God, since his own contemporaries clearly saw him as continuing the preaching of the prophets before him (Mk 8:28; Lk 9:18–19). The evan-gelists and other New Testament writers agreed with and reflected upon this assessment. The letter to the Hebrews, for example, begins with the claim that what God once spoke through the prophets is now said in Christ (Heb 1:1–2), and the gospel of John goes even further in its prologue to identify Jesus with the eternal word of God spoken in cre-ation (Jn 1:1–18). Luke goes beyond the idea of word when he connects Jesus to the pouring out of the prophetic spirit. The Acts of the Apostles not only records empowerment by the Holy Spirit at every preaching of the gospel message (Acts 2:4; 4:8, 31; 5:12; 8:17; 10:44), but links Moses and David as prophets who foresaw Jesus as their successor in manifest-ing the Spirit in acts of power (Acts 2:29–35; 3:22–23). Luke sums up the prophetic role of Jesus through both word and Spirit-filled actions in a climactic scene at the very end of the gospel when he has one of the disciples on the road to Emmaus wonder how anyone could have failed to know about "Jesus of Nazareth, a prophet powerful in *word* and *deed* before God and all the people" (Lk 24:19).

These and many other New Testament texts prepared the first generation of Christians for the realization that they in turn were to carry on the prophetic mission of Christ once they had received the gift of faith through the word and outpouring of the Spirit. Indeed almost all of the New Testament books could be considered handbooks for the spreading of the gospel. They are linked to the apostles or evangelists by *author*-ity, and deal with apostolic teaching. In this sense they also model the apostolic and evangelizing role for their readers. A partial portrait of the good news can be drawn that sharpens the link between the prophetic proclamation and the preaching of the New Testament *kerygma*. Briefly, it would include the following:

1. The prophetic divine plan for Israel emphasized divine transcendence, the universal rule of God over all peoples, and a miraculous restoration of a new Zion. Jesus expresses this in the proclamation of the kingdom of God which has arrived as a "time of fulfillment" (Mk 1:15; Lk 4:17–19). The gospels then lead the reader through how this is to be accomplished: Jesus will be a king, but a suffering messiah, a servant king; he will also be glorified and establish a new era of the Spirit, but only after his resurrection, and he will welcome all peoples into the kingdom.[25] Paul adds to this the concept of "mystery." He preaches the wisdom of God in mystery, hidden from us, yet planned by God before all time (1 Cor 2:7; Rom 16:25). It is employed even more frequently in the later letters to the Colossians and Ephesians,[26] and centers on the inexplicable freedom that God has exercised in welcoming Gentiles into the covenant given to his chosen people (see Rom 11:25; Eph 3:3, 9; 1 Tim 3:16).

2. The prophetic theme of repentance and conversion is likewise central to the gospel. It is closely tied to Jesus' announcement of the kingdom in Mark 1:15, "Repent! For the kingdom of God is here!" And it is ingrained in one of the healing traditions of the gospels where forgiveness of sins receives priority over healing of the body (Mt 9:1–8; Mk 2:1–12; Lk 5:17–26; Jn 5:14–15). It is carried on in the preaching of the early church recorded by Luke in the Acts of the Apostles.[27] This theme of repentance is marked as an urgent requirement. Paul's early letters to the Thessalonians and the end of 1 Corinthians deal with the hope for Christ's expected return in the near future. And yet the gospels remember that "the good news of the kingdom will be proclaimed throughout the world as a witness to all nations, and only then will the end come!" (Mt 24:14). The apocalyptic passages in Mark 13, Matthew 24 and the book of Revelation fortify this sense of urgency that the

gospel must be preached before the end comes. Watchfulness is the key word (Mt 24:42; 25:13; Mk 13:36–37). The reason for this urgency is that when the master does return, he will only recognize those that already know him. This is the import of Jesus' parables of the wise and foolish virgins (Mt 25:1–13), the seed cast on good ground (Mk 4:1–20) and the marriage feast (Lk 14:16–24). It is also the point in both the Emmaus story in Luke 24:13–35 and Jesus' farewell prayer for his disciples in John 17:20–26. It also forms the background to Paul's theology of dying and rising with Christ (Rom 6–8) and the unity of the body of Christ (Rom 12:3–8; 1 Cor 12:12–26; Eph 1:22; 2:15–18; 3:6; 4:15–16). Paul sums up this prophetic urgency when he insists that all who call on the name of the Lord will be saved, yet how will they call on one in whom they do not believe? And how will they believe unless someone preaches? And how can they preach unless they are sent (Rom 10:13–15)?

3. Like the message of Second Isaiah, the good news is always the promise of salvation to those who need a savior. The Johannine tradition speaks of this divine plan of salvation in the language of God's love revealed in Jesus (Jn 1:16; 17:22–24; 1 Jn 4:7–21), summed up finally in 1 John 4:8: "God is love!" Paul, too, can speak of love motivating the divine plan of redemption. His treatise on God's love in Romans 8 ends with the ringing declaration that nothing "can separate us from the love of God that comes to us in Christ Jesus our Lord!" (Rom 8:39). This spirit of joyful confidence is rooted in the conviction that God now welcomes all people into the covenant, Jew and Gentile alike, and all are equal there: men and women, slave and free (Gal 3:28; Rom 10:12). The theme of God's universal love is so strong that Paul wrestles constantly with the fear that the Jewish people might be cut off from the covenant if they cannot know Christ, but he refuses to even consider it possible (Rom 9–11; Gal 2:12–3:13). Luke addresses the universality of God's plan by showing that the Holy Spirit can come down on born Jews (Acts 2:1–4, 4:31), converts (Acts 8:14–17), hated persecutors like Paul (Acts 9:17), and Gentiles (Acts 10:44) alike. It is indeed a promise of salvation to the poor, the blind, the prisoner, the mourner and the brokenhearted (Lk 4:18–19 citing Is 61:1).

4. We noted above that the Old Testament idea of witness had both the components of testifying and of putting one's life on the line. Disciples are commanded to go forth without possessions to preach only what words the spirit provides in precisely these terms in Jesus' mission charge recorded by all the synoptics (Mt 10:5–42; Mk 6:7–13; Lk 9:1–6). The final commission to evangelize at the end of the gospels of Matthew and Luke also stress the tasks of the witness to testify by word and deed (Mt 28:16–20; Lk 24:48). Acts is built around the spread of the gospel to the

ends of the earth by those who are charged as witnesses (Acts 1:8). Even the choice of a new apostle emphasizes that he must have been a witness to the risen Lord (Acts 1:15–26). The Johannine tradition, too, favors the language of the witness tradition. The whole of the farewell speech of Jesus to his disciples in John 14–17 can be read as a subtle explanation of how Jesus gives witness to the Father, how the Father gives testimony on behalf of Jesus, and how the disciples are to carry this witness to others.

In light of what was said above about the close connection between the suffering role and the witness role in the servant texts of Isaiah, we should not be surprised that the language of witness occurs forty-four times in John and thirty-four times in Luke–Acts. It brings together the best prophetic insights into the reason for the death and resurrection of Jesus the servant and the urgency to testify to it as the good news of God's plan of salvation for all people who will heed it and become part of the kingdom. Indeed, in this statement we find all four of our themes brought together as one.

## THE GOSPEL AS A MODEL FOR EVANGELIZATION

Evangelization as a biblical category making use of the preceding insights can be described as both the proclamation of the good news of salvation in Christ to all parts of the world (Mt 28:16–20; Lk 24/Acts 1) and also the strengthening and building up of the community in the "way" (Acts 9:2) by living the implications of the gospel as the apostles bore witness to it (Acts 2:42–47; 4:32–35).[28] This corresponds to the broad definition of evangelization provided by the synod of 1974 which combines the command to teach and baptize all nations (Mt 28:19–20) with the need to proclaim anew the gospel to the believing community to vitalize and deepen its own life in Christ.[29]

In "On Evangelization in the Modern World," Paul VI went on to outline a sketch of the essential biblical foundations for making evangelization a formative part of our membership in the church today: (1) it must be associated with the mission of Jesus himself as portrayed in the gospels; (2) it proclaims human liberation, especially from sin and its effects; (3) those who are evangelized are to be identified with the "kingdom" of God; (4) it requires untiring effort, even suffering; (5) it builds a community, the church, which is one with Jesus as evangelizer.[30] In short, this description reflects the gospel outline of Mark's story of Jesus, who (1) preached that the kingdom of God was close at hand (Mk 1:15), (2) called for conversion of heart while he healed the sinner and physically bound (Mk 2:1–12), (3) invited disciples to share his mission (Mk 3:13–19), (4) taught them the meaning of his cross and their sharing in it (Mk 8:31–38), and (5) formed of them a community sharing his very life and self at the last supper (Mk 14:22–26).

If the gospel story itself is the model for evangelizers, then the lesson seems to be that we need to become more steeped in biblical categories and biblical modes of thinking if we are to become more evangelically aware.[31] Since this must avoid the pitfall of a literalism or fundamentalism and be adapted to and articulated in contemporary ways of thought, I would like to offer some thoughts toward developing a spirituality of evangelization based on the Bible.

If we take the four themes that have emerged from our reflections on the total scriptures, we can draw two sets of models, one for personal growth, the other for the mission or task of evangelization. The first might be called the *content* of our biblical spirituality, the second the *means* by which we share it with others.

### Model One: Personal Appropriation of the Prophetic Message

1. The divine plan is the vision of the whole. We read scripture in order to see the rich diversity of divine action through the long ages of Israel and the early church, and to realize that these are stories, poems, laws, oracles, letters that have come out of real people's experience of God in their lives. With this in mind, we should look forward to the contradictions and differences in historical narratives or gospel parallels and expect to find in each narrative or account the nuance that will reveal something new about God's presence to our lives. We will want to read the scriptures regularly and as widely as possible, not seeing it as drudgery, but as an adventure of discovery that will teach us each day more about our faith and ourselves as a part of God's plan. We are *disciples*, always learning from the master.

2. The call to conversion challenges me to investigate my life plan against the lessons of scripture. I will need to consider reorientation of my values and priorities. If I have learned, how do I put it into practice. The Bible is full of stories of heroes of faith with clay feet whose ways can help me learn what God expects and what God rejects. They range from an Abraham to a David to a Ruth or Esther or Daniel and on to a Peter, Mary of Bethany or Paul himself. But for the Christian, each and every one points to one person, Jesus of Nazareth, the Christ and Lord. Conversion will mean reading and meditating on the scriptures in order to make a commitment to Christ, to become a follower of Christ, and to be like Christ. When we discover further that the message of Jesus centers

on the cross and resurrection, we discover that our model is to be the *servant*, in all of its biblical dimensions, but especially in light of the servant texts of Isaiah as they are embodied in the gospel account of Jesus.

3. To receive "good news" suggests that our proper response is joy and enthusiasm: It is the pearl of great price or the treasure in the field for which we would sell everything else to possess it (Mt 13:44–46). Other injunctions describe this longing: "Hunger and thirst after holiness" (Mt 5:6); "Unless you become like a little child you will not enter the kingdom of heaven" (Mt 18:3); "Come to me, all you who are weary and find life burdensome, and I will refresh you" (Mt 11:28); "Anyone who does not take up the cross and follow me cannot be my disciple" (Lk 14:27). If we develop an understanding of the message of scripture as good news, we begin to see all things from a balanced perspective: there is room in creation for happiness but also for suffering. Either way, however, we are impelled to share our joy and give comfort to those who suffer. Our desire for the treasure always includes an urge to share it. Perhaps we could meditate on the model of the greatest of the preachers of good news, Paul the apostle, who reveals his passionate concern for both the message and its recipients in every letter. Especially, his balanced attitude as the messenger of good news comes out in his words to the Philippians, "I have learned to eat well or go hungry, to have much or to have nothing—in him who is the source of my strength, I have strength for everything!" (Phil 4:12–13). Our model is the apostle.

4. A witness must testify. The meditative reading of scripture raises for us many questions of how we can best express our commitment to Christ, our conviction that the gospel is good news and that others can see as much in them as we do. That is, we need to sharpen our beliefs and values so that they will be a part of our public self. Jesus warned his disciples not to be a light under a bushel basket (Mt 5:14–15). This is pointed advice to a church that is commissioned to evangelize the world. Pope Paul VI points to the twofold command to witness by our lives and by proclamation.[32] The biblical books are filled with examples of both throughout, but we might especially recall the Lukan summation of Jesus' ministry, that he was powerful in word and deed (Lk 24:19). Finding the balance of personal holiness and public witness will always be difficult. But for this reason, Jesus' disciples never stand as individuals, lone rangers, outside of the community. As a church, they work together to share their life and worship and to support one another in bearing testimony while remaining steadfast. Reflection on the role of witness

then should lead to a deeper commitment to active participation in the church.

*Model Two: Sharing the Prophetic Message*

1. The evangelizer will have to open up a vision to others. To do this in scriptural categories will mean asking people to look into their own experience and begin to see it as a journey in which God has been present. Each person is already a disciple of life. All of us can be drawn to seek more from it than we already possess, to note our lacks and unfulfilled hopes for ourselves, and be invited to explore the biblical story so that we can relate its experience to our own.

2. The task of conversion calls forth the persuasive power of the believer. If we reflect on the miracle stories of healing and forgiveness throughout the gospels, the discussions and confrontations between Jesus and his opponents in Matthew and John, and the passionate pleadings in Paul's letters to the Corinthians, Galatians and Thessalonians, the approaches will stand out by which we can invite others to live by values other than their normal short-range, secular goals in life. The New Testament might be considered in toto a literary genre of persuasion. But the gospels and the Pauline correspondence both keep a remarkable balance between confronting the personal decisions of hearers about their own lives and confronting their social and religious views as a nation or community. In both cases, emphasis falls on the central significance of the cross and on empowerment by the Holy Spirit. We are thus brought back to the Isaian role of the servant. The New Testament in its proclamation of the gospel message is suffused with both the strength of its conviction and the humility of its service to others. The embodiment is Jesus, and the lessons are for all evangelizers.

3. Bringing the gospel as good news can best be accomplished by relating its message to the everyday experience of people. For this, reflection on the parables in the synoptics will have particular power. Parables contain both general examples of human experience and an unexpected catch that opens the eyes to new possibilities. The father's unexpected sense of total welcome and forgiveness for a prodigal son illustrates this (Lk 14:11–32). In another way, the sermon on the mount in Matthew 5–7 contains numerous challenging but unexpected descriptions of life as a disciple, e.g., the beatitudes; the contrast sayings: "you have heard it said . . . but I say . . ."; the sayings on prayer, fasting and almsgiving. If bringing good news is an apostolic role, then these types of

biblical texts can be read or discussed with the goal of showing the hearer that God is already at work in their experience, and that accepting faith will open up a greater possibility for giving meaning to that experience.

4. The final category of witness with its note of testimony should remind us that those who call on the name of the Lord will be saved (Rom 10:13), and that the first Christian community was described as devoting itself to study, prayer, the eucharist and praising God (Acts 2:42–47). They gave thanks to God readily (Acts 4:24–26; 11:18), and never ceased proclaiming the name (Acts 5:40–41). Paul, too, usually opens his letters with praise and thanksgiving for God's work among the churches (Rom 1:8–9; 1 Cor 1:4–9; 2 Cor 1:3–7; Phil 1:3–11). At the very least, our witness of word and action must be characterized by a spirit of prayer that places praise and thanksgiving of God before our own immediate needs and concerns. The marks of a witness are confidence in the truth and trust in God's help (Mt 10:5–20; Acts 4:8–12). This translates into a sense of peace for the individual and the community, but a peace marked by passionate concern for the lack of peace and the lack of right order in the world. Ultimately, our evangelization preaches a gospel to both the individual searcher and to the world order.

## CONCLUSION

*Disciple, servant, apostle* and *witness* are biblical concepts that offer real opportunity to the evangelization effort to relate the outer mission of the church to spread the gospel with the inner spiritual growth of the individual. This short reflection hardly exhausts the wide range of possibilities that biblical reflection offers us for exploring our evangelizing mission as a church. Hopefully, however, it suggests a few possibilities and invites still more.

## NOTES

1. Jay Dolan, *The Immigrant Church: New York's Irish and German Catholics, 1815–1865* (Baltimore: Johns Hopkins University Press, 1975), 132. See also Gerald Fogarty, SJ, *American Catholic Biblical Scholarship: A History from the Early Republic to Vatican II* (San Francisco: Harper & Row, 1989), 3.
2. See Michael R. Welch and David C. Leege, "Dual Reference Groups and Political Orientations: An Examination of Evangelically Oriented Catholics," *American Journal of Political Science* 35:1 (February 1991), 28–56, especially 31.

3.  The Notre Dame Study of Catholic Parish Life is available in a series of reports based on the statistical samplings done in 1983–84. For its overall scope and goals, see David C. Leege and Joseph Gremillion, "The U.S. Parish Twenty Years after Vatican II: An Introduction to the Study," *Notre Dame Study of Catholic Parish Life, Report 1* (Notre Dame: University of Notre Dame, 1984). The statistics can be found summarized in Joseph Gremillion and Jim Castelli, *The Emerging Parish: The Notre Dame Study of Catholic Parish Life Since Vatican II* (San Francisco: Harper & Row, 1987), 149.

4.  The Notre Dame Study suggests that parish religious education programs that focus on adult catechesis show significant interest in Bible study, sometimes as the result of specific programs such as RENEW. See Susan R. Raftery and David C. Leege, "Catechesis, Religious Education and the Parish," *Notre Dame Study of Catholic Parish Life, Report 14* (Notre Dame: University of Notre Dame, 1989), 6–7.

5.  See Michael Welch and David Leege, "Dual Reference Groups and Political Orientations," 30, 39.

6.  David C. Leege, "Parish Life Among the Leaders," *Notre Dame Study of Catholic Parish Life, Report 9* (Notre Dame: University of Notre Dame, 1986), 5.

7.  David C. Leege, "Catholics and the Civic Order: Parish Participation, Politics, and Civic Participation," *Notre Dame Study of Catholic Parish Life, Report 11* (Notre Dame: University of Notre Dame, 1989), 7.

8.  *Ibid.*

9.  The Third General Synod of Bishops, *Evangelization in the Modern World: Synod Working Paper,* published in *Origins* 4 (August 29, 1974), 147–53.

10. Pope Paul VI, "On Evangelization in the Modern World" (Washington, D.C.: United States Catholic Conference, 1976).

11. "On Evangelization in the Modern World," nn. 6–16, are particularly valuable. The closing report of the Third General Synod is cited by the pope in affirming that evangelization "constitutes the essential mission of the church" (n. 14).

12. Texts of Vatican II documents and the English titles for the documents are taken from Walter Abbott, SJ, ed., *The Documents of Vatican II* (New York: Guild Press/America Press/Association Press, 1966). "Lumen Gentium" is found on pp. 14–101.

13. *Ibid.,* 660–68.

14. *Ibid.,* 584–631.

15. *Ibid.,* 111–28.

16. See Eugene Smith, "Response to the Document 'Ad Gentes,'" Abbott, *Documents of Vatican II,* 633; Calvert Alexander's "Introduction" to the document points out the "decidedly scriptural approach" taken by this and other council documents (p. 581).

17. The term "evangelization," for example, occurs in n. 6 of "Ad Gentes" in an isolated context with no follow-up. The comprehensive use of the term to explain the nature of the church's mission in Catholic circles has re-

ceived major impetus from the synod of 1974 which took as its topic the evangelization of the world, and the subsequent apostolic exhortation of Pope Paul VI, "On Evangelization in the Modern World," issued December 8, 1975. A sign of this change in terminology is the fact that the *New Catholic Encyclopedia* (New York: McGraw-Hill, 1967) contains no treatment of evangelization at all but over seventy pages on "mission, missionary work, and missiology."

18.   See notes 3 and 4 above for recent statistical studies. The emergence of Catholic interest in scholarly insights about the Bible is reflected in numerous recent books. See, e.g., Raymond Brown, *Biblical Exegesis and Church Doctrine* (New York: Paulist Press, 1985), or, still more recently, his *Responses to 101 Questions on the Bible* (Paulist Press, 1990). For popular biblical study, see Daniel Harrington, "The Bible in Catholic Life," *The Catholic Study Bible* (New York: Oxford University Press, 1990), RG 16–30.

19.   See Robert Funk, Bernard Scott, James Butts, *The Parables of Jesus, Red Letter Edition: A Report of the Jesus Seminar* (Sonoma: Polebridge Press, 1988), which sets out the judgment of an imposing body of scholars on the authenticity or lack of authenticity of each of the gospel parables. Popular reporting of up-to-date biblical scholarship is represented also by *U.S. News and World Report*'s cover story for Easter 1990, "The Last Days of Jesus" (April 16, 1990), 46–53.

20.   It must be remembered that our ancestors one hundred and fifty years ago had relatively few sources of information about the biblical world beyond the testimony of the Bible itself so that it was naturally viewed as the primary history resource for its time period. With over a million tablets and other written sources discovered in the last hundred years from the lands of Babylon and Egypt alone, as well as innumerable others from neighboring cultures, we now know factually a much different picture of many events recorded in the Bible and can understand better how biblical authors were making use of such events to proclaim religious truth or even reinterpret their own past scriptures. Church authority has encouraged Catholic biblical scholars to make use of such knowledge in their studies, beginning with Pope Pius XII's encyclical "Divino Afflante Spiritu" (1943) and continuing in statements of the Pontifical Biblical Commission up to the time of the council. For good treatments of these documents, see Raymond Brown, "Appendix," *Biblical Reflections on Crises Facing the Church* (New York: Paulist Press, 1975), 109–18; and Joseph Fitzmyer, SJ, *Scripture and Christology: A Statement of the Biblical Commission with a Commentary* (New York: Paulist Press, 1986).

21.   Michael Welch and David Leege, "Religious Predictors of Parishioners' Socio-political Attitudes: Devotional Style, Closeness to God, Imagery and Agentic/Communal Religious Identity," *Journal for the Scientific Study of Religion* 27 (1988), 536–52, especially 546–48.

22.   *Ibid.*, 548.

23.   See the "Introduction" to the Fourth General Synod document, "The Evangelization of the Modern World" (note 9 above), and a fine discussion,

"What Is Catholic Evangelization?" in Patrick J. Brennan, *The Evangelizing Parish* (Allen: Tabor Publishing, 1987), 5–22.

24.   See Dt 6:10–19; 7:1–15; 11:26–32; 30:15–20.

25.   See Mt 16:13–18; Mk 8:27–38; Lk 9:18–36; Jn 3:14–16; 18:33–37. Especially the sermons of the apostles in Luke's Acts of the Apostles are constructed as summaries of the early church's preaching, what is commonly called the "kerygma" ("proclaimed message"): Acts 2:14–36; 3:11–26; 11:16–41.

26.   Eph 1:9; 3:3, 4, 9; 5:32; 6:19; Col 1:26, 27; 2:2; 4:3.

27.   See note 25; add also Acts 5:31; 10:43; 17:30.

28.   This sense of evangelization as the nourishment of a faith already received is already found in those New Testament texts such as 1 Peter addressed to believing communities. It is also built into the structure of the gospel of Matthew where the evangelist has gathered the teachings of Jesus that articulate the life in the kingdom of God into five large sermons or "books" that correspond to the five books of the law of Moses in the Pentateuch: Matthew 5–7; 10; 13; 18; 24–25.

29.   Synod document definition; see note 9 above.

30.   Pope Paul VI, "On Evangelization in the Modern World," nn. 6–14.

31.   See note 5 above.

32.   Pope Paul VI, "On Evangelization in the Modern World," nn. 41–42.

## DISCUSSION QUESTIONS

1. Have you experienced any change in the use of the Bible in the Catholic Church in the last twenty years?

2. What new directions for recovery of the Bible in the church did the Second Vatican Council begin?

3. What are the major Old Testament themes that relate to evangelization that can be found in the prophets?

4. How does the New Testament proclaim that all Christians must be evangelizers?

5. Can you construct a model for your own life in which evangelization plays an important role?

## FOR FURTHER READING

David Bohr. *Evangelization in America.* New York: Paulist Press, 1977. See especially section 1, "Biblical Perspectives," 11–43.

Patrick Brennan. *The Evangelizing Parish.* Allen: Tabor Publishing, 1987.

Eugene LaVerdiere. "Using the Bible in Evangelization—How?" *Catholic Evangelization in the United States of America,* July/August 1988, 42–43.

Pope Paul VI. "On Evangelization in the Modern World." Washington, D.C.: USCC Publishing and Promotions, 1976. This is the most important source for these reflections. Its biblical and ecclesial contextualization is a model for all evangelizers.

John Scullion. *Isaiah 40–66.* Old Testament Message Series. Wilmington: Michael Glazier, Inc., 1982.

# MODELS FOR AN EVANGELIZING PARISH
## Carol A. Gura

Recently I have spent some time helping with my eldest daughter's wedding and have been struck with the radical changes that have taken place in the church since my own marriage twenty-seven years ago. The three one-hour pre-Cana talks on the "rhythm" method and budgeting have been replaced by experiences in deeper communications skills presented in the Engaged Encounter. Couples today spend time planning and selecting readings and music to fit the theme for the liturgy, while we left all that to a priest who said mass with his back to us. Even the invited guests reflect a tremendous shift. Our wedding guests were mostly of one ethnic grouping and the traditions of Middle Europe were strictly adhered to, while the guests celebrating my daughter's marriage came from many countries and cultures. The shock is not so much the change, but the short period of time over which these changes have taken place.

While most of the American church has settled into comfort and ease with the wide-sweeping changes since Vatican II, let us not get too comfortable. As we move into the next millennium, we must brace ourselves for yet more change. The twentieth century United States culture moved rapidly from an agricultural to an industrial to a technological society, yet the church, particularly the local parish, lagged behind. We continue to evangelize for an industrial culture, while most of the "thirty-something" crowd and the new generation of young Catholics never experienced that culture. They were born and raised in a fast-paced, technological world. Ongoing change in our methods of evangelization are necessary to meet the needs of a people faced with the complexities and challenges of the twenty-first century. In this article we will examine some trends which will affect evangelization in the decade of the 1990s and attempt to draw up some corresponding models for parish evangelization.

## TRENDS FOR THIS DECADE AND THE NEXT

*Global Awareness and Pluralism*

As a nation, and as a church, we have begun to view ourselves as a global village. Karl Rahner interpreted Vatican II as the Catholic Church's first moment of self-actualization as a world church. In other words, the universality of the church was realized when, for the first time, a worldwide episcopate gathered, the vernacular was accepted, and the universality of salvation was proclaimed. This moment in church history continues as the Catholic Church becomes more and more sensitized to its world responsibility.

The emergence of numerous achievements in communications from fax machines to satellite dishes has indeed linked our lives to the lives of the most remote populations. A global economy is imminent. Global awareness extends to concern for the planet in all the forms ecology has taken in most recent years. This global awareness pervades the United States in a unique manner, as new populations of immigrants cross our borders, enriching the melting pot we have always proclaimed. The tensions over whether to move toward a mosaic or tapestry of cultures or to pasteurize or melt all cultures into a new predominating culture will permeate this next decade.

Parishes can no longer close their eyes to the Asians and Hispanics, our most recent immigrants; to the native Americans, whose land and culture we sought to destroy; or to the African-Americans we enslaved. Even those parishes insulated in uni-cultural suburbia must allow the enrichment of these cultures to impact their communities because their parishioners will rub elbows with this cultural explosion in the workplace. Currently, corporate America is running seminars and workshops on the multicultural, changing workplace and its implications for management, collaboration and supervision.

The trend toward a more global view will call forth from the evangelizer and the evangelized a conversion from a parochial vision, which sees "my parish as a kingdom unto itself," toward a more global or even cosmic vision, where collaboration, listening and learning are essential. It will call forth commitment to rethink old habits of waste and destruction as we move toward a stewardship of the earth's resources based on a spirituality of creation.

*Spiritual Revival*

John Naisbitt and Patricia Aburdene, in their recent book, *Megatrends 2000,* project a religious revival as well as a renaissance in the arts as key trends for this decade.[1] My own work among young adult, inactive Catholics has convinced me of their spiritual quest and thirst, even when they have dropped church practice.

There are many reasons for this growing spiritual hunger, from the coming of the millennium and its "end of the world" popular religiosity to the freedom of people in the United States from war and work. With more leisure comes more time to ponder the great questions of what it means to be human.

Currently, ninety-four percent of the United States population believes in God.[2] Yet mainline churches are the "losers" in this spiritual surge as "new age" groups and fundamentalist churches attract growing numbers of the young, many of whom are former Catholics. The seekers are attracted to smaller, decentralized fellowship groups, as they search out a link between everyday life and the transcendent. The simplistic formulas for good and evil preached by the fundamentalists have an appeal. In the "new age" phenomena the attraction is to the self-actualization and inner guidance found in meditation. Both groups, at opposite ends of the spectrum, are making use of the latest in telemarketing and telecommunications to spread their message.

As we seek to evangelize and recapture the imaginations of the young and not-so-young spiritual seekers, we must recover our rich traditions of spirituality found in the mystics and contemplatives. Personalizing and gathering small groups around the scriptures will appeal to the quest for belonging. As we are converted from the large, centralized parish plants to small communities rooted in the gospels and in human compassion, we will authentically evangelize this next generation.

## Valuing Women's Experience

The qualities that women bring to the marketplace reflect the trends of a new corporate leadership model. In many corporations, the authoritarian management model is being replaced by a model which seeks to bring out the best in people, respect individual talents, encourage self-management, and empower people by sharing authority. All this is noted as a significant trend for this decade by Naisbitt and Aburdene.[3]

The propensity of the American bishops toward consultation, dialogic methods and empowerment of the laity reflects the same dynamic. We are moving away from old autocratic leadership styles to more collaborative teams of management. The qualities needed to make this shift, claim Naisbitt and Aburdene, are inherent in women and are being taught to men through corporate seminars and training courses.

The implications for this trend in the church are multiple and controversial. Will authentic leadership roles in the church be passed on to women, trained for ministry? As the clergy crisis reaches its peak in this next decade, what models for collaboration, team ministry, shared responsibility and empowerment will emerge? It is a very creative moment in the church as we seek new solutions to the crisis in leadership.

As larger and larger numbers of women continue to move into the work force out of necessity, we need to respond as a church community. This response includes: advocacy and provisions for child care as well as elder care; development of personnel policies for maternity leave, time-shared jobs and equal wages for church employees; careful planning and consulting on time demands for parental involvement in sacramental preparation programs and school-related events; and support, encouragement and training for a family perspective in parish life. This all calls for a conversion from paternalism and even feminism, which excludes, to a partnership which is inclusive.

*Addictive Systems*

The greatest contribution of the United States in the last half of this century has been the twelve-step program. Begun by Bill W. and Dr. Bob in Canton, Ohio, with the recovery program known as A.A., this simple, self-help spirituality has birthed recovery from many addictions. Groups for eating disorders, narcotics addictions, dysfunctional family systems, co-dependency have all sprung from this one-day-at-a-time recovery program. The amazing fact is that there are no dues, no properties owned, no hierarchy of leadership, and yet this program has universally helped people of all ages, from all walks of life, and from all cultures. There is a spirituality in the program which calls for a dependency upon a "higher power," who many call God. Some have further observed that for our current generation the twelve-step program is a new way of naming sin.

The most recent development over the last ten years has been the awareness that whole systems are addicted. Whole systems need redemption. As a church we are constantly committed to being evangelized or converted. As we name our own sins, open ourselves to conversion and work for change, parishes, dioceses and church structures will be healed. This conversion is vital to the reconciliation of the alienated both within our midst and outside our communities. The willingness of the church to admit human weakness heralds and proclaims the authenticity of our evangelizing efforts. "The church is an evangelizer, but she begins by being evangelized herself."[4]

These four trends are by no means complete, but represent major patterns which demand a shift in thinking, interacting and planning for the future of the parish. It is important to keep these trends in mind as we look to the practical question, "How can the mission of evangelization be effective for the future of the church in the United States?" The task before us is to develop models for parish evangelization which will meet the needs of people in a technological world where rapid growth and change is apparent. Yet at the same time we are to remain faithful to the sacramental life and tradition of the Catholic Church. This demands balance, reflection, understanding of the human situation, and the wisdom of the Spirit. To guide the creative process it is essential that we begin with the source of authentic evangelization, Jesus, as presented in the gospels.

## SCRIPTURAL MODELS FOR EVANGELIZATION

### Jesus' Mission

Jesus' mission is clearly stated in Matthew's gospel: "Reform your lives! The kingdom of heaven is at hand" (4:17). It is further developed by Luke:

> God has sent me to bring good news to the poor, to proclaim liberty to captives, recovery of sight to the blind, and release to prisoners, to announce a year of favor from the Lord" (4:18–19).

As our lives are reformed, turned around, we begin to see the power of the good news of God's kingdom for the world's poverty, captivity, blindness and bondage in all its forms. This is the challenge and call of each parish community, of each baptized person.

### Jesus' Ministry

Jesus' meeting with the Samaritan woman at the well of Jacob signaled his stance toward other cultures and religions and toward women. A pluralistic sense, multicultural openness and inclusive attitudes needed for the church of the future can be discovered in this brief conversation with this woman. Through the encounter Jesus uncovers the thirst of all humankind and responds with living water. We discover that, in spite of outward appearances, self-sufficient posturing, and belonging to the wrong group, all are thirsty, restless for the "hound of heaven."

This encounter also reveals the power of the evangelizing moment. As Pope Paul VI states, " . . . the person who has been evangelized goes on to evangelize others. Here lies the test of truth, the touchstone of evangelization. . . ."[5] The woman goes back to her town to share her excitement: "Come and see someone who told me everything I ever did! Could this be the messiah" (Jn 4:29)? Her method of evangelization is a question which invites the dialogue to continue, a question which invites the others to discover for themselves. She learned well from the master! Dialogue and the freedom to choose are essential for the process of evangelization to continue in this historical moment.

The encounters of Jesus with his apostles, the sick, blind and lame, Martha, Mary and Lazarus, Nicodemus, the widow and the rich young man all hold the attitudes and actions we need to adapt for evangelizing in our time and place. They demand our reflection for all they can reveal to us.

### Model of the Early Church

The early Christians took their master's mission seriously and developed communities which would support and empower their task. Their model included their commitment: "to the apostle's instruction, and the communal life, to the breaking of the bread and the prayers" (Acts 2:42). Four elements were integral parts of the early Christian communities: the scriptures, at first an oral storytelling of Jesus' life; the community, where all was shared; the eucharist, Christ made present in the breaking of the bread; and the prayers, where decisions and crises were faced with the laying on of hands, fasting and prayer.

Paul further developed the evangelizing model for communities throughout his journeys in the Gentile world. Both Acts and the letters of Paul present the model for church growth. The good news was preached and proclaimed, often followed by signs and healings; leaders were discerned, appointed and prayed over, and Paul moved on; letters of encouragement, admonishment and guidance were sent to the communities; and Paul revisited those communities when possible.

## PRINCIPLES FOR PARISH EVANGELIZATION

Study of the trends listed above and reflection on the scriptures reveal some basics for creating an evangelizing parish in our day. The new evangelization called forth by "Christifideles Laici"[6] requires parishes to strengthen and develop models which include the following principles:

1. *The mission of the parish is to build God's reign.* We, as parish, must continually reflect on the question, "Why are we evangelizing?" It is very easy to settle for a narrow vision. "On Evangelization in the Modern World" constantly reminds us that, in the broad view, evangelizing to

bring about the reign of God is the fullest motive for all our efforts. The yeast of life, the pearl of great price, the seed which grows into a large tree are all images of the breadth and depth of evangelization.

To stop short of that goal, settling for creating comfortable, warm and welcoming communities as the end of this great commission, is not enough. In this society, the invitation, the welcome and the sense of belonging which evangelization draws forth is a difficult and important accomplishment. Yet once this happens, the work of the "new evangelization" is just begun.

To evangelize with the mission of co-creating to build God's reign is a real challenge. In God's reign, no one culture dominates, but all cultures form a tapestry of giftedness. In God's reign, there is no oppression, there are no addictive systems, for freedom pervades. In God's reign, peace, balance and harmony dwell in the presence of total, unconditional love and reconciliation. A reflection on the gospels, particularly the parables, reveals the challenges we all face in evangelizing to bring God's reign to fruition.

2. *The parish is committed to ongoing renewal.* An evangelizing parish is first open to its own ongoing renewal. Individuals and parishes must be exposed to the parts of the gospel that have been hidden, with an openness to ongoing conversion. Many programs offer backdrops for conversion and renewal: Cursillo, Marriage and Engaged Encounters, Christ Renews His Parish, RENEW, TEC, Missions, Life in the Spirit, and numerous retreats and days of recollection. Yet to prepare for this new evangelization we must go beyond programs.

Internal, authentic renewal, conversion of individuals and faith communities are a matter of the Spirit. We can set up environments for the Spirit to work effectively through us and must offer continuous prayer for the Spirit to work among us. We are called to be open to free dialogue with the cultures of the world and the religious ideas they uphold. We must enter into this dialogue open to conversion to a fuller truth. As we embark on the pilgrimage toward a church come of age under the unpredictable Spirit, as Father Patrick Brennan reminds us, we need to reimagine church, particularly as expressed locally in parish life.[7]

3. *The goal of the parish is the transformation into communities of disciples.* Father Thomas O'Meara defines ministry as "public activity done by a baptized follower of Jesus, using charisms of the Spirit present in each personality to help us realize the kingdom or reign of God."[8] This definition describes the ministry of the disciple. Volunteers will no longer be able to do this task. We need disciples to take up the public task of building this reign of God by developing their fullest potential and using their unique gifts for evangelization. We need disciples to evangelize

more disciples. "Go out, making *disciples* of all nations. . . ." Volunteers make a time commitment to work at a task for a limited time, without pay. Disciples work and minister for a lifetime.

Thus, while first we evangelize by inviting, we must remember that we are not inviting spectators or supporters, but disciples. Disciples happen when our evangelizing efforts bring about authentic conversions. This is the challenge of the next step in evangelization.

4. *The life of the parish is rooted in the good news.* The centrality of the proclamation of the good news is vital, not only in homilies but also in sacramental preparation processes, in adult religious formation, and in opportunities for parishioners to witness. Jesus' reconciling action of dying and rising unites us once again with the creator, making us co-creators in building God's reign through the action and persistent presence of the Spirit. This news is "good" precisely because it speaks to our personal and communal stories of dying and rising with and in Christ. It has the power to fill us with hope in desperate times. This good news, which has the power to transform lives, is critical for our current cultural environment.

5. *The parish is committed to bringing the Good News to the poor.* As the scriptures recount, Jesus came to preach this good news to the poor. Where is the poverty in our country? The cities certainly remind us that poverty still exists in the wealthiest country on the planet. The infant mortality rate, the numbers of homeless, those still suffering malnutrition in a country where waste dominates, are all traces of pervading poverty which must be eradicated. The church, made present in the local situation through its parishes, is and must continue to respond with a preferential option for the poor. In this very real way, the good news is being lived out.

Furthermore, there is a more pervasive and subtle poverty which exists. The spiritual poverty produced by preoccupation with material possessions, the human poverty of isolation and loneliness, the poverty of the next generation deprived of a basic education, occupational skills and an appreciation of the arts, and the poverty of the earth, raped of her natural resources, are all waiting to hear and feel the effects of the good news.

## PARISH MODELS FOR EVANGELIZATION

### Model A: The Parish Council

In this model, the parish council is that "visioning" and reflecting body in the parish focused on continually assessing needs, encouraging the parish ministries to respond in the light of the parish mission, and evaluating the movement and direction of the life of the parish. This relatively new parish council structure and focus adapts itself well to the mission of evangelization.

The members study and reflect upon "On Evangelization in the Modern World," and incorporate its principles into the parish mission and goals. All ministries, rooted in the gifts or charisms of the parishioners, are directed toward the evangelizing mission and are evaluated and refined according to the principles of evangelization.

A second variation of this model is based on the more traditional parish council structure. An evangelization commission is developed, along with the other commissions, and works as a catalyst and resource for all the parish ministries in their evangelizing mission. The evangelization commission empowers the community out of their baptismal call to proclaim the good news to all, while offering various programs and processes which evangelize.

*Model B: RCIA*

Another model for evangelization in today's parish is integral to the Rite of Christian Initiation for Adults. In the parishes where RCIA permeates all of the sacramental preparation and the life of the parish, the transformation, conversion and evangelization of that parish community is ongoing. RCIA provides a process: belonging, storytelling, relationships, ritualization, celebration and dialogue. In applying and adapting this process to all parish ministries, the essentials of evangelization are at the heart of the parish. Ministries of outreach must be refined and made a regular part of RCIA. The development of Re-Membering Church, a process for alienated Catholics, is a direct result of the creative movement to link evangelization and RCIA. The possibilities for evangelization are endless when RCIA is developed as a process rather than a program.

One small parish, located in the city, struggled to increase and maintain its membership. RCIA was still in its developmental stages when a new pastor, committed to the process, arrived. His first major change was to install an immersion pool for baptisms. The pastoral minister was trained and encouraged to work with children in the school, ninety percent of whom were not Catholic. She developed a children's catechumenate for the school children who were interested in the faith. Through the children's interest, parents began to inquire and the number of adult catechumens grew. When the parish community experienced the initiation of these children and their parents at the Easter vigil, the immersion pool was a catalyst for many conversions. Long-time Catholics realized the full impact of their own baptism, death to new life, as the newly initiated came sputtering out of the waters, clothed in their white garments. The community was inspired and motivated to share their experience and translate it into the action of inviting neighbors and family members to "come and see."

*Model C: Small Christian Communities*

The recent trend toward development of small Christian communities in the large U.S. parishes represents a new potential for yet another evangelization model. The parish is challenged to discover ways to help groups which are already gathering to move toward a transformation into communities focused on evangelization. Other parishioners are inspired and motivated to come together to share the good news and discover realistic means of proclaiming this gospel in the marketplace, thus forming additional small communities. Small communities challenge their members to move from reflection and prayer to witness, action and discipleship. Where these communities commit themselves to evangelize, this model will emerge with new force and new possibilities for reaching the beneficiaries of evangelization.


IMPLICATIONS FOR THE EVANGELIZATION TEAM

The evangelization team, a catalyst for evangelization in the parish, will influence the future directions of the process of conversion. However, the team cannot work in isolation. The members will need the support, challenge and collaboration of the parish staff, the parish council and the leaders of all parish groups and organizations. In the models described above, the team will need to have an understanding of RCIA, small Christian communities and new parish council structures. Serious reflection and discussion will lead to strategies and action plans which begin the creative process of developing new models for parish evangelization.

Since the evangelization team cannot and must not take on all of the work, they will need to refocus their direction. The following may be of help in examining the renewed role of the team:

1. The team must come to know the parishioners, the faith community and the larger territorial community in a personal and relational way. This can be done through telephone surveys, personal visits, one-on-

one contacts, sacramental contacts, and contact at times of crisis. The contact must remain dialogic, wherein the evangelist is first a listener and, when appropriate, is willing to share his or her story.

2. The team needs the freedom and the wisdom to develop creative responses, plans and actions to respond to the individual, parish and community needs they uncover. For this task, they will need to search, read and study the work of other parishes and other denominations in all parts of the country. They can then adapt and make the necessary changes to fit their environment.

3. The team would benefit most if it regularly gathers the leaders of other ministries in the parish for dialogue and creative development. The most essential of these ministries include: RCIA, small community leaders, social justice groups, Re-Membering Church community, the bereavement group, the divorced and separated group, spiritual development committees, adult enrichment groups, and family ministry leaders.

4. The team, focused on the pluralistic nature of our society, will necessarily raise the consciousness of the congregation to the multicultural richness of other cultures and religions. This will require time and energy for discovering speakers, liturgical expressions and artistic experiences which will enrich the life of the parish.

5. As new models for collaborative leadership develop, the team will need to alert the parish staff, the parish council and other leaders to new methods of operation and leadership styles. The educated laity of today require that shared responsibility become part of parish life. The evangelization team itself will need to be sure it is leading the parish in this more dialogic and collaborative style.

While each parish has its unique story and style, my experience has been that all of the ideas and issues mentioned in this article are practically operational, in some form, in many parishes across the country. The parable of the sower and the seed is the best metaphor for the direction the church in the U.S. has begun. The seeds of RCIA and small communities have been sown, sometimes in good soil, sometimes among the rocks; the seeds of collaboration have sometimes fallen among the thorns of frustration; the seeds of liberation and justice action have fallen on the road and have been somewhat trampled; the seeds of the good news have fallen on hearts of stone as well as on hearts of flesh. Yet the sower's basket is filled, to the brim and running over, with new seed. Parishes are fertilizing and plowing new soil to receive these seeds. The new laborers, lay and clergy, young and old, are waiting in the fields for the rich harvest.


## NOTES

1. John Naisbitt and Patricia Aburdene, *Megatrends 2000: Ten New Directions for the 1990s* (New York: William Morrow and Company, 1990).
2. *Ibid.*, 275.
3. *Ibid.*, 216–29.
4. Pope Paul VI, "On Evangelization in the Modern World" (Washington, D.C.: United States Catholic Conference, 1976), n. 15.
5. *Ibid.*, n. 24.
6. Pope John Paul II, "Christifideles Laici" (Washington, D.C.: United States Catholic Conference), n. 35.
7. Patrick J. Brennan, *Re-Imagining the Parish* (New York: Crossroad/Continuum, 1990), 3–8.
8. *Ibid.*, 17–18.

## DISCUSSION QUESTIONS

1. Does your experience verify these trends? How? Would you add any other trends you have observed?

2. What key issues for evangelization can you elicit from additional stories in the scriptures?

3. Retell your experience of the renewing power of RCIA and/or small Christian communities.

4. In what practical ways can the good news transform the liberation and justice issues of our day?


## FOR FURTHER READING

Patrick J. Brennan. *Re-Imagining the Parish.* New York: Crossroad/Continuum, 1990.

Vincent J. Donovan. *The Church in the Midst of Creation.* New York: Orbis Books, 1989.

John Naisbitt and Patricia Aburdene. *Megatrends 2000: Ten New Directions for the 1990s.* New York: William Morrow and Company, 1990.

# THE NEED FOR EVANGELIZATION TRAINING

Susan W. Blum

"A serious preparation is needed for all workers for evangelization" (Pope Paul VI, "On Evangelization in the Modern World," n. 73).

In 1927 Edward L. Thorndike revolutionized the adult education movement by reporting for the first time his findings which directly opposed the prevailing belief that "You can't teach an old dog new tricks." His findings scientifically proved that *adults can learn.*

Today the major challenge regarding the training of Catholic evangelizers remains basically the same as that facing the earliest adult educational theorists: Can "old" Catholics learn new approaches, methods, styles and attitudes for sharing their faith? Can an "old" system adopt a new consciousness, awareness, mindset and lifestyle of contemporary evangelization? Reduced to its simplest form, the question becomes, "Can old Catholics (or the old institutional church) learn new tricks?"

*Case:* Sarah Jones is a middle-aged Cleveland housewife. Her neighbor's teenaged son just committed suicide. Sarah wants to tell her friend about the way Jesus consoled her and how her faith strengthened her during times of personal crisis in her own life. But Sarah is afraid . . . Catholics aren't supposed to share their faith . . . it's a private matter . . . it's awkward . . . and, besides, it's not "the done thing."

*Case:* Hernando Gomez works in the oil fields of southwest Texas when there is work available. How does he share his deep faith in a loving, caring God when poverty surrounds him in the midst of an economically and educationally depressed area?

*Case:* Sally Oates is a field representative for a Fortune 500 company and is jetting to San Francisco for a national sales meeting. Her seatmate, a total stranger, notices the crucifix she is wearing and mentions that he has not been to mass since his divorce six years ago. His eyes moisten as he shares how much he misses the eucharist and asks if the church has changed its stance on divorce and remarriage. Sally doesn't know how to reply.

*Case:* Father Larry Smith has been given the opportunity to study on a year's sabbatical leave. He wants to study evangelization. Where does he go for his training? How does he spend his year?

*Case:* After months of deliberation, a local parish council decides that their needs will best be met by employing a full-time director of evangelization. Also, a local bishop and diocesan council decide to hire a diocesan director of evangelization. How will they know whom to hire? What are the capabilities, credentials and education required for these positions? Where would these people have been trained? Are degrees required? In which fields?

*Case:* Jeannette Johnson was recently hired as a parish director of evangelization, and Steve Jones was hired as her diocesan counterpart. They both want to initiate training programs immediately. What's available? What works? What's appropriate for their parish/diocese?

*Case:* A large, prestigious Catholic university initiates a degreed program in evangelization on the undergraduate and graduate levels. They are seeking a director for their newly formed Institute of Evangelization. Whom do they hire? What curriculum is developed? What courses are offered? Who teaches these courses? What qualifications do the instructors need? What are the requirements for completion of the degrees?

## LEVELS OF TRAINING

The desired outcomes of evangelization training programs must offer a wide range of levels of competency, based on the needs of the ecclesial community, the sponsoring organization and the individual. For our purposes here, three levels of competency are discussed: *professional* evangelizers (multi-level leadership, diocesan/parish directors of evangelization, professional trainers of evangelization, higher education personnel); *institutional* evangelizers (professional or lay evangelizers involved in formal diocesan/parish programs); *relational* evangelizers (laity involved in informal, personal evangelistic encounters).

The level of the professional evangelizer speaks for itself and, obviously, will require a much more sophisticated and specialized academic/ training/educational program than now exists.

Institutional evangelization is defined as the process in which one participates in parish or diocesan-wide, structured, time-specific and location-specific projects such as the RCIA, Come Home for Christmas/Easter, Alienated Catholics Anonymous, Re-Membering Church, RE-NEW, Christ Renews His Parish, Cursillo, Marriage Encounter weekends, charismatic conferences, parish missions, open houses, census programs, and mass media appeals. These programs are usually planned by professionals and implemented through diocesan or parish lay committees. Specific training in the content or context of the particular program or project is necessary for the institutional evangelizer *in addition to training in relational evangelization,* which forms the underlying foundational basis as a prerequisite for all three levels of evangelization. Professional or institutional evangelizers will not be effective without mastery of relational evangelization theory and skills and the ability to teach them to others.

In contrast to the structured, institutional approaches, relational evangelization is defined as the process in which an individual explicitly shares with others his or her personal relationship with the Lord Jesus Christ. The characteristics which distinguish relational evangelization are that it is implemented on an informal, one-to-one, personal basis on the grassroots level, predominantly by laity during interpersonal encounters with friends, family, co-workers, neighbors and even strangers.

Relational evangelization occurs anytime, anyplace, under any circumstances. The laity have an infinite number of opportunities for personal, "over-the-coffee-cup" evangelistic encounters. In scriptural terms, relational evangelization calls the laity to "search out and invite others from the hedgerows to the banquet table" (Lk 14:21–23).

Relational evangelization includes not only the basic presumption of an "evergrowing love" for the ones evangelized ("On Evangelization in the Modern World," n. 79); witnessing to them through the "wordless witness" of lifestyles (n. 21); inviting them into deeper conversion (n. 23); or integrating them into the local faith community (n. 23). Relational evangelization also requires "a clear and unequivocal proclamation of the Lord Jesus" (n. 22).

"There is *no true evangelization* if the name, the teaching, the life, the promises, the kingdom and the mystery of Jesus of Nazareth, the Son of God, are not proclaimed" (n. 22, emphasis added).

Relational evangelization is the most elemental and basic form of evangelization, and all evangelization training opportunities must be built on the strong foundation of relational evangelization training.

## TRAINING OPPORTUNITIES

It was from the specific exhortation from Paul VI for "serious preparation for evangelizers" that the virgin territory of adult religious educational programming in evangelization training emerged. Currently, there is a wide variety of formal training programs for evangelization in North America. More than forty formal programs or training organizations were represented at the 1990 annual conference of the Association of Coordinators of Catholic Schools of Evangelization, co-sponsored by Evangelization 2000 and the Paulist National Catholic Evangelization Association.

Six specific evangelization training models are "showcased" and discussed in detail later in this essay. However, a general survey of existing training models reflects the wide variety of goals, purposes and methods currently offered.

The notion of three separate but complementary and supportive levels to evangelization training (professional, institutional and relational) is clearly observable when the purposes, objectives and curricula for existing training programs are examined. While overlapping occurs in all of them, clear lines can be drawn between those "schools" which concentrate mostly on theological and foundational principles resulting in the formation of professional or institutional evangelizers and those which include these foundational principles but focus on the practical skills required for one-to-one relational evangelization.

Unfortunately, there is a dearth of professional-level, academic training for evangelizers. I know of no Catholic university which offers a degreed program in evangelization as many Protestant universities and seminaries do; I know of no Catholic university which even offers a specialized "major" of evangelization within a degreed program; and, until a few years ago, I knew of no Catholic university or seminary which was even offering a single accredited course in evangelization. For three years the Paulists offered a course through the Washington Theological Union in Washington, D.C., and courses have been offered at Mt. St. Mary Seminary in Cincinnati and Mary Immaculate Seminary in Allentown, Pennsylvania. The challenge remains in higher education circles to design and develop accredited graduate-level curricula in evangelization training.

Training courses geared to both the professional and institutional evangelizers include the Paulists' Evangelization Training Institutes in Washington, D.C., and a variety of national or regional programs offered by specific groups such as the National Council for Catholic Evangelization, the North American Forum on the Catechumenate, and the

National Service Committee of the Charismatic Renewal as well as "Rebuild My Church," a program designed specifically for leadership at the University of Steubenville.

Most of the training for institutional evangelization, however, occurs on the diocesan level. For instance, the excellent training programs of the archdiocese of Indianapolis and the diocese of Cleveland both devote the majority of time during the first year of their programs to intensive studies of Paul VI's document and to institutional methodology (such as studying the demographics of the parish neighborhoods or participating in parish-wide census-taking or educational programs). The archdiocese of Boston's program states its purpose as "intended to provide parishes with resource persons for parish-based evangelization efforts."

The diocese of Providence provides a comprehensive training program for "Total Parish-based Evangelization." Like most other diocesan programs, outreach training is included somewhere in the training process but within the larger curriculum of "evaluating parish leadership, worship, activities, programs, attitudes; determining needs for an evangelization committee; training leaders; developing an evangelizing community; and, finally, outreach processes," as described in the Providence program.

A sampling of programs known to emphasize relational evangelization training on the grassroots level includes Denver's Catholic Evangelization Training Center; Miami's Good News/Buena Noticia Outreach Ministry; Michigan's Duns Scotus Friary's Franciscan School of Evangelization; San Antonio's SINE (System of Integral New Evangelization) program; the University of Steubenville's Evangelization Training Program; the Daughters of St. Paul's Parish Visitation Program; and our own national/international training programs, Mission:Evangelization and Share Your Faith.

Remembering that the needs not only of the ecclesial community and of the individual but also of the specific sponsoring organization are considered in program development, each of these programs has its own unique flavor, charism and specialization. For instance, the Duns Scotus program offers a wide range of programs centering around inner healing, scripture and prayer. Their semester-long "Called to Witness" course promotes outreach training within the context of their Franciscan spirituality.

The University of Steubenville's programs emphasize home visitation, reflecting a Catholic adaptation of the highly successful and effective Protestant model, "Evangelism Explosion." SINE specializes in "neighborhood evangelization," with small base community formation a priority.

The Catholic Evangelization Training Center in Northglenn, Colorado, offers a comprehensive three-year program with the dual purpose of "training each parishioner to be an effective evangelizer and to form an evangelizing community of the parish."

In researching training resources for this article, a delightful serendipitous finding was the Daughters of St. Paul's "Parish Visitation Program to Give the Whole Christ to the Whole Parish." These resourceful and imaginative sisters (whom I thought only sold books!) have developed an effective program for visitation training for three separate parish situations. "Plan A, B or C" is selected and then custom-designed to meet one of thirteen goals for the visit, which are outlined as options with accompanying suggested implementation methods for each one.

There is a wide range of differences in terms of location, length of training, format and cost among these programs. Participant costs for materials range from voluntary donations at Duns Scotus to $15 for Mission:Evangelization, $25 for Miami's program and $95 for the Denver program. The cost for the five-day Paulist Institute is $295, and the Steubenville week-long program is $250. Some of these programs are residential, requiring travel to their specific sites; others use an itinerant "Have Bible, Will Travel" approach and will come to your parish, diocese, seminary or university.

In addition to these general training programs, there also are programs designed for specific populations such as LAMP Ministries (to evangelize the poor) and NET (for youth evangelization). Several specific programs have also been developed specifically for Hispanic or black evangelization. Addresses for additional information concerning any of the programs mentioned are included at the conclusion of this essay.


## SHOWCASE OF SIX EFFECTIVE PROGRAMS

A more detailed understanding of six specific programs operational in the United States today is provided by gleaning descriptions and comments directly from the promotional brochures or material offered by these programs.

### National Council for Catholic Evangelization

The NCCE National Evangelization Training Workshops and Seminars are informational, practical and process-oriented workshops presented by teams of four or five professionals in evangelization. They are held throughout the United States and Canada, sponsored and hosted by any diocese or group interested in a developmental and experiential approach to training evangelists. Publicity, registration and on-site preparations are the responsibility of the host diocese or group.

Two three-day seminars are offered. "Catching the Evangelizing Spirit: First Steps" develops the broad perspectives and implications of Catholic evangelization by exploring a theological understanding of evangelization, presenting practical tools, and providing opportunities for personal growth and conversion. "Developing Evangelization Teams: Continuing the Journey" focuses on the qualities of an effective evangelizer and how to develop, form and support evangelization teams, and it explores needed skills and resources.

NCCE also offers two one-day seminars. "Creating a Vision for Catholic Evangelization" presents an overview of Catholic evangelization and a vision for creating an evangelizing parish. "Skills for Evangelization Teams" develops skills for the work and ministry of an evangelization team.

The NCCE seminars and workshops are designed with parish teams as the focus; however, any group of church professionals and volunteers who wish to develop and expand the ministry of evangelization would benefit.

*Paulist Evangelization Training Institute*

This five-day institute, offered three times each summer at St. Paul's College in Washington, D.C., is designed to equip lay people, religious and clergy with the basic ideas, tools and methods of evangelization from the perspective of North American Catholicism. The institutes are taught on the popular level and are intended for people starting in the field of evangelization on the parish, diocesan or other programmatic levels.

The curriculum exposes people to the range of theological ideas and practical issues that form the background of contemporary evangelization and operates at three levels: theory, practicum and laboratory. The institutes are based on the view that there is a distinct Catholic vision of evangelization because of the distinct Catholic theology of salvation and spiritual growth through involvement in the community of believers. The institute experience is contexted in the Paulist tradition of evangelization as well as the church's prayer (Liturgy of the Hours and eucharist).

*Diocese of Cleveland*

A multimedia approach to evangelization training is offered by the diocese of Cleveland's Evangelization Office. "Share the Good News: A

Prayer and Reflection Guide on Evangelization in the Modern World" is a seven-part guide which helps parishioners studying as a group to understand the implications and inferences of "On Evangelization in the Modern World" (EMW). This study guide would best be utilized in a parish interested in establishing an evangelization commission, or to give an existing evangelization commission fresh inspiration and vision.

Each session focuses on a different chapter of EMW, offering prayer services, quotations from scripture and EMW, and discussion starters. In addition, homework assignments are given to enable the group to begin to assess its own parish. Flexibility for a group's unique circumstances is built into the study guide, and the instruments developed for understanding, assessing and planning parish-based evangelization activities are very practical.

Another resource offered by the Cleveland Evangelization Office is a slide-tape presentation, "Becoming an Evangelizing Parish," which is intended to help parishes identify what is and what is not happening in evangelization in the parish. With a good variety in the one hundred color slides and a superb script, followed by suggestions for group discussion, this presentation would be valuable for a parish in its beginning stages of understanding evangelization.

A third resource from Cleveland is a forty-page workbook, "Dynamics for Creative Evangelization," by Father Mark A. Latcovich. This workbook is designed to be used to help parishioners discover their need for self-evangelization and to point them to ways of sharing their faith with others.

### Good News/Buena Noticia

Good News/Buena Noticia offers a three-pronged approach to evangelization training which originated in the archdiocese of Miami: Good News/Buena Noticia I, II and III. The second and third courses (both ten-session courses) respectively address the apologetics and scriptural basis of evangelization. However, it is Good News/Buena Noticia I that is the "basic training course."

This fifteen-week program centers on the practical training of lay evangelizers, primarily as home visitors, training them to share the experience of God in their lives in a simple and attractive manner congruent with Catholic tradition. It utilizes role-playing, lectures, small group sharing, on-the-job training and many other educational techniques to enable participants to deepen their own faith and strengthen their commitment to Christ and to his church. Additionally, Good News I assists the Catholic evangelizer to identify the most frequently encountered resistances and questions in the process of evangelization and to deal with them effectively.

While Good News/Buena Noticia I has usually been offered in archdiocese of Miami parishes, having trained more than 2,400 men and women since its inception, it is now available for parishes, dioceses or movements upon the request of bishops, pastors or diocesan directors. It has been presented in Chicago, Los Angeles and the Dominican Republic.

*Mission:Evangelization*

Mission:Evangelization is a fifteen-session training program in relational evangelization skills which has been used in more than three hundred parishes in the U.S., Canada, the Caribbean, South Africa and the Far East. More than twelve thousand lay evangelizers have been trained. Mission:Evangelization offers a multimedia curriculum designed to engender: (1) foundational principles and accurate understanding of current Catholic theology and teaching, and (2) mastery of relevant specific competencies in relational evangelization. These competencies are taught within the context of home visitation preparation, although it is emphasized that they are generalizable to any one-on-one evangelistic encounter.

The program is usually offered on the parish level although it has been presented diocesan-wide and in several universities and seminaries with graduate-level accreditation. The course is usually facilitated locally by a parish staff member, however, and is based on the training manual, Mission:Evangelization, which has been translated into Spanish, and is supplemented by videotaped presentations.

A research-based, systematic methodology is presented in the initial ten classroom sessions, followed by five "on-the-job" training sessions.

While Mission:Evangelization is highly popular and effective, many pastors or parish evangelization coordinators have suggested a "condensed version" since they found many of their parishioners were interested in training but unwilling to commit to a fifteen-week program, especially in the context of home visitation. As a result of these grassroots evaluations and input, a five-week research-based course, Share Your Faith, has been developed which stresses a "no-nonsense" behavioral approach to evangelization training that is practical, relevant and immediately applicable. It is not intended as a comprehensive course in Catholic evangelization but as a competency-based program which results in the mastery of fifteen specific evangelization skills used by ordinary lay people in the ordinary events of their day-to-day lives. Share

Your Faith is accompanied by a facilitator's guide and optional video presentations.

### SINE (System of Integral New Evangelization)

SINE is the most comprehensive and complex training opportunity available today, resulting in the training and transformation not just of individual evangelizers but of entire parishes. SINE is "not an organization or institution, not a movement or association, and not merely a method" but a basic, organic and holistic pastoral model or system for parishes which seeks to transform the parish from being a "religious service station, a primarily sacrament-oriented parish," into a missionary parish, an evangelizing community.

With its roots and history in Mexico, SINE offers a complex and systematic training program which results, on the operational level, in a comprehensive pastoral plan for the parish. This plan integrates the basic elements of the Christian life and all the dimensions of the mission of the church, including: (1) the *kerygma,* catechesis and Bible study; (2) the formation of communities and social services; (3) liturgical celebration and spontaneous prayer; (4) the charismatic experience and the ecumenical dimension; (5) the apostolic commitment of all the faithful; (6) the care of special groups like family, youth, the sick and those in need of rehabilitation or liberation.

The training is offered in sequential steps, beginning with a full-day workshop in which the theological foundations and the pastoral plan of SINE are presented. Secondly, the SINE I Seminar is a four-day seminar with sixteen talks, presenting the entire vision and explaining each step of the pastoral plan, offering practical ways to implement it. Third, an evangelization retreat follows, offering a basic, intensive spiritual experience of Christian foundations. These first three steps are offered to the pastor, assistant priests, nuns and committed laity.

The second phase of training is offered to a group of about one hundred and twenty laity who will serve as the first collaborators in the community. These training experiences include evangelization missions, evangelization retreats and training workshops, and are given in the parish or diocese, at the SINE Training Center in Mexico City, or in the Regional Office in San Antonio, Texas. SINE is now working in twelve countries in more than five hundred parishes, with thirty-two parishes involved in the United States.

## CONCLUSION

Amazing inroads have been forged in the field of Catholic evangelization training. None of these pioneer programs existed ten years ago! All have experienced revision as they have been "refined and tested as gold" in the fire of "hands-on" experience. There is no question that thousands and thousands of "old Catholics" are willing and eager to learn "new tricks."

The greatest needs, however, concern two aspects of our original question: Who is going to teach these "old Catholics," and what is the essence, the content, the thrust of the "new tricks"? The two most critical needs today are the need for academic training on the professional level and the need for empirical, evaluative research of existing programs. It is time for a Catholic university to develop a degreed program in Catholic evangelization on the graduate level to form and certify professional, specialized evangelization educators.

Secondly, most of the existing programs remain unevaluated in terms of effectiveness of their long-range goal of providing service to the church, resulting in Paul VI's dream of "the transformation of all strata of society." Such an evaluation would encourage a reasoned, logical investment on all ecclesial levels of human and financial resources into evangelization training programs which are cost-effective, time-tested and proven.

As the consciousness of American Catholics progressively is raised concerning their right and responsibility to evangelize and as an awakened laity recognizes the need to become articulate, informed and committed evangelizers, the need for effective low-cost, locally available, grassroots training programs will increase. Dioceses and parishes today would be wise to take advantage of those programs which utilize the multiplicative process of "training trainers," thus assuring leadership on the local level in the future.

Paralleling the growth and development of the religious education field, I envision that in the future we will see: professional, degreed directors of relational evangelization in nearly every parish and every diocese; Catholic publishing houses flourishing with an abundance of viable and creative evangelization training resources; the formation of national and regional associations of credentialed, professional evangelization trainers/educators; and extensive parish-wide adult evangelization training programs.

There is no doubt that an urgent need for evangelization training exists today on all levels. It will be our conscious, concerted efforts to fulfill that need which will play a vital role in the revitalization of the church and the transformation of the world. May those who come behind us find us faithful!

## DISCUSSION QUESTIONS

1. What is the greatest need for evangelization training in your parish or diocese? For you personally?

2. What training opportunities are available which are appropriate for your parish or diocese? For you personally?

3. What barriers or obstacles prevent appropriate evangelization training for your parish or diocese? For you personally? How can these obstacles be transformed into opportunities?

## RESOURCES

Archdiocese of Boston Training Program, 159 Washington St., Brighton, MA 02135.

Catholic Evangelization Training Center, 10620 Livingston Dr., Northglenn, CO 80234.

Catholic Evangelization Training Program and Rebuild My Church, Franciscan University of Steubenville, Franciscan Way, Steubenville, OH 43952.

Duns Scotus School of Evangelization, Duns Scotus College Seminary, 2000 W. Nine Mile Rd., Southfield, MI 48075.

Evangelization Training Program for Total Parish-based Evangelization, Diocese of Providence, 1 Cathedral Square, Providence, RI 02903.

Good News/Buena Noticia, Inc., P.O. Box 707, Hollywood, FL 33022-0707.

Lamp Ministries, 2704 Schurz Ave., Bronx, NY 10465.

Mission:Evangelization and Share Your Faith, c/o Isaiah Ministries, 3211 N.W. 121 Lane, Coral Springs, FL 33065.

NCCE (National Council for Catholic Evangelization), 7494 Deron Lane, Manassas, VA 22111.

NET (National Evangelization Teams), 1190 Oakdale Ave., West St. Paul, MN 55118.

Parish Evangelization Team Training, Archdiocese of Indianapolis, P.O. Box 1410, Indianapolis, IN 46206.

Parish Visitation Program, Daughters of St. Paul, 50 St. Paul Ave., Boston, MA 02130.

Paulist Evangelization Training Institute, 3031 Fourth Street, N.E., Washington, DC 20017.

Share the Good News, Diocese of Cleveland Evangelization Office, 1031 Superior Ave., #751, Cleveland, OH 44114.

SINE (System of Integral New Evangelization), 11230 West Ave., Suite 2106, San Antonio, TX 78213.

# MEDIA FOR THE SAKE OF THE GOSPEL
Rosemary Jeffries, RSM

How many times have you heard or read the parable of the gospel where it says, "Do not light your light and keep it under a bushel! Put it on a lampstand for all to see." No doubt these words have made sense to you, maybe even inspired you. Certainly lights are meant to be seen, not hidden, and surely the light of Christ's word is meant to be seen, not hidden. Evangelization following this logical maxim is simple. This essay on communications and evangelization will explore how simple putting the light on a lampstand might be in our contemporary culture.

When I read the words of this parable, I often imagine the remote lighthouse set out on a cliff as a light to direct seafarers on their way. Lighthouses are an integral part of our American history. Many of these beacons still provide strategic lights to those at sea despite the advances of radar and new maritime technology. These lights guide thousands of travelers who usually never see the weathered walls of the lighthouse itself or ever think about the people who keep the lighthouse in operation.

The image captures for me the connections between communications/media and the task of evangelization. Pope Paul VI in "On Evangelization in the Modern World" describes the church as a sign of Christ and the depository of the good news to be proclaimed. "It is the content of the gospel, and therefore of evangelization, that she [the church] preserves as a precious living heritage, not in order to keep it hidden but to communicate it."[1] The church, like the lighthouse, is both sign and communicator. The importance of the message of the gospel is essential for evangelization, yet communicating the sign receives equal emphasis in this document. "The content of evangelization must not overshadow the importance of the ways and means."[2]

As the lighthouses that dot our ocean and lake shores are positioned for optimum visibility to bring light to those traveling the seas, the means for evangelization also need to be positioned for optimum visibility. Pope Paul VI realized that positioning the gospel in the modern world demands understanding the present-day culture.[3] In particular he states, "Evangelization loses much of its force and effectiveness if it does not take into consideration the actual people to whom it is addressed, if it does not use the language, the signs and symbols, if it does not answer the questions they ask, and if it does not have an impact on their concrete life."[4]

## THE MEANS OF EVANGELIZATION

How can the message of the gospel be made visible to the American culture in sign, symbol and language that will respond as well as inspire the diverse population of this country? The document offers three major ways of evangelization: through one-to-one communication, through preaching and through media.[5]

The first two ways provide strong personal methods to communicate the gospel message. Millions of Catholics in thousands of parishes are busy in these areas of activity. Yet the numbers of "unchurched" continue to climb. In 1978, forty-one percent of Americans reported that they did not attend church or synagogue. By 1988, forty-four percent claim this disaffiliation.[6] The same Gallup poll, however, showed that Americans have become more spiritual during the same period. For example, in 1988, eighty-four percent of Americans claimed that they believe in the divinity of Christ, compared to only seventy-eight percent in 1978. Also, thirty percent of the "unchurched" in 1988 claimed that religion was important in their lives.[7]

Media, the third way of communicating the gospel, functions more like the lighthouse. It radiates a communication of light to unknown numbers of people in need of a sign of hope. The media are certainly a useful tool for evangelization in today's American culture, which is often considered to be in the middle of a media revolution. Americans consume more media entertainment than citizens of any other country in the world. The average American home has television on about seven and a half hours a day. Children watch more hours of television than they spend hours in a classroom.[8] Television is the primary "storyteller" and often the backup baby-sitter. Additionally, Americans consistently consume other forms of media at work, in the car, and while shopping as a means of entertainment as well as information.

## THE MEDIA CULTURE

To use modern media to communicate the gospel message to the American public seems obvious. The use of media for the purpose of evangelization is not a new idea. However, it is an idea that needs updating and readjustment. The media options of today's American culture are different from the media options available when "On Evangelization in the Modern World" was released in 1975.

For example, in 1975 less than one percent of American households had VCRs. By 1989, nearly sixty-five percent of the households had VCRs.[9] In 1975 only nine million households subscribed to cable television. By 1989, forty-nine million of the nation's households had cable.[10] Cable systems grew from offering twelve channels of choice in the beginning to offering as many as eighty or more channels to today's subscribers. People can shop through cable TV; their houses can be secured through it; and they can do their banking through some systems. Information systems for business, media and other organizations today use satellite transmission regularly to connect, while in 1975 satellite transmission was just beginning to be popular.

The hunger for information is underscored by the tremendous increase in TV news. Not until the early 1960s did the network news increase from fifteen minutes to a half hour.[11] Today the network television stations present two hours of evening news and hour-long morning news programs. During the day news updates and midday reports fill broadcast hours. Finally, half-hour late news recap and two-hour late evening news analysis fill out the menu of news offerings. Information and entertainment opportunities are both more extensive and pervasive.

In print communications, options have also increased in the recent past. In 1975, 9,657 periodicals were published. By 1989, 11,556 periodicals directed at every segment of the American population were printed.[12] Newspapers catering to local cities and townships offered additional print options. Though some long-standing publications like Look, Life, The Saturday Evening Post and some older daily newspapers folded in this period, the overall growth has been amazing.

The message of the gospel is in stiff competition with multiple messages of the modern media menu of offerings. It is in competition with instant transmission of information and media directed at specialized interests. The message of evangelization found in Pope Paul's exhortation, however, suggests that to reach the "strata of humanity" there is a need to use elements of culture.[13]

Since the American population supports the diversity of media, the work of evangelization in this media culture would seem to be served best through what professional communicators would call a "media mix." For example, a gospel message directed at the unchurched needs to be available in print ads for newspapers or selected magazines as well as in broadcast formats for network or cable television, for radio or for video-cassette. The message also needs one-to-one follow-up from an evangelization minister. The message could also be enhanced and explicated by the preached word at a special event sponsored by the local parish. Mixing media formats provides a number of ways that a particular individual will hear the message or be reminded of the message. A media mix also provides the individual with a way to take a closer look by connecting with an evangelization minister or remain distant while deciding a course of action. Some individuals clip ads or take down toll-free numbers and respond months later.

## EXAMPLES OF NATIONAL MEDIA CAMPAIGNS

Let us consider some examples of national efforts to use this media mix approach.

### "For God's Sake Campaign"

In 1989 the Catholic Communications Campaign sponsored by the Catholic bishops of the United States launched a national media effort called "For God's Sake Do Something."[14] This effort included print ads and TV spots that depicted current social problems such as homelessness and caring for the frail elderly. They carried the message to the reader or viewer that voluntary help is needed. The ads invited the consumer to respond to a toll-free (800) telephone number and "do something." This was an ecumenical endeavor sponsored by Catholic Charities USA, the Council of Jewish Federations, and Lutheran Social Services. People were trained to respond to each call. They would take a monetary pledge for one of the sponsoring agencies, or connect the caller with an opportunity to do volunteer work in their area. In some cases they would connect the caller with the help they requested.

As with any national campaign using an 800 number, the variety of calls is very wide. Being prepared to connect people with local resources for giving or receiving help has been essential to the credibility of this type of effort. The one-to-one facet of this campaign demanded careful coordination, but groups cannot be in the business of advertising assistance if they cannot deliver help when it is requested.

Due to the ecumenical nature of the campaign, major media outlets such as *People, Newsweek, Ladies Home Journal,* and *Fortune* magazine as well as major TV networks—ABC, CBS, NBC, FOX—and many local stations and publications offered public service space and time to run the ads. These ads conveyed a message of the church caring for the poorest persons in our society, and they encouraged people to accept their responsibility to care for their neighbor also—a classic gospel message.

This campaign was developed by media professionals who donated their time. The production costs amounted to approximately $150,000 but the contributed public service space amounted to more than $5,000,000. More importantly, this campaign reached millions of people who received a message of care and God's love. While only a portion of the people seeing the ads used the 800 number (more than 3,000 calls in the first eight months), many more heard the message and might have volunteered or helped in their local area without ever calling the 800 number. The value of such an effort is hard to document purely with numbers responding. These spots are still running on some stations.

*Mercy Image Campaign*

In a similar way, the Sisters of Mercy of the Americas in 1989 launched a national print and radio campaign. The purpose of this ongoing effort is twofold: to reimage religious life in the public media, and to make the invitation to religious life known to women who might consider this lifestyle. The campaign's objectives determined the need for a more focused audience. Women between the ages of twenty-five and thirty-nine with some professional career became the target audience for this effort. Focusing the audience also influenced the choice of media, namely radio rather than television, and print ads for selected magazines, newsletters and some newspapers.

The Mercy Image Project is directed at purposes that enhance the life of the religious order. It also carries a message of commitment to God and God's people. The ads feature individual Mercy sisters in their professional workplace with copy describing their dedication to serving people while being women committed to prayer and community. The stories are real stories about real sisters.[15]

For the national effort the ads carry an 800 number. The calls to this number have resulted in people asking for more information as well as seeking help. During the first four months thirty calls of the one hundred and twenty-five to the 800 number were serious inquiries about religious life. The others ranged from donations of baby clothes to the call of a mother of seven seeking help with food and clothing. Like the "For God's Sake" campaign, the Mercy Image Project has persons answering the phones trained to handle calls for help as well as calls for further information about religious life. Callers are usually connected with a sister in their own area to meet their particular needs.

This ad campaign was produced with the help of media professionals in research and production. It also received public service space and time in *Business Week, Ad Week* and numerous radio stations. Ads were strategically placed in a few select professional magazines—*Nursing '89, Social Work Journal, Catholic School Teacher*—to reach the target audience (women between twenty-five and thirty-nine years of age in some profession).

This campaign functions on the local level as well as the national level. Sisters in twenty-five major locations of the order covering thirty-seven states conduct local efforts using the same spots and ads but replace the 800 number or the national contact name with a local contact name and telephone number. The creativity of the local campaigns is greatly enhanced by the help of local media (newspapers, radio, magazines, cable TV, etc.). These local efforts extend the national effort in hundreds of ways.

For example, in Buffalo the sisters arranged in February 1989 to have a week set aside in the city called "Mercy Week" complete with proclamation from the mayor, banners, local TV coverage and a celebration with the diocesan church. In St. Louis and Pittsburgh, radio spots attracted the interest of the major daily papers which printed feature stories on local sisters. In St. Louis this connection with radio has resulted in the order co-sponsoring a career day for women with the station and the local Mercy Hospital. In Pittsburgh, TV and radio coverage on local talk shows has encouraged other religious congregations to work together with the Mercys in a joint media campaign directed at reimaging religious life.

Ads were also placed in hospital and educational institution newsletters reaching at least 400,000 co-workers during the first four months. A videotape produced for small group use provided local sisters with another media to use in parishes and schools while their local media efforts were in operation.

*Elements of a Successful Campaign*

In these national campaign examples, it is important to note that both efforts called on media professionals to develop and shape the creative material. Having professional-quality material helped in securing public service space and time.[16] Engaging the help of professionals in the media to plan and execute the campaign is key to a successful campaign.

Though the media world almost seems too slick for the gospel message and not the most comfortable place for the gospel messenger, experience suggests the opposite. The people who work in the media for the most part are good individuals who care about others and the needs of society. They are people who admire commitment. Media people are in the business of bringing information, entertainment and inspiration to the public. Offering media professionals the opportunity to help evangelize is in its own way a form of evangelization.

People in the media want to use their craft in meaningful ways. Often church-related projects provide a unique opportunity for that. People who work in the media are challenged by the same family and personal problems that all people face; consequently, the opportunity to interact with a church minister often meets some of their personal needs as well.

Another key element in the examples used so far is the assumption that people who need the gospel message or an invitation to a life-challenging vocation are often not in the church pew or in close contact with religious ministers. Finally, a successful campaign needs to provide for credible follow-up.

The campaigns described reached wide audiences and made provisions for careful follow-up responses. These last two elements are essential keys to utilizing the media for the sake of the gospel in a responsible way. Returning to the lighthouse image for a moment, using media means reaching an audience that is wide and diverse. However, it also reaches some individuals who require careful assistance in making their way to help. Lighthouses also require skilled personnel maintaining their proper functioning.

## LOCAL EXAMPLES

Media can be successfully used by individual parishes or organizations or religious congregations. Some parishes in highly urban areas like New York City, Chicago, Los Angeles, etc., are faced with very expensive media rates and very stiff competition. A sixty-second radio spot in New York City might cost about two thousand dollars while the same spot in Belmont, North Carolina, will cost about twenty dollars. The number of charities or churches seeking public service space in the smaller locations are fewer. Being heard amidst the thousands of charities and causes that compete for attention in a major metropolitan area is much more challenging.

I offer these next two examples of local efforts to underscore the importance of creativity mixed with knowledge of the audience and the media environment.

First, St. Paul's Church in New York City realized that they could never afford to pay for media advertising. At the same time they realized that there were hundreds of people in the city who were "unchurched." They capitalized on their location by placing a TV monitor on the corner of their church property. With the help of media professionals they produced a videotape inviting people to inquire about the faith. This tape played at various times of the day and night. The thousands of people who passed by this location on the street at least knew that the church cared enough to invite them. Some stopped and really listened to the tape. For those who showed more interest or seemed in need of help, people from the parish were standing in the vicinity of the TV monitor to offer more information or assistance. A wide audience was reached yet great attention was given to follow-up.

Placement in a smaller city or suburban/rural area is much more affordable. Here the important factor is knowing which media to use, when to place the media, and planning for adequate follow-up. Local media professionals are usually more than willing to help. In fact, they might be members of the parish. Making the effort to meet with the local media and seeking ways that they and the parish, organization or religious order can work together for the good of the civic community are key to a successful local effort.

For example, in Trenton, New Jersey, the local radio station, WHWH, worked with diocesan personnel to set up a "Family Food Fund." The station personnel suggested ways of getting the message out while the diocesan personnel provided the coordination needed for distribution. With the help of the radio station management, the local daily paper also joined the effort. The mixed media approach of radio spots and newspaper ads, as well as announcements in parish bulletins and reminders from the pulpit, assured optimum exposure for the effort. The effort attracted help from a wider audience than the Catholic community, while the Catholic Church and the sponsoring media were credited with caring for community needs.

Radio stations, cable TV stations and local papers are interested in community-minded projects and are usually willing to work with local groups. Often they are willing to co-sponsor projects that benefit the local area such as Thanksgiving food drives, clothing drives, funds for the homeless, etc. Here the cooperative effort benefits everyone. The media provide free advertisement for the drive while the parish or organization provides the needed follow-up responsibilities. The media are perceived as being community-minded while the church organization increases its presence in the local community as a caring institution.


## THE COMMITMENT TO EVANGELIZE THROUGH MEDIA

These examples of national and local efforts describe commitment of time, energy and money to utilize media for the sake of the gospel. If you are a member of a parish or religious order, or are a priest or bishop, you might be saying to yourself, "It's a great idea to use media for evangelization, but . . ." Let me list a few of the usual excuses:

"I don't know anything about media so I'll leave it to someone else."

"The time and money needed is too much for our budget and limited staff."

"We could spend a lot of money and get no response or not the responses we want."

There are a hundred reasons why church personnel find using media difficult.

As a church communicator for the past fourteen years, I have heard the excuses from bishops, pastors, religious superiors, parish ministers and friends who question the demands of money and time to use media. Consistently, the questions always suggest that using the media does not really work.

I understand the limitations of money and time but I am convinced that using media is a cost-effective investment of money and time for evangelization. Where could any church project communicate with more than seven million people for less than one cent per person as demonstrated in the two national examples? Though some of the responses to the request for volunteer help or the invitation to religious life were off the mark, I would still say that using the media really worked. Millions of people were touched at least by a message of God's love at work through individual people.

The national examples I used were both under-funded. They met success through contributed time, money and energy. Media professionals offered important assistance, media outlets offered public service space and time, and the church and religious order coordinators volunteered their time in addition to already full schedules. No doubt, media efforts take the time, energy and money that most church-related organizations are short on.

## FAITH IS THE PRIMARY ELEMENT FOR A CHURCH CAMPAIGN

The most critical element for a church effort at media and evangelization, however, is faith. Media efforts can be evaluated by counting numbers of responses or by measuring increase in attendance or donations depending on the purpose of the campaign. Counting is a typical method for evaluating media efforts, but counting numbers does not provide the whole picture for evaluating an evangelization campaign of any sort. How can anyone measure how a message of God's love or a message of personal commitment worked in the heart and mind of the viewer? The examples given illustrate that millions of persons heard or saw the ads. Though few responded in the ways provided by the campaigns, many might have responded in ways that remain unrecorded.

Media efforts require faith that the word of God can take root quietly as well as obviously and are an extension of the preaching that is the core of spreading the gospel. Often the results of media on the audience are intangible. Like the lighthouse, using media reaches a wide, anonymous audience who benefit in ways never known to the persons responsible. Evangelization through media, like the lighthouse, puts the light on a contemporary lampstand for all to see.

Not providing the lighthouse for sea travelers would be irresponsible. Likewise, I believe that using media for the sake of the gospel carries the same responsibility. My belief echoes the strong belief of Paul VI: "The presentation of the gospel message is not an optional contribution for the church. It is the duty incumbent on her by the command of the Lord Jesus, so that people can believe and be saved."[17] In a society of forty-four percent "unchurched," we, the church of that same Lord Jesus, need to try new ways to put our light on a lampstand for all to see.

## NOTES

1. Pope Paul VI, "On Evangelization in the Modern World," (Washington, D.C.: United States Catholic Conference, 1976), n. 15.
2. *Ibid.*, n. 40.
3. *Ibid.*, nn. 2, 6, 20, 40.
4. *Ibid.*, n. 63.
5. *Ibid.*, Chapter IV.
6. John Naisbitt and Patricia Aburdene, *Megatrends 2000: Ten New Directions for the 1990s* (New York: William Morrow and Company, 1990), 275.

7. *Ibid.*
8. Jack Trout and Al Reiss, *Positioning: The Battle for Your Mind* (New York: McGraw-Hill, Inc., 1981), 11–13.
9. U.S. Bureau of Census, *Statistical Abstract of the U.S.: 1990,* 110th edition (Washington, D.C.: Department of Commerce, 1990), table 914.
10. *Ibid.*
11. Desmond Smith, "TV News Did Not Just Happen—It Had to Invent Itself," *Smithsonian* 20 (January 1989), 88.
12. U.S. Bureau of Census, *Statistical Abstract of the U.S.: 1990* (Washington, D.C.: Department of Commerce, 1990), table 927.
13. Paul VI, "On Evangelization in the Modern World," nn. 19–20.
14. Information about this campaign can be obtained from the Catholic Communication Campaign, Department of Communication, United States Catholic Conference, 3211 Fourth St., NE, Washington, D.C. 20017.
15. Information about this campaign can be obtained from Rosemary Jeffries, RSM, Director of the Mercy Image Project, Mount Saint Mary, 1645 U.S. Highway 22, Watchung, N.J. 07060.
16. The Federal Communication Commission has deregulated broadcasting, reducing the regulations regarding the reservation of public service time for non-profit use. Yet, given good relations with the media and a well-thought out campaign that ultimately serves the community, media outlets will provide public service. Often a combination of paid and public service is the most attractive to offer to the media outlet.
17. Paul VI, "On Evangelization in the Modern World," n. 5.

## DISCUSSION QUESTIONS

1. What is the central message you feel is important for the young adult audience, fifteen to twenty-five, often referred to as the "lost generation"?

2. How would you use a "media mix" in your parish or diocesan work of evangelization to reach the lost generation? Be specific in response: i.e., name stations, papers, etc., and the strategies to these outlets. (Choose another specific audience, e.g., elderly, sixty to seventy-five, if the younger group does not fit.)

3. Why do you think people spend so much time involved in media consumption? Does it provide a substitute?

## FOR FURTHER READING

"Communications, Media and Spirituality." *The Way Supplement* 57, Autumn 1986.

Francis P. Frost, Ph.D., ed. "A Vision All Can Share: Toward a National Plan for Church Communications." Washington, D.C.: USCC Department of Communication, 1982.

Pontifical Commission for the Means of Social Communication. "Communications: A Pastoral Instruction on the Media, Public Opinion and Human Progress." For the application of the Second Vatican Council's "Decree on the Means of Social Communication." Washington, D.C.: United States Catholic Conference, 1971.

Jack Trout and Al Reiss. *Positioning: The Battle for Your Mind.* New York: McGraw-Hill, Inc., 1981.

———. *Marketing Warfare.* New York: McGraw-Hill, Inc., 1986.

———. *Bottom-up Marketing.* New York: McGraw-Hill, Inc., 1989.

# IV
## New Fervor

# COME, HOLY SPIRIT!
# THE DIVINE SPIRIT AND EVANGELIZATION
George E. Griener, SJ

Pope Paul VI's apostolic exhortation "On Evangelization in the Modern World" speaks of the Holy Spirit as the "principal agent" and "goal" of evangelization. The Spirit alone, says Paul VI, "stirs up the new creation, the new humanity toward which evangelization should tend with that unity in variety which evangelization wishes to achieve within the Christian community."[1]

The pope sketched a rich and fascinating description of evangelization's relationship to the Holy Spirit. It presumes an integral link between God's Spirit, effective proclamation of the gospel, and a new order of creation. As we shall see, it also expands the notion of evangelization in a significant way.

This essay reflects on the Holy Spirit as "agent" and "goal" of evangelization, seeing this as intimately linked with the "new creation." Let me begin where most of Christian theological reflection has begun, in the lived faith of the Christian community at worship. Our faith is nourished and sustained through images. Two visual images, both drawn from the liturgy of the Easter season, both rooted in scripture, express for me the action of the Holy Spirit in the life of the church.

## EASTER IMAGES OF THE HOLY SPIRIT

The first image comes from an Easter vigil service. The liturgy of readings, which traces the history of salvation, begins with Genesis and the story of creation. But instead of being proclaimed in solemn tone from the pulpit, this time the creation narrative was exuberantly dramatized in the sanctuary to the joyful music of a modern American liturgical composer.[2] "God" was perched on a ladder in the center of the sanc-

191

tuary, and creation began as God blew a mighty wind across the deep. From a bag, the divine creator pulled out the stars and the moon, creatures of the sea, fauna and flora, wildlife and animals. And finally from the earth God raised up a human couple, Adam and Eve. God, taking in all this from the top of the ladder, seemed to enjoy creating very much! Creation was not just a majestic moment, it was also a joyful expression of love! And we sang, praising that love.

The Hebrew word *ruah,* translated in the New American Bible as "mighty wind," also includes the notions of breath or spirit or life principle. Other translations of Genesis render it as "God's Spirit hovering over the water." The Nicene Creed speaks of the Holy Spirit as "Lord and giver of life." Creation is anchored in the joy-filled depths of God's own life, and comes to realization through God's word and Spirit.[3] The imaginatively dramatized "creation" account at the Easter vigil seemed to illustrate aspects of our belief in a way that many words could not. The rest of our faith—with its reflections on sin and death, on promise and love, on the suffering and resurrection of Jesus—finds its foundation in the mystery of God's life-giving, creative love. As the letter to the Romans assures us, this love has flooded our hearts through the Holy Spirit.

The second image comes from the other end of the Easter season, the celebration of Pentecost. While we entered the church, three persons were in the sanctuary holding lighted candles. The Latin hymn "Veni Sancte Spiritus," "Come, Holy Spirit," was sung in the background. As we began the opening song, "Send Down the Fire of Your Justice,"[4] the three exchanged their candles for flaming torches and began to dance, first in the sanctuary, then down the aisles of the church until flames seemed to dance over the heads of the whole assembly.

The dancing fire brought back memories of the Easter vigil, the paschal candle and the expanding glow of Easter light as worshipers lit their own candles. But the dancing flames also stoked images of the life-giving breath or Spirit of God racing over the deep, drawing life and light from the darkness. Our celebration of the risen Christ, which we had begun weeks earlier at the vigil, was coming to its end, or, better, to its *fulfillment:* the energy of the risen Lord was being poured out on us, the church.

It was an expressive, vibrant image: the Christian community aflame with the power of the Spirit. Those of us celebrating that Pentecost morning had been anointed, set afire with the power of God, sent to make Jesus known, Christ present in a world rooted in the creative energy of God's Spirit and the loving form of God's word. All creation groans and yearns for transformation, Paul once wrote, a transformation in the Spirit whose beginning we were celebrating once again.

## RENEWED AWARENESS OF THE HOLY SPIRIT

Awareness of the Holy Spirit has become more ingrained in the consciousness of Catholics than was the case a generation ago. I liken it to the experience of looking up a word in a dictionary, or locating on a map a country you think you have never heard of, only to find, in the subsequent days or weeks, that you see that word or hear about that country over and over again—in the papers, on the news, even on quiz shows! And you begin to wonder whether you simply hadn't "recognized" it before! Now that your ear is "attuned," now that your consciousness has been "raised," you hear it over and over. Catholics are finally becoming "attuned" to the Holy Spirit!

Almost a century ago Pope Leo XIII wrote an encyclical on the Holy Spirit, "Divinum Illud Munus," but it didn't have great impact on Catholic consciousness or spirituality. However, in recent years, especially after the Second Vatican Council, it seems that we hear about the Spirit every time we turn around! Paul VI even spoke of the church living "at a privileged moment of the Spirit." In 1986 John Paul II published an encyclical, his own personal reflection on the Holy Spirit.[5] This new interest isn't a phenomenon associated with only some minority group in the church; it reflects a more profound understanding of the mystery of God's action in the world—through God's word, made flesh in Jesus Christ, and through the ongoing activity of the Spirit.

Many factors have deepened our awareness of the role of the Holy Spirit in the church: historical and biblical studies; the Rite of Christian Initiation of Adults, with its immediate liturgical link between baptism and the seal of the Spirit (which we are used to calling "confirmation"); the three eucharistic prayers, with their emphasis on the role of the Spirit in the transformation of the altar gifts and the creation of the community; the broadened appreciation of the many gifts and talents and ministries of the people of God, whose origin is the Spirit; the understanding of Pentecost, not as the end of the Easter season, but as the culmination of the Easter event; and the impact of the Catholic charismatic movement.

## GOD'S SPIRIT IN SCRIPTURE

In Hebrew scripture, God's *ruah*/wind/breath/spirit broods over the waters of creation (Gen 1:1), drives prophets to speak in the name of the Lord (Is 61:1–3), anoints the kings of Israel to rule with justice (1 Sam 10:1–6), empowers leaders and judges with wisdom (Num 11:

16–30). The Spirit will come to rest on God's messianic chosen one "with wisdom, understanding and knowledge, might and fear of the Lord" (Is 9:1–7). And as a sign of the last days of fulfillment, the *eschatos*, the Spirit will rest on all without distinction of gender or rank in society, filling them with hope, vision and dreams of God's reign (Jl 3:1).

The New Testament portrays the life-giving Spirit as initiating the "new creation" through Jesus of Nazareth. The Holy Spirit generates new life in the Virgin Mary, hovers over Jesus at his baptism, sends him out into the desert, anoints him with the task of spreading news about the reign of God. For Paul, the Spirit's activity in Jesus reaches its fulfillment by raising him from the dead, making him the first fruits of the "new creation."

In John's gospel, Jesus promises to send another counselor or advocate who will keep the community grounded in faith, truth and love. Luke sees the Spirit gathering together the disciples, dispersed after the death and resurrection of Christ, uniting them into a community through prayer, interpreting scripture, sharing the bread and mutual service. The Spirit encourages them to live and proclaim the good news of God's plan and presence in the world, empowering them with wisdom and strength when their message encounters resistance and rejection. That same Spirit creates openness in the hearts of those who hear the gospel: "No one can say, 'Jesus is Lord,' except in the Holy Spirit" (1 Cor 12:3).

The Holy Spirit of love and truth bonds together the local churches spread across the Mediterranean coastline. If Jesus remains with this rapidly expanding network of local churches—which later generations would call dioceses—then it is through the power of his Spirit. The Spirit welds these communities into a tangible sign, something like a sacrament, or, to use an image of the eastern church, an *icon* of God's presence and action in the world. The human community, fragmented through strife and sin, is being reunited, created anew through the Spirit, and the church is the visible sign or proof of this divine action.


## BROADER CONCEPT OF EVANGELIZATION

Hand in hand with a renewed appreciation of the Holy Spirit, there has also been in the church a deeper understanding of evangelization. Michael Amaladoss sees a paradigm shift in the theology of mission since Vatican II, from "the missions" to "the mission" to "evangelization."[6] If "the missions," understood as the "foreign missions," regarded success in the numerical or geographical extension of the church, "mission" became an essential element of being church, an ongoing responsibility to proclaim the gospel.

Ongoing reflection on the Spirit in the life of Jesus has taken us to a still deeper understanding of his task—the proclamation of the reign of God. The focus of Jesus' preaching was not primarily himself, but the reign of God. The "reign" would signal the "end time," or the "new creation," but its impact overflows into the present. Human suffering of all kinds moved Jesus to forgive the sinner, eat with the outcast, heal the sick, console the poor, touch those who longed to be touched by God.

Our world, where so much human suffering and misery can be traced to the decisions and choices of other human beings, has moved Christians to understand the mission of Jesus more integrally. The 1970 bishops' synod concluded that "action on behalf of justice and participation in the transformation of the world fully appear . . . as a constitutive dimension of the preaching of the gospel or, in other words, of the church's mission for the redemption of the human race and its liberation from every oppressive situation."[7]

Mission, now understood as evangelization, looks to promote the reign of God and all that entails. So Paul VI could write: "Evangelizing means bringing the good news into all the strata of humanity, and through its influence transforming humanity from within and making it new."[8]

Evangelization calls forth and encourages within a given culture or society those goods and values whose roots lie in the creative action of the Spirit. It names and challenges cultural prejudices and values which oppose the understanding of humanity symbolized in the biblical concept of God's reign. This stance can demand a prophetic witness, which in the Judeo-Christian tradition is supported by God's Spirit: "We believe in the Holy Spirit, Lord and giver of Life . . . who has spoken through the prophets."

Walter Brueggemann says that "the task of prophetic ministry is to nurture, nourish, and evoke a consciousness and perception alternative to the consciousness and perception of the dominant culture around us."[9] This is very close to what Pope Paul had written as the task of evangelization: "It is a question . . . of affecting and as it were upsetting, through the power of the gospel, humankind's criteria of judgment, determining values, points of interest, lines of thought, sources of inspiration and models of life, which are in contrast with the word of God and the plan of salvation."[10]

The pastoral letters of the American bishops, drawn up in consultation with a wide range of Catholics and specialists, and addressing such questions as war and peace, the economy, the death penalty, the concern to respect life through opposition to abortion or euthanasia, have been attempts by the Catholic community of the United States to promote an inner transformation of American society.


SPIRIT OF HOLINESS: INTEGRAL TRANSFORMATION

The truth of the gospel message is preserved and proclaimed in the teachings and creeds of the church, in the explicit proclamation of the gospel, but also in the life of integrity, compassion and love which these communities embody and manifest. Paul VI spoke of "the living witness of fidelity to the Lord Jesus—the witness of poverty and detachment, of freedom in the face of the powers of this world, in short, the witness of sanctity," all made possible in the "consolation of the Holy Spirit."[11]

This "witness of sanctity" might be described as the attractiveness of integrated, generous, loving human beings who can live in hope and faith in the final mystery of their lives. This attractive witness makes the faith credible and desirable—and begins with each of us. I was about to say: with each individual. But "individual" transformation or conversion through the Spirit always occurs in the context of the believing community. Personal holiness, personal integrity, is always situated within and made possible by a network of other persons. The spiritual transformation which the Spirit of holiness accomplishes in me affects not only a private, moral component of my life, but also my relation to the community of faith, the church.

Evangelization includes explicit invitation to others to join this community of faith and hope, includes the building up of a community, the church, where gospel values and vision are preserved, articulated, heard, cherished, concretized and celebrated. Evangelization includes proclaiming the word in the power of the Spirit, and giving thanks for that word in the Spirit. There we encounter the risen Christ, the first fruit of the "new creation."

For my conversion to Jesus to become integral, the Spirit has to change my perception of who I am and how I relate to the larger social and political realities of which I am a part. The "witness of sanctity" which evangelization presupposes touches many levels of my personality: moral, religious, intellectual, political. Transformation, which flows from openness to the word of God in the gospel and the Spirit of God in grace and the world, embraces a new moral appreciation of what is right and wrong, a new intellectual manner of understanding the world, a new religious appropriation of my relation to God, and a new political stance toward civic and international responsibilities. There is also what Robert

Doran calls "psychic conversion," a transformation and reappropriation of the images and symbols through which I interact with the world around me.[12]

The integrity and authenticity of Christian transformation is evaluated or discerned in ongoing dialogue with the community of faith, and against what tradition calls "the gifts of the Spirit." This expanded understanding of conversion dovetails with a transformed concept of the notion of evangelization, and with a new appreciation of the role of the Holy Spirit in the history of salvation.

## SPIRIT OF TRUTH: ROOTED IN THE PAST,
## ATTENTIVE TO THE PRESENT, OPEN TO THE FUTURE

The truth of the gospel is not a "fact," like the volume on the Great Lakes or a chronology of the Napoleonic wars that needs only to be handed on without distortion or error. The truth of the gospel is one whose content embraces and transforms the whole sweep of history, to its end. It always strains forward to its fulfillment. The Christian community celebrates the birth, death and resurrection of the Christ, but also calls: Maranatha! Come, Lord Jesus! Truth is eschatological, finds its fulfilled uncovering at the end of history, is uncovered in the course of history: "It ain't over 'til it's over," a baseball great was fond of saying.

Salvation, described by Paul as a new creation, is in actuality the completion, the fulfillment of that event of God's love begun when God's breath uttered the word, Let there be light! No wonder that the Easter season opens with the reading from Genesis at the vigil, and comes to completion with the outpouring of the Spirit on Pentecost.

A community, as the American philosopher Josiah Royce reminded us, has a past and a future. It is a community of memory and recollection, and a community of expectation and hope. This is true of the Christian community. The truth of the gospel is not merely a narrative of some past event, it is also promise of what is yet to be unveiled.

Fidelity to the message of Jesus entails ongoing contact with the community of faith, the church. In that community of faith and love, whose inner heart is the Spirit of Jesus, we come to understand the gospel; we stay in vital contact with the history of the community, its memory, its tradition, its scripture texts and credal formulas, as well as its tradition of prayer, liturgy, and religious expression in art, music, architecture, poetry and literature. The faith is handed down and born anew not only in the formal documents of the community, but also in the richness and variety of expression found in its many cultural manifestations. There is a beauty in that tradition which speaks of and bears witness to God's own.

An attentiveness to the present, to the "signs of the times," promotes an ongoing "incarnation" of the faith, an appropriate expression of and lived witness to the faith, but also of the living context in which faith finds its content. To believe in God is always to believe in God within the concrete context in which I believe. To know what it is to say "yes" to God is discovered anew in the concreteness and specificity of my life.

The Spirit of truth keeps us in contact with the faith by sustaining our contact with the world we live in, nudging us away from flight, from apathy, from dullness and insensitivity. If we are unable to resonate in some way with the experience of the world around us, we will never be able to make the word of God's love credible to that world. "The joys and the hopes, the griefs and the anxieties of the world of this age, especially those who are poor or in any way afflicted, these too are the joys and hopes, the griefs and anxieties of the followers of Christ."[13]

This attentiveness to the present can mean discovering the activity of the Spirit beyond the borders of what we traditionally call Christianity. Martin Luther King, Jr. related that it was reading about Mahatma Gandhi, listening to his message of peace, which allowed King to discover a new power to love, to discover the socially transforming dynamic of non-violent charity. King had been attentive to the Spirit in the world and had discovered a new depth to his own faith. As Christians dialogue and interact today with Jews, Muslims, Buddhists, Hindus and people of other beliefs, we should be willing, to borrow an expression of John Dunne's, to "cross over" to the side of the other and learn from his or her experience, then return enriched by the encounter.[14]

A community exists not only on memory, but on expectation and hope as well. In a given cultural context, that is, in the immediate world around us, that process can take the form of reflecting critically on the values, structures, mores, presuppositions of our culture, and then "imagining" alternatives to that complex, or of imagining transformative extensions of that complex which make more tangible and credible the presence of God's love.


## SPIRIT OF LIFE: GIVER OF THE NEW CREATION

Perhaps we are coming to see what calling the Spirit the "goal" of evangelization might mean. The Christian community, grounded in faith in the love of God revealed in Jesus Christ, strains forward toward the fulfillment of God's will for the cosmos: an integral expression of love and beauty as that cosmos, formed and shaped through the wisdom, commitment and imagination of the human community acting under the graceful influence of the Holy Spirit, reaches its final expression.

Christian faith sees the world as having its roots and source in God's love, as that love was expressed through the divine word and Spirit. But the world is also unfolding toward the final expression of that love, urged and moved forward by the Holy Spirit, so that the world we live in, with its gracious natural beauties and with the variety of human expression found in its myriad cultures, becomes the concrete symbol—one could almost say "the body"—of the Spirit.

In this unfolding expression, we share an important, essential role. If evangelization aims at the full expression of the Spirit, then the Spirit is at work in us, prompting fidelity to the message of Jesus, an attentiveness to the "signs of the times," and a creative, even *imaginative* openness to the future of that process.

The future comes into existence by the ongoing imagination of the human community, imagining what is not yet, "seeing" what isn't there, realizing the divine phantasies of what is possible. "When I pour out my Spirit on all mankind your old men shall dream dreams, your young men shall see visions" is the way the prophet Joel describes it. To the extent that these visions and dreams are inspired by the Spirit, they have the Spirit as their cause and agent; to the extent that they are realized in the world, in cultures, in the relationships between human beings, in the social, political and economic structures that form the context of so much of our personal interaction, the Holy Spirit is "incarnated" there, indeed becomes the goal of evangelization. The "new creation, the new humanity" that comes about finds its source and its goal in the Spirit.[15]

Dreaming in the Spirit has little to do with mindless daydreaming or wishful thinking. It is hard-nosed dreaming, critical dreaming with the facts and statistics of the world before us. It means envisioning alternative ways of making sense of the data, alternative solutions to the problems, alternative structures to local society, or to the international economy. It means imagining alternative ways for human beings to live with each other on this planet, ways which respect the dignity of each human being and the sovereignty of God. Such dreaming cannot be set aside for moments of idle pastime, but must become second nature to the way we encounter the world and live out our commitment to Jesus.

If surveys are correct, many of our contemporaries oscillate between apathy and anxiety: apathy, resulting from resignation in the face of the magnitude of the world's problems; anxiety, a natural response to the mortal threat posed by those problems. Evangelization often means providing images, symbols, traces of hope which result from a new, alternative, faith-filled interpretation of the facts and data and statistics of the situation.

We are also beginning to appreciate how closely connected evangelization and a renewed earth really are. John Paul II's 1990 Peace Day message emphasized responsibility for the environment and ecology as integral to the Christian vision of "the new creation."[16] Perhaps it is a sign of the times that the 1989 San Antonio World Conference on Missions and Evangelization celebrated "The Earth is the Lord's" as one of its topics, and that the 1991 Seventh Assembly of the World Council of Churches in Canberra, Australia, adopted "Giver of Life—Sustain Your Creation" as its sub-theme.

"In the beginning . . . God's Spirit brooded over the deep." The salvation, which it is our joy and responsibility to live and proclaim, brings this beginning, this creation, to its fulfillment and goal. It brings about God's love by touching us individually, touching every dimension of ourselves and our world as well: the social, political, economic and environmental levels. If God's love has been poured into our hearts, that love should overflow into the whole world around us. "Lord, send out your Spirit, and renew the face of the earth!"

## NOTES

1.  Pope Paul VI, "On Evangelization in the Modern World" (Washington, D.C.: USCC Publications Office, 1976), n. 75. The English translation in the USCC version of the exhortation seems to reverse the meaning of the text here, rendering it "the new humanity of which evangelization is to be the result," whereas the Latin text reads: "Jure pariter affirmari potest Eum esse etiam finem ac terminum omnis evangelizationis: unus enim novam creationem operatur, humanitatem nempe novam, ad quam evangelizatio ipsa tendere debet per illam unitatem in varietate, ad quam predicatio necessario provocat in communitate christiana" [AAS 68 (1976) 66].
2.  Marty Haugen, *Tales of Wonder* (Chicago: CIA Publications, 1989).
3.  Yves Congar, "The Word and the Spirit Do God's Work Together," in his *The Word and the Spirit,* trans. David Smith (San Francisco: Harper and Row, 1986).
4.  Haugen, *Tales of Wonder.*
5.  Pope John Paul II, "The Lord and Giver of Life," *Origins* 16 (June 12, 1986), 77–102.
6.  Michael Amaladoss, SJ, "Mission: From Vatican II into the Coming Decade," *International Review of Mission* 74 (1990), 211–20.
7.  "Justice in the World," Synod of Bishops, Second General Assembly, No-

vember 30, 1971, n. 8. Text available in *The Gospel of Peace and Justice: Catholic Social Teaching Since Pope John,* presented by Joseph Gremillion (Maryknoll: Orbis Books, 1976), 513–29.

8. Paul VI, "On Evangelization in the Modern World," n. 18.
9. Walter Brueggemann, *The Prophetic Imagination* (Philadelphia: Fortress Press, 1978, 1983), 13.
10. Paul VI, "On Evangelization in the Modern World," n. 19.
11. *Ibid.,* nn. 41, 75.
12. Robert Doran, *Psychic Conversion and Theological Foundations: Towards a Reorientation of the Human Sciences* (Chico: Scholars Press, 1981).
13. Second Vatican Council, "The Church in the Modern World," n. 1.
14. John Dunne, *The Way of All the Earth* (New York: Macmillan, 1972). The Third Synod of Bishops, discussing evangelization in October 1974, urged dialogue with non-Christians in order to come to a deeper understanding of the gospel. Cf. n. 11 of the synod document.
15. Leonardo Boff, "The Mission of the Holy Spirit: Transformation and New Creation," in his *Trinity and Society* (Maryknoll: Orbis Books, 1988), 189–212.
16. Pope John Paul II, "Peace with God the Creator, Peace with All of Creation," *Origins* 19 (1990), 465–68.

## DISCUSSION QUESTIONS

1. How does the New Testament describe the role of the Holy Spirit in the life and ministry of Jesus? How is Jesus the "first fruits" of the new creation?

2. What has been the development of the notion of mission and evangelization since Vatican II?

3. Pope Paul VI describes one of the functions of evangelization as transforming cultures from within. What impact does that have on the concept of evangelization when cultures and societies are so varied and different?

## FOR FURTHER READING

David M. Coffey. "A Proper Mission of the Holy Spirit." *Theological Studies* 47 (1986), 227–50.
Yves Congar. *The Word and the Spirit.* San Francisco: Harper and Row, 1986.
Donald Gelpi. *The Spirit in the World.* Wilmington: Glazier Press, 1988.
Jürgen Moltmann. *God in Creation: A New Theology of Creation and the Spirit of God.* San Francisco: Harper and Row, 1985.

# THE EUCHARIST: SUMMIT AND FONT OF CHRISTIAN EVANGELIZATION

Richard N. Fragomeni

## INTRODUCTION

In the apostolic exhortation "On Evangelization in the Modern World," Pope Paul VI presents new images of evangelization to the Roman Catholic Church. This important teaching, published in 1975 to commemorate the end of the Holy Year of Reconciliation, introduces an understanding of evangelization which integrates the dynamics of justice and the reconstituting of the social order into the foundational identity of Christian ministry. As the text points out, working toward human liberation is not foreign to evangelization; rather such work is central to the Christian task as it finds its ultimate fullness in the reign of God. One significant element of evangelization, therefore, is the life of the Christian community. It is the community becoming compassion as it awaits in joyful hope the advent of Christ and proclaims the freedom which the risen one brings to the fullness of creation.

Within this horizon, the text speaks of the liturgy as the premier activity of evangelization for the formation of a community of compassion. The sacramental life, culminating in the celebration of the eucharist, is the driving force which brings ongoing formation and strength to Christians to live lives of justice and to work for social liberation. The preaching of the word within the eucharist, as well as on other occasions in the community, is given special significance. The liturgical homily is considered prophetic speech which invites the community to envision the world anew. The eucharist, as summit and font of the life of the community, is imaged as the wellspring of evangelization. The evangelical power of the eucharist calls the community to live the mystery of faith and to become itself the sacrament of justice. Thus the eucharist, in word and sacrament, evangelizes the community into justice as the evangelizing community becomes the living liturgy of justice for the regeneration of the world. Such a vision raises important questions for the celebration of the liturgy.

If the eucharist forms and evangelizes the community to become compassion, what areas of the present liturgical renewal can become more clearly images of justice and signs of the reign of God? If liturgy is indeed formative of an evangelizing community, what elements in the celebration, especially of the Sunday eucharist, could best appropriate this vision of evangelization offered in "On Evangelization in the Modern World"? In response to these questions, this essay will examine various ways in which this vision of evangelization offered by Paul VI can be more consciously appropriated in the eucharistic celebration.

Several areas will be considered. First, we will examine the death of Christ and how it can be more clearly the focus of our gatherings. Second, the ministry of hospitality will be reviewed as a vital source of parish formation in evangelization. Third, preaching and liturgy planning will be considered as vital to the integration of evangelization and liturgy. Music and musical texts are primary modes of communication in the liturgy and formational of the community's consciousness. This will be the fourth concern of the essay. Finally, we will look at the role of art and environment and its function in the process of forming a community of compassion.

## "YOU PROCLAIM THE DEATH OF THE LORD UNTIL THE LORD COMES AGAIN"

From the earliest tradition, it can be seen that Christians gathered to keep the memory of Jesus Christ as he had commanded at the last supper. From the writings of St. Paul, it is clear that the relationship of this memorial to Christian life was critical. We are offered the same sense from the Acts of the Apostles, where the breaking of the bread is intimately joined to the mandate for a discipleship of equality lived within the community of compassion. Thus, from the beginning the memory of Jesus kept over bread and wine was considered the summit and fountain of Christian life and witness. At the table the memorial of the death of Jesus was kept and the fledgling community was fortified in its dangerous new way of being.

In the earliest scriptural account of this gathering, Paul warns the Christians at Corinth not to make the gathering a sham by excessive greed and self-indulgence, creating distinctions in the community and forgetfulness of the body. His concern was significant. The Lord's sup-

per could easily become a countersign, thus losing its force of energy for
the building up of the body. What is also obvious from this text is that the
gathering was a mode of proclaiming the death of the Lord until the day
of the Lord's return (1 Cor 11:26). The celebration of the eucharist, as it
was later to be known, was therefore the source of the unity and mutual
service for the community and the place where the memory of the death
of the Lord was proclaimed unto the future.

We observe several things from this. First, the gathering of the
Christian community was at the center of the formation and maintenance of Christians in communion with Christ. Second, according to the
Pauline testimony, the proclamation of the death of the Lord was the
foundational message of the eucharistic gathering. In the memory of
Christ crucified, the community discovered its identity and received the
force to live in such a way that they constituted a witness to an alternative
vision in the world around them. This way of life, a living evangelization,
if you will, was indeed cause for violent actions against the Christian
community, so that the life of Christians was completed by the testimony
of martyrdom. One could trace this phenomenon as developed in the
first four centuries of Christianity. Martyrdom became the great sign of
evangelical faith and a total association of the Christian with the death of
the Lord. It was called a second baptism by Tertullian and was considered a witness to the validity of the community's claim to follow the
message of the gospel.

Central to the proclamation of the death of Christ and martyrdom
was communion with Christ, realized perfectly in martyrdom but also
known in the sacrifice of daily life lived as a Christian and fortified by the
breaking of the bread. One image used to understand this communion
with Christ and the death of the Lord was *pascha*. As the tradition grew,
two distinct modes of understanding pascha emerged. To this image I
want to give particular attention because it offers, I believe, a fertile
ground of exploration for a conscious inclusion of the dimensions of
evangelization and justice in the eucharistic celebration.


## THE IMAGES OF THE PASCHA

Study of the understanding and commemoration of the death of the
Lord, which evolved into our present Easter triduum, in early liturgy and
theology gives us some insight into the use of the pascha image. We see
two distinct interpretations of this image of the death of Christ. These
two interpretations have been classified as the pascha–passio and the

pascha–transitus; the first related etymologically to the Hebrew word meaning suffering, and the second as passage, or transition.

A summary of these two approaches to the death of Christ can be taken from the text *Unsearchable Riches: The Symbolic Nature of the Liturgy* authored by David N. Power.[1] The author takes up these two modes of interpretation and claims that the earliest interpretation explains the death of Christ with the focus given to the passion and the explicit emphasis on the suffering of the Lord. It is encapsulated in the image of the pascha–passio or the passion as suffering.

> The tradition which takes Pasch as passion points more explicitly to the suffering Lord and to his experience of God in suffering. The resurrection symbolizes the victory of that death, of the victory of life in death itself. In Johannine terms, the hour of death is the hour of Jesus' glorification; glory is manifested on the cross and the cross is its symbol.[2]

This interpretation leads the Christian to discover in the cross of suffering the hope of glory and resurrection, since the cross itself is the victory over death. Resurrection, therefore, is not something apart from the cross but that which is discovered in the very reality of embracing it. Martyrdom, the consummate act of communion with Christ, was indeed the proclamation to the world of the strength of the Christian gospel. The image of the pascha–passio gave strength to those facing martyrdom.

From early on, in relating the eucharist to the common Christian life, the fostering of other images emerged. In an age of more confident expansion and governmental support and approval of Christianity, martyrdom no longer was an issue. Thus, the view of the death of Christ was seen differently. There is evidence that a second understanding emerged: the image of the pascha–transitus, or the death as a passing over. Power gives this summary:

> The tradition which associated Pasch with passage understands the resurrection as the anti-pole of death. Jesus passes through death to life and to glory. The death is more the condition of glory than its manifestation; the victory is given in the raising to life, not in the death itself.[3]

In this interpretation, when martyrdom is no longer a struggle for the community, pascha–transitus invites the Christian to see the daily temptations and trials against the soul as that which must be conquered.

The children of God seek to be pure in the things of this life so as to pass into spiritual fulfillment in the promise of eternity.

Power contrasts these two images and their relation to the living of Christian life:

> The starkness of the Johannine glory, given in death itself, may be difficult to assimilate for those who wage constant war against temptation and weakness, and who are more in the position of children seeking milk than of martyrs giving witness in their own lives to the death which they commemorate.[4]

It is not difficult to see how these two distinct modes of understanding the pasch of the Lord not only influenced the life of the Christian in the world, but also the very shape and meaning of the eucharistic celebration throughout the centuries. In time, with the developing notions of sin and redemption, the image of the pascha faded away and gave way to the image of Christ's death as expiatory sacrifice. Hence, the eucharist was celebrated more as the commemoration of Christ's sacrifice to the Father than as the celebration of the pasch.

What we have explored thus far can be summarized as follows: (1) The gathering of Christians for the eucharist is the center of Christian life and is the experience of communion in Christ. (2) At the gathering, the memory of the death of the Lord is proclaimed. (3) The image of the pascha is a key image to interpret the death of Christ and the life of the Christian. (4) As the community developed, various interpretations of the pascha were brought forward. These interpretations reflected the cultural and social conditions of Christian acceptance and in turn influenced the shape of the liturgy and the community's self-understanding.

What implication does this discussion have for an integration of justice and liberation in the contemporary celebration of the eucharist? Both the image of the pascha as transitus and later the image of expiatory sacrifice seem to foster a spirituality and sense of Christian life devoid of engagement in the arena of social change and liberation. Now, with the understanding of evangelization and justice brought forward by Paul VI, there is a call for something more: the life of Christians caught up in the struggle for liberation. Echoing the Second Vatican Council, "On Evangelization in the Modern World" sees as constituent to the gospel a solidarity with the oppressed and the victims of injustice in the social, political, economic, ecclesial and environmental realms. This shift in understanding evangelization suggests the potential for conversion that the reappropriation of the image of pascha as passio can bring about for the celebration of the eucharist and the Christian life. The image of pascha–passio invites a consciousness of communion with Christ as vitally linked with the witness of justice, even to martyrdom.

We already see signs of interest between liturgy and justice. Christian communities are gradually sensing the original linking between the gathering, the Christian life of compassion and communion with Christ. It seems important to suggest that the community could be assisted in consciously appropriating Paul VI's vision of evangelization by a forceful retrieval of the pascha–passio. This image in preaching, art, catechesis and as root image for parish planning could give new focus and driving force to a community seeking to live the gospel authentically.

## THE MINISTRY OF HOSPITALITY

In recent years, parishes have taken seriously the call of such parish liturgical reformers as Sulpician Eugene Walsh[5] who have insisted that a significant ministry of the liturgical assembly is one of hospitality. Parishes with able staffing or volunteers have attempted to create an atmosphere of welcome at the community gatherings. We have noticed that the ministry of greeters emerged which either replaced or amplified the work of the ushers. There is a growing sense of hospitality at social gatherings after mass, the invitation to greet those close by during the celebration and the attempt at name tags to bring a sense of closeness during the celebration of the eucharist. In this present practice, hospitality seems to mean intimacy, warmth and the escape from isolation and individualism common in modern social living.

In view of "On Evangelization in the Modern World," can hospitality be something else? Can we extend our understanding of hospitality at the eucharist to become a more comprehensive outreach to the oppressed and poor in our neighborhoods and cities? For instance, we have soup kitchens and outreach ministry to the homeless. What if our ministry of hospitality, rather than only going out to the poor, worked on bringing the poor into the regular Sunday gatherings? What if at the Sunday eucharist the community were to bring the poor, the homeless and the alienated from the soup kitchens to join in the gathering? Such an experience would be, no doubt, the occasion to raise serious questions about neighborhoods, Christian responsibility, our interconnection with the economy, the difference between need and want and the place where eucharist and Christian life converge. Such communities, gathering for the eucharist this way, would be invited to ask questions such as: Do we feed the poor and give them no shelter? To what extent do we share the gospel? What about our baptismal call to evangelization?

The call of evangelization moves hospitality from a gentle cordiality of like-minded people to an eating and drinking with the poor, the crippled, the beggar, and with those unable to reciprocate the invitation to the dining room table.

But the questions go on. What of the alienated because of sexual orientation, divorce, remarriage, a physical or mental handicap, not to mention the hospitality of justice afforded to women in church and society?

If the vision of evangelization is to be realized, the celebration of the eucharist must be a place for everyone to be at home. It is the source and summit of Christian life to the degree that all are welcomed. Parish planners do well to go beyond the understanding of hospitality as cordial warmth into the real challenge that faces us today—the call to evangelization and the engagement in deeper realms of hospitality which engage in concerns for human rights and belonging.

## PREACHING AND LITURGY PLANNING

The status of preaching has taken a significant turn in the past twenty-five years. The liturgical homily has replaced the sermon and the manuals of dogma as the focus and orientation of preaching. Homiletics courses are now part of the ordinary curriculum for ministry with the latest in video equipment and communication techniques for presbyteral, diaconal and lay formation of preachers. Homily services and lectionary studies have blossomed, and the desire to preach well and with enthusiasm for the faith is growing. In view of Paul VI's invitation, there is a further step for preachers and for those whose ministry brings them to craft language at the eucharistic assembly.

In a recent text, *Finally Comes the Poet: Daring Speech for Proclamation*,[6] Walter Brueggemann suggests that the language of the poet is what best brings forth the memory of Christ, the imagination of the hearers of the word and conversion into a life of justice. The poet speaks the forgotten and keeps alive within the assembly the hope of God's reign, offering an alternative to restlessness, greed, guilt, oppression and fear.

Brueggemann's insights invite homilists to speak grace and not duty, opening to the Christian community the hope of a world that is given as gift by the death of Christ. In other words, he suggests that to move a community to being compassionate, the preacher–poet speaks not in moralistic tones of shoulds and musts, but in an evocative language that offers to the heart the irresistible vision of a different world given by God. Thus the homily will speak the words of grace as heard in the ministry of Jesus and in the struggles for justice in the memories of the forgotten ones. Preaching will comfort with the words of conversion. It images humanity and the world that robs oppression of its power in the cross of Christ.

This type of preaching puts a great challenge to preachers. Homily preparation needs a new rooting. Rather than simply subscribing to a variety of homily services and preparing the preaching alone, homilists are well advised to pay attention to the document *Fulfilled in Your Hearing,* published by the National Conference of Catholic Bishops,[7] which encourages homily preparation with members of the assembly. A serious preparation of the homily with a group from the parish will allow the voices of pain to be identified, the places where grace can be preached to be named, and the poetic task of offering an alternative world to be encouraged.

Preaching is not public biblical exegesis. It is a poetic narrative which tells the Christ story and the human story as the passion story of human liberation from sin and injustice, which alone is the place where the resurrection can be proclaimed.

Along with the preaching ministry, liturgy planning has become an important concern for parishes. "On Evangelization in the Modern World" can have an impact on the role of liturgy planners as they too create and shape other moments of word in the eucharistic celebration. Several ways of integrating a clearer focus of evangelization emerge. First, much more attention can be given by liturgy planners to the writing and proclamation of the general intercessions. In these prayers the community is allowed to be one in prayer and memory with those in need. Parish liturgy teams do well to avoid the missalette versions of the intercessions which give vague references to the quests for liberation. Indeed, in their vagueness, such versions contribute to the denial of suffering that must be brought forward in hope in a community of compassion.

Second, in a related area of the proclamation of the word outside of the eucharistic assembly, liturgy planners can integrate the vision of "On Evangelization in the Modern World" within the celebrations of parish reconciliation. Communal penance services, as they are commonly called, have special importance during Advent and Lent, if not more regularly. These celebrations urge the community to discover its own sin and to proclaim the traces of God's mercy in the face of Christ. Time could be given to the construction and proclamation of litanies of sin and mercy. These litanies give voice to the compassion and mercy of God and an invitation to the sinner to discover true humanity around the eucharistic table, the source and summit of peace and recovery.

A third concern for liturgy planners and those who preach the word is the devotional life of the community. Devotions can lead the assembly to a profound entry into compassion and a life of evangelization. Devotions, devoid of all sentimentalism and nostalgia for the past, are still important for the conversion life of the parish. Liturgy planners and homilists could plan devotions as they arise from the cultural and spiritual needs of the assembly. Of significant note is the renewed devotion to the passion of Christ that is to be found in various Hispanic communities. This devotion, closely linked to the struggle with liberation and human suffering, sees in the dead Christ the ancient articulation of hope within the pain which emerges in the struggle for justice. Creativity in this area has not yet emerged. It remains an enterprise for the creative liturgists among us.

## MUSIC AND EVANGELIZATION IN THE EUCHARIST

Not unlike preaching, the ministry of music can be considered a ministry of the word. As such, it plays a significant role in the formation of the religious imagination of the eucharistic assembly. By melody and poetry, the assembly is called to keep the memory of Christ and to sing the songs of justice. In order to better integrate this vision of evangelization in the ministry of music, several challenges arise.

First, the vast majority of contemporary liturgical music and texts is composed by white, middle class males. While publishing houses are attempting to integrate into the current repertoire music from the African-American and Hispanic communities, the bulk of the music emerges from the dominant voices of the culture. Publishing houses seem to promote composers of this sort and hesitate to make public and encourage the work of women, racial minorities and the music and texts which arise from the struggles of the voiceless, gathering human suffering into the memory of Christ. Perhaps this is the challenge of parishes and dioceses. Local, regional and national groups could promote the creation of texts and melodies which arise out of the struggle for human dignity and the quest for liberation, giving special attention to the fine texts emerging from women's communities.

Second, the role of the cantor is emerging as a necessary and vital part of the contemporary liturgical renewal. Not only is this ministry one of musical hospitality, but it also is a prophetic role of giving voice to the assembly which has been voiceless for centuries. The cantor can take the assembly into places where it has never been, namely, into the euchology or blessing prayers of the church. Predominantly seen as the prayer of the presbyter, the eucharistic prayer, for example, can truly become the voice of the assembly by acclamations of thanks, led and encouraged by the cantor. This great prayer, which proclaims the death of the Lord, can be prayed musically in such a way as to keep it from being the sole prayer of the presider.

Above all, music is a mode of evangelization par excellence. If song is praying twice, then it is also a double call to conversion of the human heart: the place of all change and the starting point of evangelical activity. Can such a powerful source of transformation well up with images of struggle for life, informed by the death of Christ and calling the eucharistic gathering to become the new creation?

## ART AND ENVIRONMENT

Much contemporary church art and furnishings are purchased from catalogues of distributors of religious goods. The most common image of Christ in these catalogues, making its way more and more into the assembly space, is that of Christ as the resurrected one, usually superimposed on a cross. This image portrays Jesus as happily inhabiting new life, the passion over and the glory of resurrection achieved. This image invites the assembly into a communion with Christ in an other-worldly existence, supporting a common belief that the social ordering and relationships of this world are acceptable. This representation of Christ and its implications are important to consider in our discussion of evangelization and liturgy. Several questions emerge. Is it enough for images of Christ to bring an assembly into an other-worldly existence? Rather, should not the image of Christ on the cross evoke the suffering present in human reality and the hope that the death of Christ offers? It seems that if the image of Christ is such that it denies the pain of the cross and therefore is not connected to the suffering of this life, there is something false in the image. It would be interesting to consider the ways in which a community's image of the pascha influences and is influenced by the art of the eucharistic gathering place.

Another significant question concerns the plurality of images of the crucified one. Could it be possible to image the crucified one by placing on the cross a Christ who is black or Hispanic? Could the image of Christ thus evoke in the assembly the vision of justice and compassion which in this world calls out for the transformation that the good news of Jesus proclaims?

A second concern of environment wherein the liturgy could integrate the concerns of social ordering and compassion is that of the placement of the assembly. The disposition of place and how people are related to one another in communion with Christ is a significant image which shapes Christian consciousness. How do we configure ourselves around the table? Who sits where? How is power configured? Where do the poor sit? I believe a story can assist thinking about such questions.

In a Washington, D.C. parish, African-Americans were at one time limited to seating in the back of the church. They sat on simple wooden benches, while the white community sat on fine pews in the front of the assembly. When the parish came to be a predominantly black assembly, and the memory of oppression was not to be forgotten but transformed, the wooden benches were taken from the back of the church and brought to the front. These benches now serve as places of honor for catechumens, guests, and those celebrating noted occasions. The reversal of this ordering remains a loud environmental symbol to that eucharistic community and speaks a solidarity with those who continue to be alienated by racial and cultural bias. It is a visual lamentation to the suffering which remains and an invitation to compassion.

## CONCLUSION

This article suggests that an understanding of evangelization, as given by Pope Paul VI, influences the ways in which we celebrate the eucharist. Such an understanding invites us into a celebration which more closely associates the community of compassion with Christ's suffering and its victory over death. In union with Christ's death, the eucharist invites our communion with suffering humanity. The essay has suggested ways in which the celebration can become an ever-deepening source and summit of Catholic evangelization that seeks to change the world in the power of Christ's death until all tears are wiped away and salvation dawns like the morning star.

## NOTES

1.  David N. Power, *Unsearchable Riches: The Symbolic Nature of the Liturgy* (New York: Pueblo Publishing Co., 1984), 154–58.
2.  *Ibid.*, 155.
3.  *Ibid.*
4.  *Ibid.*, 156.

5.  See Eugene A. Walsh, SS, *The Ministry of the Celebrating Community* (Pastoral Arts Associates of North America, 1977).
6.  Walter Brueggemann, *Finally Comes the Poet: Daring Speech for Proclamation* (Minneapolis: Fortress Press, 1989).
7.  *Fulfilled in Your Hearing: The Homily in the Sunday Assembly* (Washington, D.C.: United States Catholic Conference, 1982).

## DISCUSSION QUESTIONS

1.  As your parish celebrates the eucharist each Sunday, what images of the death of Christ strike you? What do these say to the way we live the Christian life?

2.  How involved should Christians be with questions of injustice? Does this resonate with your perceptions about and celebration of the eucharist?

3.  Is the celebration of the eucharist in your parish one of hope? What is the hope generated in the celebration?

## FOR FURTHER READING

Edward M. Grosz, ed. *Liturgy and Social Justice: Celebrating Rites—Proclaiming Rights.* Collegeville: The Liturgical Press, 1989.

Ralph A. Keifer. *The Mass in Time of Doubt: The Meaning of the Mass for Catholics Today.* Washington, D.C.: Pastoral Press, 1983.

Bernard J. Lee, ed. *Alternative Futures for Worship—Vol. 3: The Eucharist.* Collegeville: The Liturgical Press, 1987.

Mark Searle, ed. *Liturgy and Social Justice.* Collegeville: The Liturgical Press, 1980.

# EVANGELIZATION 2000: A GLOBAL VIEW
## Tom Forrest, CSsR

The most extraordinary happening in the history of the world occurred almost two thousand years ago. The infinite creator of the universe inserted himself into our human history by being born as a man. God took on our human nature, not to share our comforts, but to carry our sorrows and sins to the cross. This utterly unique and loving action of God marked the beginning of the world's salvation in Christ, and as such dwarfed every other event in human history.

Jesus Christ was born of a virgin named Mary, and he died for us on Calvary. But unlike other great heroes of the past, *Jesus Christ is alive!* He rose from the dead and liberated all people from the self-centered and devastating slavery of sin (cf. Jn 8:32, 36; 14:16). The desire of Christ's heart as he died for us remains the same: to save the world by winning followers to his way of forgiveness, goodness and love, and he mandates us to help him in this task. The year 2000 offers us a God-given, God-graced moment for doing this, a time to do something great and glorious for Christ and his people. To let such an occasion slip by unused would be the waste of a spiritual treasure not to be equaled for another thousand years.

The world knows very well how to announce, commemorate and celebrate its special anniversaries. Nations, and at times the entire globe, recognize birthdays and anniversaries of special patriots, great thinkers and leaders, explorers, inventors and artistic geniuses. Society rightly feels an obligation to commemorate these people and their great contributions to human progress. We still have vivid memories of the planning and preparation that went into such extraordinary events as the centennials of the Statue of Liberty, the Australian Constitution, and the bicentennial of the French Revolution. On those occasions there were enough fireworks to start a small war, and enough joy and shouting to signal the end of one!

The year 2000 is a time to celebrate and commemorate Jesus Christ.

The date itself is totally and exclusively Christian. A.D. 2000 literally means in the year of the Lord 2000, that measure of time since the coming of Christ. What could be more appropriate than for us, as Christians, to focus the world on the true meaning of that coming! No one ever has, or ever will, equal the impact on history of this carpenter from Nazareth, executed as a criminal at the early age of thirty-three, yet still inspiring thousands to live and even die for him, his followers outnumbering the disciples of any other cause!

EVANGELIZATION 2000 was born out of a simple plan aimed at motivating and inspiring Catholics throughout the world to prepare for this two thousandth birthday of Jesus Christ. On June 29, 1984, a letter was sent to Pope John Paul II suggesting a Decade of Evangelization in anticipation of the year 2000. Once at the Vatican, and then for a second time at Castel Gandolfo, we were invited to have supper with His Holiness and to talk about these ideas. Prior to our second meeting with the pope, a detailed plan of the proposal was sent to Cardinal Casaroli, the papal secretary of state.

In this proposal there was no suggestion of a super organization or central control. Rather it emphasized a unity of spirit in a common desire to give Jesus Christ a more Christian world as the best two thousandth birthday gift possible. At that time ideas were offered regarding a second Worldwide Retreat for Priests and a Catholic fellowship of evangelists. The meeting ended with the holy father saying that he would find the best way to move the project forward.

As a result, an office for EVANGELIZATION 2000 was opened in Rome, and several regional offices have since been established around the world. Except for the planning of retreats and helping to establish an association of coordinators of schools of evangelization, the task of these offices has been motivational rather than organizational. They attempt only to inspire by sharing the spirit and goals which direct the Decade of Evangelization.

Admittedly, winning the world for Christ is an ambitious goal and one that it would be presumptuous of any individual or group to claim capability of doing. EVANGELIZATION 2000 began with an uncomplicated idea and adopted a simple strategy. Depending on an outpouring of prayer and the efforts of many, it seeks to announce Christ to the world with a power that leads to conversion and transformation. It strives to motivate Catholics to support Pope John Paul II in the "undertaking and promotion of this 'new,' this second evangelization, the necessity of which all churches and episcopates of this continent are becoming ever more clearly aware" (to the bishops of Poland on their "ad limina" visit, December 19, 1987).

Our response to the holy father's call, if it is to bear fruit, requires a united effort. Only such an effort, united in the sense of generous cooperation without any spirit of competition, can prove effective (cf. Jn 17:21). Genuine evangelization is undertaken for the glory of God and for the good of all people—and not for self-interest. Since God cannot be over-glorified, and since hundreds of millions still need to hear the good news, there is more than enough work for all without any need of competition.

Although EVANGELIZATION 2000 began with a simple idea, the task of evangelization is far from simple. In today's world there are five thousand million people speaking innumerable languages and living in a bewildering variety of cultures. If preaching the good news "to every creature under heaven" (Col 1:23) called for the easy efforts of only a few, it would have been accomplished centuries ago.

Twenty-four sections of "On Evangelization in the Modern World" (nn. 17–39) are required to define evangelization and state its content. To remain simple and effective, EVANGELIZATION 2000 focuses primarily on only one part of evangelization, *kerygma*, the initial proclamation of Christ as only savior of the world. This is by no means the whole task of the evangelizer, as "On Evangelization in the Modern World" states very clearly. But making known the loving person, wondrous words, and astonishing works of Christ is the indispensable starting point and power source from which the church must build and be built. The ongoing formation of the people of God (the focus of movements such as the neo-catechumenate) and the transformation of today's social realities into a kingdom of love (the focus of social justice programs) must necessarily follow.

The scriptural text that gives EVANGELIZATION 2000 its strategy for global evangelization is Matthew 10:7: "As you go, make this announcement: 'The reign of God is at hand.' " There are 970 million Catholics in the world. In varying numbers they are on every continent and in every country. The primary effort of this initiative is to bring home to each of them the truth that "as they go," they too have the God-given task of carrying with them the good news of Jesus Christ.

## THE TRUE MEANING OF THE OCCASION

Birthdays are the most common occasions between family and friends for expressing appreciation and love. Of all family members and friends, no one has done more than Jesus Christ to win our gratitude, admiration and love. He is more than just another great thinker to be packaged with Aristotle, Buddha, Freud and Einstein. He is the "wisdom of God" (1 Cor 1:24), the definitive, God-given answer to the timeless question of how to live a good life. He is an artist beyond Picasso, Rembrandt or Michelangelo because his life itself surpasses in beauty anything ever captured on canvas or in stone. He is the master who tutors us in the sublime art of living as God's children. He is the architect of the universe, the timer of the stars and designer of the human mind, the very center of human history. He is supreme as:

- *Storyteller.* His parables of the prodigal son and the good Samaritan are better known than any tale of Shakespeare.

- *Teacher.* When still a boy, "all who heard him were amazed at his understanding" (Lk 2:46–47). "Crowds were astonished" and "spellbound," and even enemies wondered, "Where did this man get this wisdom" (Mt 7:28–29; 13:34–35; 22:33)? His sermon on the mount is the most quoted synthesis of wisdom in the world. When Paul echoed that wisdom, even a Roman proconsul was "astonished at the teaching of the Lord" (Acts 13:6–12).

- *Model of goodness.* "Though he was in the form of God . . . he emptied himself, taking the form of a servant. . . . He became obedient unto death, even to death on a cross" (Phil 2:6–8). "Greater love than this has no man, that a man lay down his life for his friends" (Jn 15:13).

- *Leader.* He said, "Follow me," and people left their nets, money tables and homes, to follow him even to death. The wind and the sea and even the dead obeyed him (cf. Mk 4:39–40; 5:41–42; Lk 7:14).

- *Wonder-worker.* His birth itself was a wonder (cf. Mt 1:18–25). "Astonished beyond measure," people exclaimed, "He has done all things well; he even makes the deaf to hear and the dumb to speak" (Mk 7:37). He could multiply fish in the basket of a boy or in the nets of fishermen (cf. Lk 5:5–7; 9:16–17). When these same fishermen were made fishers of all people, they could work similar wonders simply by speaking his name (cf. Acts 3:6; 4:10, 30; 9:34).

As the two thousandth anniversary of his birth grows near, more and more people will be asking:

- How could this destitute man from such a despised town in Galilee, who never wrote a book, led an army or owned anything, become the best-known figure in all of history?

- How could the gospel story of his life outsell—millions of times over —any other book ever written?

- While communism disintegrates within the century, how can his church remain the most ancient and enduring of all social structures?

These are the questions the world will soon be asking. The right answers can change the world! EVANGELIZATION 2000 is an effort to help put those answers on the tip of every Catholic tongue. "Reverence the Lord Christ in your hearts, and should anyone ask the reason for this hope of yours, be ever ready to make answer" (1 Pet 3:15).

## A UNITED EFFORT TO PREPARE THE RIGHT GIFT

The year 2000 will be the *most extraordinary commemorative event* in Christian history. It offers a challenge that calls for an historic Catholic and Christian response.

The fact is that this particular desire of Christ—a world that knows and follows him, a world evangelized—is so costly that the entire church, the whole Christian family, must contribute the way entire nations contribute for their celebrations. Doing less for Christ would label us as stingy with the God who gave us everything.

For the church, the year 2000 must be lived as a very special family event with everyone in the family playing his or her part. Getting this to happen is what EVANGELIZATION 2000 is all about.

- Others go out *shopping* for that special birthday gift. For Christ, we have to go out *evangelizing*. The gift is a new believer.

- Others go out to purchase their gift with *money*. We go out in *courage and faith,* leaving behind anything that distracts from total confidence in the power of the Holy Spirit. "The gift you have received, give as a gift. Provide yourself with neither gold, silver nor copper" (Mt 10:8–9).

- Others use a *kiss or touch* to convey their love. We convey our love for Christ by *touching others with his love.* This love motivates us to distribute not only bread for the body, but the bread of life as well. "I am the bread of life. . . . If anyone eats this bread, he shall live forever" (Jn 6:48–51).

• Others record their love stories with *letters and poems.* The unrivaled love story of Christ is written in the pages of the *gospel.* Uncountable copies of that book have already been distributed. Our task is to write its message on human hearts!

Astonishingly, EVANGELIZATION 2000 has, at times, been accused of dreams too grandiose, a kind of megalomania in mission. If anything, all our efforts as yet lack the dynamism and daring that the task requires. It is hard to believe that "humbly" doing less is the ideal and that the largest church in Christianity fulfills its mission with only modest efforts. Exactly what can be considered doing too much for a brother and friend who died for us on a cross, and who is truly our God?

These are some of the efforts of EVANGELIZATION 2000 aimed at inspiring Catholics to this task:

• *Worldwide Retreat for Priests.* Successful church efforts need the support of bishops and priests. In September 1990, five thousand priests and bishops participated in a retreat in the Papal Audience Hall of Vatican City on the theme "Called To Evangelize" (described in detail later in this essay). EVANGELIZATION 2000 is also conducting numerous other retreats around the world for bishops and priests on the same theme.

• *Worldwide Prayer Campaign.* EVANGELIZATION 2000 depends on prayer as the most vital of all its preparatory efforts. The Prayer Campaign is now in communication with four thousand contemplative communities and fourteen hundred intercessory prayer groups around the world. A prayer book titled "Prayers for the New Evangelization," published in five languages, is in circulation stimulating prayer support and helping to instill evangelization into the Catholic conscience.

• *Association of Schools of Evangelization.* It is unfair to tell people they must evangelize without teaching them *how!* For many Catholics, "evangelization" only generates images of street-corner preachers brandishing Bibles like terrorists with guns. ACCSE/2000, an international association, is comprised of coordinators of Catholic schools of evangelization. The purpose of the association is to facilitate and accelerate the spread of schools dedicated to training Catholics for the specific task of evangelization. They do this through mutual support and encouragement, and through the generous sharing of ideas and resources. For training the evangelizers of the future, there are plans to send youth teams around the world to bring the challenge of the Decade of Evangelization to young Catholics.

- *LUMEN/2000.* We are mandated to carry the good news to every creature. Radio and television are among the best communication tools in the world today. LUMEN/2000 inspires a spirit of cooperation and mutual support among Catholics using mass media for the proclamation of God's word. Its first goal is to help improve the quality and content of Catholic programming.

- *Publications.* Since the Bible is the first tool in the hands of any evangelist, efforts are under way to inspire the establishment of a worldwide Catholic distribution service to help make the Bible available to the poor and persecuted. The magazine, *NEW EVANGELIZATION 2000,* goes to every bishop of the world and to all active Catholics who request and promise to read it. One prayer book for evangelization ("Prayers for the New Evangelization") has been produced, with others to come.

- *Continental and Regional Offices.* In addition to the office in Rome, continental offices of EVANGELIZATION 2000 now exist in the United States, Singapore, Spain, Mexico, Argentina, Peru, Brazil and Australia. These offices are primarily centers of communication. EVANGELIZATION 2000 decides and controls nothing on local levels since the task of pastoring always remains with the bishop. We function only where our help is requested and desired.


## EVANGELIZATION 2000 AROUND THE WORLD

*Latin America*

Latin America is on the eve of celebrating five hundred years of evangelization. The first missionaries braved travel in the frail boats of Christopher Columbus bringing the good news to what was then called the new world. Five hundred years later that new world is on the verge of a new evangelization. This time, though, the task depends upon the rich spiritual resources and determination of Latin America itself.

The five hundred year old faith of that continent can no longer be called "new." More Christians live in Latin America than on any other continent. Both politically and spiritually, the final decade of this millennium will prove to be an historically critical moment for the nations of Latin America. In its efforts in Latin America, EVANGELIZATION 2000 is working hard to promote an evangelization so new in its fervor, expressions and methods that it can be an answer to the needs of that continent.

EVANGELIZATION 2000 has met with the Episcopal Council of Latin America (CELAM) and with eleven of the regional episcopal conferences. Bishops of Mexico have listed EVANGELIZATION 2000 among their three major evangelization programs. During 1990, the staff of EVANGELIZATION 2000 has spoken at, or collaborated with, more than one hundred congresses, conferences, retreats and evangelistic events throughout Latin America.

Schools of evangelization are spreading rapidly throughout the continent. At a meeting of the Association of Coordinators of Catholic Schools of Evangelization in Guadalajara, Mexico in April 1990, twenty-four delegates participated from fifteen countries of Latin America. Latin America sent close to one thousand priests to the Worldwide Retreat for Priests in September 1990.

Ushuaia on Tierra del Fuego, Argentina, is the southernmost point of the inhabited world. An appropriate name for that spot is the "End of the Earth." From there, EVANGELIZATION 2000/Latin America celebrated the launching of the Decade of Evangelization on December 20, 1990. This date was chosen because at Ushuaia it is a day of twenty-four hour sunshine. This is seen as a symbol of Christ, the eternal light that we wish to carry from there to the "furthest boundaries of the earth" (cf. Acts 1:8).

*Asia*

Because of the rich variety and strength of its many cultures and religions, Asia/Oceania poses an exciting challenge to the Catholic Church. Efforts of EVANGELIZATION 2000 are not intended to destroy what is beautiful in any cultural tradition. The only goal is to show how all humanity can be restored in Jesus Christ. At this particular moment in history, the peoples of Asia/Oceania appear wonderfully responsive to the gospel message. Present efforts are only the prelude of greater things yet to come.

EVANGELIZATION 2000 has conducted a number of retreats specifically for Asian priests and bishops. According to Archbishop Leonardo Legaspi, chairperson of the Philippines Bishops' Conference, the two retreats given for bishops of the Philippines resulted in evangelization becoming "the basic uniting force of all the items that will be dealt with in the upcoming plenary council of the Philippines Catholic Church." EVANGELIZATION 2000 was named the directional "spirit" of that council. Nearly seven hundred priests from Asia and Oceania attended the 1990 Worldwide Retreat for Priests in Rome.

There is a continental branch of ACCSE/2000 with members from seven Asian countries. At the opening of a School of Evangelization in the Philippines, Archbishop Antonio Mabutas of Davao City said: "Schools like this are giving us a Catholic—a truly universal—ecclesial vision." New schools of evangelization are foreseen in the Philippines, India, Sri Lanka, Indonesia and Oceania, with additional outreach to the Pacific Islands.

Because Asia has the youngest population in the world, youth plays a significant role in any effort to evangelize. Young people in India have begun a three year preparation program for the Decade of Evangelization. A group in the Philippines has caught the spirit of the decade with the catch-phrase, "YOUTH 2000." In regions made unsafe by political and social unrest, young men and women are asked about their willingness to proclaim the gospel, even at risk to their own lives. They respond by saying, "In situations like these, there is a special need for making Christ known."

*Europe*

Recent events in Europe offer us a field ripe for the harvest! The fall of communism opens up to us a vast opportunity to spread the message of Jesus among people who have been deprived of the good news for the past forty years. Of the two thousand places allotted for Europe at the Worldwide Retreat for Priests, about three hundred were filled by bishops and priests coming from eastern European countries. New religious freedom in Czechoslovakia made it possible for over one hundred priests to attend the retreat. These priests received financial assistance from the Witnessing to God's Love Foundation in Holland, and Catholics in Japan also sent some financial aid to assist with expenses. In addition, many priests made individual donations to help their brother priests in third world countries attend the retreat.

Because more than half of the four thousand contemplative communities reached by EVANGELIZATION 2000 are in Europe and because numerous other religious communities, intercessory groups and individuals have joined the effort there, new regional centers for the Prayer

Campaign have been established in England, France, Italy and Spain, with another center soon to open in Poland.

The European meeting of ACCSE/2000 in 1990 hosted representatives of twenty-three schools from thirteen countries. Delegates attended from Poland and East Germany. The 1991 meeting of ACCSE/2000-Europe was held in Berlin, April 15–19, 1991.

EVANGELIZATION 2000 has promoted numerous events in Europe including the Spanish Leaders' Conference in Madrid, a week-long conference on "Families Evangelizing Other Families" in Ploërmel, France, the Northern European Conference in Dublin, Ireland, and a Symposium on the "Goals of EVANGELIZATION 2000" in Göteborg, Sweden. The magazine *NEW EVANGELIZATION 2000* is distributed throughout Europe in six languages (English, French, Italian, Portuguese, Spanish, and Polish).

*Africa*

The disintegration of communism as a godless economic system in eastern Europe is also affecting the African continent. In West Africa, Benin has declared that it will no longer pursue an atheistic socialist program. There are hopes of similar changes in Angola, Ethiopia and Mozambique. With doors like these opening in many African countries, there are signs that great things can happen if, like the prophets of old, we too readily respond: "Here I am, Lord. Send me!"

The first countries of Africa to be associated with EVANGELIZATION 2000 were Ethiopia, Ghana, Ivory Coast, Kenya, Lesotho, Liberia, Nigeria, South Africa, Uganda and Zambia. Representatives of these countries coming from both Anglophone and Francophone Africa have met at conferences held in Ivory Coast, Kenya and Nigeria.

Eight hundred priests and bishops from Africa and the Middle East participated in the September retreat, among them priests from the different Oriental rites of Egypt.

Bishops from twenty-three African countries have shown interest in beginning schools of evangelization in their dioceses. The second meeting of ACCSE/2000-Africa took place in Nakuru, Kenya, Jan. 22–27, 1990, with thirty-one delegates from Ethiopia, Ghana, Kenya, Lesotho, Nigeria and Tanzania. The January meeting focused on new ways to foster the spread of schools throughout the continent. At present ten African countries, in association with ACCSE/2000, have already established some type of school of evangelization.

AECAWA (Association of Episcopal Conferences for Anglophone West Africa) has invited EVANGELIZATION 2000 to conduct a retreat on evangelization for its bishops. With hopes for similar retreats in all seven ecclesial regions of Africa, this first one took place in Nigeria, July 1990.

### Brazil

Brazil is the largest country of Latin America with one hundred and twenty-five million people, the largest Catholic population in the world. The Portuguese language distinguishes it from the rest of Latin America.

The office of EVANGELIZATION 2000 was inaugurated in May 1989 by Belo Horizonte Archbishop D. Seraphim Fernandes de Araujo. A close relationship has been maintained between the office and the Brazilian Episcopal Conference. Archbishop Luciano Mendes de Almeida, president of the Bishops' Conference, stated that EVANGELIZATION 2000/Brazil "has the full support of the National Conference of Brazilian Bishops." EVANGELIZATION 2000 does its best to collaborate with parish priests and with the different church movements, while maintaining ongoing dialogue with the more than three hundred bishops of the country.

Besides a national school of evangelization, located in Goiânia near Brasilia, there are now five regional schools and thirty diocesan schools where over eighty evangelization courses have taken place since 1988. Parish-level courses have also been a great success. Evangelizers from the Goiânia National School of Evangelization have established an outreach program in the African Democratic Republic of Sâo Tome e Principe, and in July 1990 a team went to Luanda in Angola, another Portuguese-speaking nation of Africa. Among the team members was a Brazilian bishop who was enthralled by the opportunity to both serve and learn. His first comment was, "In Brazil we sometimes feel that we have a lot to suffer, but now I can say that I have seen real suffering and know that we have a mission to help."

The National Youth Center in the city of Franca coordinates the training and activities of young evangelizers. Two Hallel National Youth Conferences have been held to date. "Hallels" are musical festivals aimed specifically at evangelizing youth. More than twenty thousand young people attended the 1989 Hallel.

The Emmanuel Community of Rio de Janeiro has united the contemplative communities and intercessory groups of the nation for the task of supporting all the projects of EVANGELIZATION 2000 in prayer.

A national event to launch the Decade of Evangelization took place in Brazilia, the capital city of Brazil, on December 16, 1990. The event was preceded by a retreat for Brazilian priests on the theme of the Decade of Evangelization, and by a meeting of directors of ACCSE/2000, the Association of Coordinators of Catholic Schools of Evangelization now spread through sixty-seven dioceses of Brazil. Thirty-five thousand participated in the day-long ceremony inaugurating the Decade of Evangelization. Among the speakers were the papal nuncio, the cardinal archbishop of Brazilia, the much-beloved Archbishop Helder Camara, and Bishop Valerian D'Souza of Poona, India. The government of Brazil issued a special cancellation stamp to commemorate the occasion, and the governor of Brazilia assisted in making the event a truly national happening. The characteristic youthfulness of the Brazilian nation was evidenced by the participation, in music and enthusiasm, of a large number of young people. A special letter of encouragement from Pope John Paul II added to the significance of the sending-forth occasion.

*North America*

Knowledge of EVANGELIZATION 2000 continues to spread in the United States and Canada by raising the consciousness of American and Canadian peoples to the importance of evangelization, fostering the spread of schools of evangelization, and encouraging a campaign of prayer.

Through its affiliation with the Paulist National Catholic Evangelization Association, EVANGELIZATION 2000 is closely allied to the National Conference of Catholic Bishops' Committee on Evangelization, the National Council for Catholic Evangelization, and the National Council of Catholic Women.

The various efforts of EVANGELIZATION 2000 are being promoted in all the publications of the Paulist National Catholic Evangelization Association. In January 1990, thirty-nine ACCSE/2000 participants gathered to share with one another the many interesting developments taking place in the United States and Canada for schools of evangelization.

More than eight thousand subscriptions to *NEW EVANGELIZATION 2000* have been received, and people are responding daily to an invitation mailed with forty-five thousand prayer brochures asking Catholics to join in a campaign of prayer for the Decade of Evangelization.

PNCEA/E2000 is working closely with the NCCB Committee that will commemorate the five hundredth anniversary in 1992 of the advent of Christianity to the western hemisphere. The contribution of Catholic evangelizers will be highlighted in this historical event.

Positive measures are being taken to capture the enthusiasm and the fervor of the Hispanic community in the United States, so that together we may see an ever-increasing spiritual renewal in our churches. We expect that this same fervor will spill over to our brothers and sisters in the Caribbean.

Christmas 1990 was the first day of the Decade of Evangelization anticipating the two thousandth birthday of Jesus Christ. EVANGELI-ZATION 2000 has made a humble beginning toward this time of dynamic new evangelization for the entire Catholic Church. With our hearts and minds united, great things can be done for the glory of God and the good of God's people!

> With the torch of Christ in your hands and full of love for all, go forth, Church of the New Evangelization! (Pope John Paul II)

## DISCUSSION QUESTIONS

1. Does the average Catholic see evangelization as an optional, pious practice or as a basic task and obligation (cf. "Ad Gentes," n. 35) of the Christian life?

2. When some are asked why they hesitate to become involved in evangelization, many answer that they are too shy and even afraid, while others say that they have never been taught anything about how to evangelize. What do you think holds most Catholics back from the task of evangelization?

3. Do you think we could be in trouble with God if, at the end of our lives, we had to admit that we never worked hard to bring others either to the eucharistic banquet table in this life or to the heavenly banquet in the life to come?

4. Evangelization has been called "the greatest act of charity, the finest expression of our love for Christ and for others." Give some reasons why you would think this to be true or untrue.

5. At the last supper Christ prayed, "Father, may they be one so that the world may believe that you sent me" (Jn 17:21). How can a spirit of unity and cooperation—as compared to jealousy and competition—among Catholics and among all Christians be a sign and even a miracle for the world, proving that Christ is truly the savior?

## FOR FURTHER READING

Pat Lynch. *Awakening the Giant, Evangelism and the Catholic Church.* London: Darton, Longman and Todd, 1990.

John Paul II. "Mission of the Redeemer." *Origins,* Vol. 20, No. 34 (January 31, 1991), 541–68.

# NOTES ON THE CONTRIBUTORS

### DR. SUSAN W. BLUM

Dr. Blum, executive director of Isaiah Ministries in Coral Springs, Florida, has been actively involved in the instruction and training of adult Catholic lay evangelizers since 1979. The founding editor of *The Catholic Evangelist* magazine, Dr. Blum is co-author of *Mission: Evangelization,* co-founder of the *Isaiah 43/Isaiah Revisited Parish Mission* processes, and author of *The Ministry of Evangelization* (Liturgical Press, 1988). She has written numerous magazine articles and training manuals based on evangelization. In 1983 she was awarded the Pro Ecclesia et Pontifice Medal from Pope John Paul II and the Paulist Fathers' National Award for Catholic Lay Evangelization.

### REV. LAWRENCE BOADT, CSP

Father Boadt, a Paulist priest, is professor of biblical studies at the Washington Theological Union in Washington, D.C., and an editor of the Paulist Press. He has authored five books and numerous articles in biblical journals.

### REV. KENNETH BOYACK, CSP

Father Boyack is the director of the Paulist National Catholic Evangelization Association and the continental director for EVANGELIZATION 2000 in North America. He serves as a consultant to the NCCB Committee on Evangelization as coordinator for the development of their National Plan and Strategy for Catholic Evangelization in the United States. Father Boyack coauthored *The Catholic Faith Inventory* with Robert D. Duggan and Paul Heusing, CSP (Paulist Press, 1986),

228

edited *Catholic Evangelization Today* (Paulist Press, 1987), and served as editor-in-chief for *The Catholic Way of Life* (PNCEA, 1990).

## REV. PATRICK BRENNAN, STL, D.Min., Psy.D. (Cand.)

Father Brennan, ordained in 1973, has served as youth minister and director of religious education at two parishes and associate pastor at three. He began the Office for Chicago Catholic Evangelization and the National Center for Evangelization and Parish Renewal in the mid-1980s. He is the author of eight books, and hosts a weekly radio show. He is on the faculty of three graduate schools and one seminary.

## REV. PETER COUGHLAN

Father Coughlan, a priest of the Shrewsbury diocese in England, has been undersecretary of the Pontifical Council for the Laity since 1980. Themes of his article are developed more fully in *The Hour of the Laity* (Philadelphia: E. J. Dwyer Pty Ltd.), his commentary on "Christifideles Laici."

## REV. FRANK P. DESIANO, CSP

Father DeSiano, ordained a priest in the Paulist community in 1972, has authored two books and numerous articles. Having served in parishes on the west and east coast, he began a new Paulist ministry, Parish Based Evangelization, to help parishes undertake evangelization projects.

## REV. TOM FORREST, CSsR

Father Forrest, a Redemptorist, was ordained by Cardinal Spellman of New York in 1954. He served for twenty-three years in the Caribbean countries of Puerto Rico and the Dominican Republic. From 1978 to 1984, he directed the International Office of the Catholic Charismatic Renewal, coordinating the first Worldwide Retreat for Priests that brought together six thousand priests in 1984. At present he is executive director of EVANGELIZATION 2000, a global effort to promote the Decade of Evangelization in response to the call of Pope John Paul II for a "new evangelization." He has preached in eighty-five countries, always giving special priority to retreats for bishops and priests.

## REV. RICHARD N. FRAGOMENI

Father Fragomeni is a priest of the diocese of Albany, New York. He holds a doctorate in liturgical studies from Catholic University and is presently on the faculty of Catholic Theological Union in Chicago.


## MOST REV. FRANCIS E. GEORGE, OMI

Bishop George, a Missionary Oblate of Mary Immaculate, was appointed ordinary for the diocese of Yakima, Washington, in 1990. Ordained a priest in 1963, he earned a Ph.D. in American social philosophy from Tulane University and an S.T.D. in ecclesiology from the Pontifical University Urbaniana in Rome. After serving as Provincial Superior of the Oblate Midwestern Province, he spent twelve years as Oblate Vicar General in Rome, from where he visited missionaries around the world. He is coordinator of the Circle of Fellows at the Cambridge Center for the Study of Faith and Culture in Cambridge, Massachusetts, and author of articles on the theology of priesthood and religious life, on missionary methods, and on ecclesial communion.


## MRS. CAROL A. GURA

Mrs. Gura is president of the National Council for Catholic Evangelization and director of evangelization for the diocese of Cleveland. Previously she was a diocesan consultant for young adult ministry, taught theology on the high school level, and was a parish DRE. She has a Master of Arts in religious studies from John Carroll University. She has written *Ministering to Young Adults: A Resource Manual* (St. Mary's Press) and several articles for *Catholic Evangelization in the United States of America*. She has presented workshops on parish evangelization and has developed two national training workshops for evangelization. She is married and has four young adults.


## REV. GEORGE E. GRIENER, SJ

A Jesuit since 1960, Father Griener studied physics (B.S.) and theology (M.A.) at Toronto, and earned a doctorate at Tübingen, West Germany. He has worked in parish ministry, taught at Loyola University in New

Orleans, and is on the faculty of the Jesuit School of Theology at Berkeley, California.

## REV. ROBERT J. HATER

Father Hater, a priest of the archdiocese of Cincinnati, is a professor of religious studies at the University of Dayton. He specializes in evangelization, catechesis and ministry. An internationally known lecturer and author, Father Hater has spoken in over eighty dioceses and has written ten books and many articles of a popular and professional nature. His latest books are *Parish Catechetical Ministry* (Benziger Publishing Co., 1986), *Holy Family: Christian Families in a Changing World* (Tabor Publishing, 1988), and *News That Is Good: Evangelization for Catholics* (Ave Maria Press, 1990).

## REV. JOHN C. HAUGHEY, SJ

Father Haughey, currently a visiting professor at the Weston School of Theology in Cambridge, Massachusetts, has written or edited seven books and numerous articles and chapters to volumes. He has been working with the business community in Charlotte, North Carolina, the last five years trying to link business and faith in a closer tandem. He has taught at Georgetown University and became part of the Loyola University Chicago Theology Department in September 1991.

## REV. KENNETH R. HIMES, OFM

Father Himes, a Franciscan, is an associate professor of moral theology at The Washington Theological Union. A regular contributor of essays to a variety of periodicals, he is co-editor with Ronald P. Hamel of the volume *Introduction to Christian Ethics* (Paulist Press).

## ROSEMARY JEFFRIES, RSM

As a Sister of Mercy in New Jersey, Sister Jeffries has been involved in church communication for fourteen years in various capacities at the diocesan and religious congregational levels. She holds graduate degrees in communication and Christian education and is currently a doctoral candidate in sociology at Fordham University, New York. Her main interests revolve around communications, culture and theology which she tries to approach with the discipline and creativity she learned in her early days as a student of art.

## MOST REV. EDWARD A. McCARTHY

Archbishop McCarthy, archbishop of Miami since 1977, was the founding bishop of the diocese of Phoenix, Arizona. He has authored pastorals on faith, prayer, love, social injustice, reconciliation, racism, and other concerns. Archbishop McCarthy has served on numerous NCCB committees, including the Administrative Committee, the Committees on the Laity, Radio and TV, Priestly Life and Ministry, and Vocations. He is presently a member of the NCCB Committee on Evangelization and chairman of the Ad Hoc Committee for the Observance of the V Centenary of Evangelization of the Americas.

## DR. WILLIAM L. PORTIER

Dr. Portier is professor of theology and department chair at Mount Saint Mary's College in Emmitsburg, Maryland. He received his Ph.D. in 1980 from the University of St. Michael's College, Toronto, with a dissertation on Isaac Hecker's Americanism. He is the author of *Isaac Hecker and the First Vatican Council* (Mellen, 1985) and works in the field of American Catholic studies.

## DR. DAVID M. THOMAS

Dr. Thomas, director of the Center for Community Leadership at Regis University in Denver, Colorado, received his Ph.D. in systematic theology from the University of Notre Dame. Part of the Center's work is the offering of a master's degree in family ministry. He has served as a theological consultant to the National Conference of Catholic Bishops' Committee on the Family. He and his wife have five children.

# INDEX